HIGHER PURPOSE

The Heroic Story of the First
Disabled Man to Conquer Everest

TOM WHITTAKER
with Johnny Dodd

LifeLine
Press

A Regnery Publishing Company • Washington, D.C.

Grateful acknowledgment is made to Ruth Wantling for permission to reprint William Wantling's "At the Market-place," from *The Awakening*.

Four Strong Winds, by Ian Tyson
© 1963 (Renewed) Warner Bros. Inc.
All rights reserved   Used by Permission
Warner Bros. Publications U.S. Inc., Miami, FL 33014

Library of Congress Cataloging-in-Publication Data

Whittaker, Tom, 1948–
Higher purpose : the heroic story of the first disabled man to conquer Everest /
Tom Whittaker and Johnny Dodd.
p. cm.
ISBN 0-89526-199-5
1. Whittaker, Tom, 1948– 2. Mountaineers—United States—Biography. 3. Handicapped—
United States—Biography. 4. Everest, Mount (China and Nepal) I. Dodd, Johnny, 1963– II.
Title.

GV199.92.W474 2001
796.52'2'0873092—dc21
[B]

2001038495

Published in the United States by
LifeLine Press
A Regnery Publishing Company
One Massachusetts Avenue, NW
Washington, DC 20001

Visit us at www.lifelinepress.com

Distributed to the trade by
National Book Network
4720-A Boston Way
Lanham, MD 20706

Printed on acid-free paper
Manufactured in the United States of America

10 9 8 7 6 5 4 3 2 1

Books are available in quantity for promotional or premium use. Write to Director of Special Sales, Regnery Publishing, Inc., One Massachusetts Avenue, NW, Washington, DC 20001, for information on discounts and terms or call (202) 216-0600.

Every good faith effort has been made in this work to credit sources and comply with the fairness doctrine on quotation and use of research material. If any copyrighted material has been inadvertently used in this work without proper credit being given in one manner or another, please notify the publisher in writing so that future printings of this work may be corrected accordingly.

For my parents, Bobs and Warren, who encouraged me to be the person I wanted to be.

For the generous people of Pocatello, Idaho, who gave me a home.

And for my girls:
my wife, Cindy, whose faith in me has been
a bright light that warms my heart;
my beautiful daughter Lizzie, the champagne of my life;
and baby Georgia, the bubbles in my champagne.

CONTENTS

Men go forth to wonder at the heights of mountains, the huge waves of the sea, the broad flow of the rivers, the vast compass of the ocean, the courses of the stars; and they pass by themselves without wondering.

St. Augustine

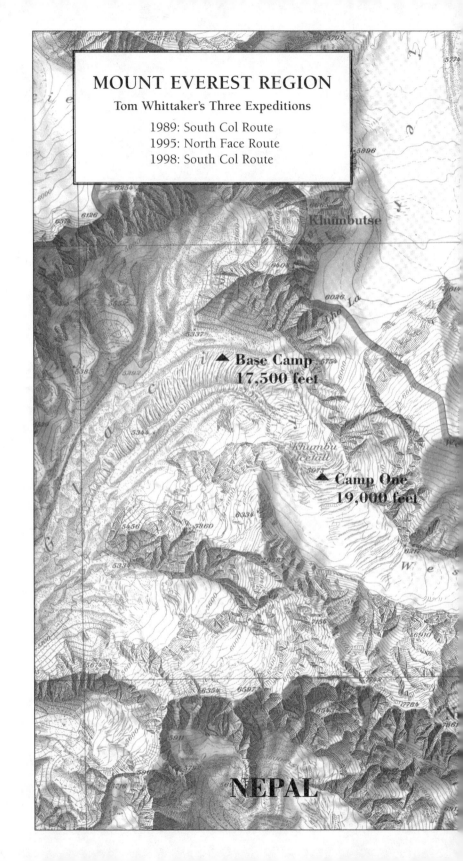

MOUNT EVEREST REGION

Tom Whittaker's Three Expeditions

1989: South Col Route
1995: North Face Route
1998: South Col Route

Khumbutse

▲ Base Camp
17,500 feet

Khumbu
Icefall

▲ Camp One
19,000 feet

NEPAL

TIBET

Advanced
Base Camp
21,000 feet

Camp Two
23,000 feet

Camp Three
25,000 feet

Camp Four
27,000 feet

T. W.
turnaround
point, 1995

MOUNT EVEREST

29,028 feet

South Summit

Camp Two
21,000 feet

T. W.
turnaround
point, 1998

South Col

Camp Four
26,000 feet

Camp Three
24,000 feet

Lhotse

Lho

Bei Peak
Changtse

CHAPTER 1
The Death Zone

Huddled inside a tent at 26,000 feet, I'm trying my damnedest not to think about the bitter wind that whips outside. Up here at Camp Four, the temperature has bottomed out at twenty below. I struggle to drag some air into my raw, phlegm-clogged lungs without setting off a spasm of coughing. No easy feat. At this extreme altitude, each minuscule movement demands an inordinate amount of effort. I busy myself checking and rechecking the pressure in my oxygen cylinders, fighting to maintain some degree of focus.

Everything in my world hinges on what happens in the next fifteen hours. I've scraped together every bit of money and equipment that could be begged, borrowed, or cajoled, called in every favor—all to prove I can pull myself up the remaining three thousand feet of Mount Everest. I couldn't do it the two other times I came to this mountain, and now the odds are starting to look ugly. According to weather reports, in less than twenty hours a cyclone will roar through this region, dumping thirty feet of snow. Anyone trapped on the upper reaches of Everest will either be buried alive or be blown off the mountain's flank, sent down the fast track to China.

Across the tent, Indra, our porter, crouches by the door and nurtures a sputtering EPIgas stove, trying to melt snow for drinking water. Above our heads, the steam freezes into a dull, glassy glaze on the blue nylon roof. His slow pace puts me strangely on edge. Not much time left. We're set to leave for the summit in five hours, at the stroke of 11 P.M. on May 19, 1998. Crouched beside me, longtime friend and CBS cameraman Jeff Rhoads checks the pressure in the oxygen cylinders, attempting to determine which bottles remain full enough to carry with us. Screwing the brass fitting into the bottle, he twists the black knob and stares groggily at the gauge—

which reveals the amount of oxygen inside—repeating the reading to himself over and over. His blistered lips move slowly, as if chanting a prayer. At this altitude, oxygen isn't a factor to take lightly.

The zipper on the fly sheet runs upward. We are greeted with the grizzly, unshaven face of Argentine cameraman Tommy Heinrich, who's covered in blood and down feathers. Tommy, here to document the expedition for one of our sponsors, grins maniacally and pushes his way inside. His presence here in the tent isn't particularly welcome. Not now. I can almost feel him sucking away what precious little focus I've managed to gather for the climb ahead. Jeff and I both know getting up to the top and returning alive will prove to be the greatest challenge of our lives.

"What the hell happened to you?" mumbles Jeff, glancing up from the oxygen gauge. Jeff, normally affable and generous, has over the course of the expedition lost his patience with Tommy. Covered by a pile of sleeping bags, I sit in silence and watch the scene unfold, my voice too hoarse from bronchitis to speak.

Tommy's small, deep-set eyes dart around the tent. He wonders if he can sleep here. He wants something to eat. He wants oxygen. He wants to talk. Indra hands him a bowl of noodles. Just watching him wolf the food down is difficult for me, as I am too nauseated to eat. The urge to drift off, far from here, tugs at me, but I am mesmerized by the scene. In between swallows, Tommy tells us how it all happened. A little more than sixteen hours ago, he left camp with Angela Hawse and Gareth Richards, my two expedition teammates, and muscled his way up the mountain's final pyramid to the South Summit. On the way down, he located the mound of snow he'd come looking for. After a few minutes of digging, he uncovered the frozen body of Scott Fischer, one of nine climbers killed on the mountain in the now legendary rogue storm of May 1996. Tommy had told us of how Scott's widow had asked him to retrieve the wedding ring Scott wore on a string around his neck.

"No matter how hard I pulled, I couldn't break the string," Tommy stammers. "So I tried using my ice axe to rip it. But . . . it felt like this . . . this hand took hold of the axe and shoved the ferrule straight through my snowsuit, down into the flesh of my forearm."

In my exhaustion, Tommy's voice sounds far away, only vaguely real. He continues his macabre tale of pulling a bracelet from Scott's arm and removing a crampon from one of his boots. He tells of stashing the belongings inside his backpack and pushing snow back over the body.

"Then," he continues, "I turned to start my descent, but when I tried to put my boot down, it never seemed to land." Tommy fell down the steep slope, tumbling several hundred feet through ice and snow, gouging holes in his down-filled suit with the axe and lacerating his face. Now, hours later, he has staggered back into camp.

An annoyed Jeff tells Tommy that he still has plenty of time to get down to Camp Three before dark, but that if he insists on staying here he'll have to find alternate accommodations with one of the seven other expeditions. Until 11 P.M., we're all booked. Tommy, too shaken to continue down with the others, wanders back outside in search of a place to sleep.

After he exits the tent, Indra stares out the zippered door. "That man, he is cursed," he whispers, shaking his head. "Many spirits, they protect the dead up here. Not to be disturbed. No Sherpa, I think, will travel on the mountain with him now."

In between the shotgun-like blasts of wind I hear Tommy pacing outside among the scores of tents erected by various climbers from British, Iranian, American, and Singaporean teams. In less than five hours, I'll trudge through this camp and head out into the darkness of the Himalayan night, trying to reach Everest's 29,028-foot summit by sunrise, then descend before the weather turns. How the hell I'll pull it off remains to be seen. I'm a wreck. In a couple of weeks I'll turn fifty—but right now, I could pass for about seventy-five. The right side of my chest feels as though a mule has kicked it, and I've begun to worry that two of my ribs are cracked from bronchitis-induced coughing spasms. To get up here to Camp Four, Jeff and I have climbed in a day and a half what would typically take four days to ascend. In the nineteen years since the car accident that trashed both my knees and cost me my lower right leg, my body has become used to my outdoor adventures, but even by Tom Whittaker standards, twelve thousand feet of climbing in three days is pushing it. As a result, my knees and stump are grumbling. I just hope that the carbon-graphite prosthesis that replaces my long-since-amputated right foot can hold up under Everest's extreme conditions.

No use fighting any longer. The combination of hypoxia (oxygen deprivation), fatigue, and a thousand frayed synapses overwhelms me and I drift away. The voices, the ones I've periodically heard over the past weeks, return. My father stands beside me as I lie in a hospital bed, the one I spent weeks in after the accident nearly two decades ago. He whispers to my mother, "Do you think he can pull through?" And she replies, "Perhaps, for his sake, it's better if he doesn't." Lights shimmer and dance gracefully on the bottom of a pool somewhere and I feel myself dropping even deeper. . . .

When the wind finally dies down, the relative quiet jars me awake. The white beam from my headlamp, I discover, has been left on. In extreme cold, where batteries don't last long, even a few minutes of use count. Scolding myself for carelessly draining the precious battery, I switch the lamp off and fumble awkwardly through my gear, not sure what I'm looking for. I need to rest, so I close my eyes and let my chin drop back to my chest.

Twenty minutes later, the radio crackles. From the mess tent in Camp One, located two vertical miles below, our Sherpa team leader barks, "Time to go! Time to go!" I struggle into my gear, then stumble outside into the inky blackness, so dark that it seems to swallow the beam from my headlamp. Off in the distance, Everest's three-thousand-foot summit pyramid looms, nearly invisible in the night but unmistakably there. Its steep ribs of stone and ice gullies are not so much seen as conjured up in a brain starved for oxygen, weary from driving a dying body up into the upper reaches of the ionosphere. Every time I see this peak—or even get close to it—the reaction never varies: excitement, intimidation, dread. Pulling my oxygen mask down over my mouth, I stagger through camp, my crampons scraping against stone. The toe of my prosthesis slams into a rock, causing my right knee to hyperextend and throwing me off balance. The pain is excruciating.

Jeff has already moved out ahead of me and is working his way up bulges of ice that serve as the doorway to the massive pyramid of rock and ice above.

"Come on, Whittaker. This way," Jeff shouts, flashing me with his incandescent third eye. I follow him, but fifteen steps later my crampon falls off.

Why the hell didn't you do a better job of attaching it to your boot, Whittaker? I chide myself.

Our three Sherpas are giving us a head start and have yet to leave camp, but in front of me I can see a string of headlamps stretching up the mountain. As soon as I reattach my crampon, I lower my head and plod upward toward the stars.

The terrain changes when I move out of the saddle of the South Col. From a jumble of rock cemented in permafrost, the ice turns into bullet-hard crystal that runs in low-angled, undulating waves. Trying to find the crampon marks left behind by other climbers proves difficult because the ice reflects my headlamp's beam back up into my eyes. Squinting, I'm just getting the hang of picking out the faint chipped trail when my crampon snags on the lip of a small fissure and pops off once again. *Damn it, Whittaker!* A tumble down this type of terrain poses an outcome too ugly to ponder.

Using my ice axe and good boot, I pick my way up to a crack in the ice and take stock of the situation. My brain is so fuzzy that it takes me a few minutes before I realize what is happening: the rubber belting attaching the crampon to the thick boot sole glued to my carbon-graphite foot has begun to fracture and split in this otherworldly cold. I curse myself for trying to save weight by gluing a Vibram boot sole directly to the prosthesis that replaces my foot. If I'd been wearing a hard-shell mountaineering boot, this wouldn't have happened.

Think, Whittaker. Pull it together, man. You've been in tighter scrapes than this. I feel as though I'm deep underwater. Somewhere inside my chest, my heart pounds at more than two hundred beats per minute, heaving against one of the water bottles I've tucked into my thick down-filled suit. Staring into the ice, I watch the light from my headlamp dance off the ground beneath me. The heavy grunts of an approaching climber slap me back into the present. A tail-ender from another expedition has caught up with me.

"You wouldn't happen to have a Swiss Army Knife, would you?" I try shouting through the neoprene of my oxygen mask, but the words barely come out. He stops and looks at me, clearly baffled by my request.

"A Swiss Army Knife," I continue, "for my crampon strap." He glances at my prosthesis, then back up at me. Hallucinations are somewhat common up here near the summit, and I can tell he's beginning to wonder if his spent brain conjured me and my artificial foot.

"You ... you don't have one?" he asks.

"Back at camp—I left it there," I reply, forcing a smile. "Trying to save weight."

He nods, looking relieved that his mind isn't playing tricks on him, then fishes the knife out from a pocket in his enormously thick coat and presses it into my mitten. I use the screwdriver to cinch down the wire bale onto my prosthesis, desperately hoping the rubber won't deteriorate any further. My hands move with the precision of a drunk, but if I took off my thick mittens my tissue would instantly start to freeze. The frigid air rips and stings a tiny patch of exposed flesh on my face. I readjust my hood as my benefactor watches me silently.

A few minutes later I'm back on my feet, slowly hoofing up the ice slope. By now, Jeff—who constantly turns to flash me with his headlamp—has built up a twenty-five-minute lead. Our Sherpas, who over the past seventy days have become my trusted friends, finally catch up. They are some of the strongest climbers on the mountain; between the three of them, they've summited Everest a total of five times. With my companions beside me, I quicken my pace. My body feels warm and, for the first time since I left the tent, I hit my stride.

Within thirty minutes the ice bulge is behind us and we enter the consolidated snow of the couloir, a snow gully leading up into an area of horizontal bands of rock. Moving like a single multi-legged animal, the four of us trudge upward. Norbu advances ahead of me to take over the lead and my gaze latches onto the back of his red overboots, which like tea cozies completely cover his plastic climbing boots. All thought dissolves as I imagine thin elastic cords stretching from my boot and prosthesis to his heels. In my exhausted mind he supplies all the energy, pulling me up the mountain with each step. I'm merely along for the ride.

Because I've traded the internal skeleton of my right leg for an external frame of carbon-graphite, trudging over such uncertain terrain becomes the most exhausting task I've ever undertaken. I'm unable to fine-tune my balance between my feet and leg muscles. With each step, I'm forced to exert nearly a third more energy than an able-bodied climber, as I struggle not only with the terrain but also with my impaired balance. Lower on the mountain, with the aid of ski poles and fixed lines, I could rely on my upper body. Up here I have to do all the work with my legs. My prosthesis, certainly one of the most advanced ever built, presents another enormous challenge. No matter the shape or the consistency of the terrain I am negotiating, my artificial foot is locked at a right angle. Each step requires extraordinary concentration. When I do make a mistake, it usually occurs with my good foot, because I'm always on red alert on my prosthetic side. Sometimes I feel as if I'm climbing with a flipper on one foot and a roller skate on the other. It would be a huge help if I could see my feet, but I can't: even with my chin tucked all the way down onto my chest, the oxygen mask bulges too far out under my eyes. With each movement of my foot, I'm stepping into blankness. All I can do is point myself in the right direction and trust that my aim is good.

Sometime around 1 A.M., after ascending nearly a thousand feet, I glance up the mountain and try to determine Jeff's position in the string of headlamps that flicker high above us. And that's when I see it. One of the headlamps detaches itself from the group and begins bounding down Everest's steep Southwest Face. Eventually it drops from sight, swallowed up by the cold and the night. The image turns my blood to ice. In the instant it takes for the tiny light to vanish, it becomes painfully obvious that anybody can fall off this part of the mountain. Even me.

Reaching my mitten up toward my throat, I feel for the pouches hanging around my neck. One holds my wedding ring, locks of hair from my wife, Cindy, and my six-year-old daughter, Lizzie, and a shard of dark gray stone from Everest's peak; another, made from a Buddhist prayer flag, contains a few grains of rice blessed by the Dalai Lama; and the third holds the ashes of a friend, which I hope to scatter from the summit.

My thoughts turn to Jeff's safety. Could it be he who took the plunge? Everybody above me appears to have stopped; the beams of light point down the slope, but no one is descending. Eventually the headlamps turn back and continue moving up. Trying to understand what is happening, I can think of only two scenarios: either somebody dropped a piece of equipment, or the situation is so utterly hopeless that there's no use going back.

Following the lead of the climbers above, I start my ascent again—but I can't dismiss the image of the falling headlamp. If somebody went off the edge, I reason, he'd plummet a vertical mile before cratering into the ice like a meteorite. But what if he didn't drop over the ridge? What if he stopped short of the edge? He couldn't possibly last more than a few hours in this ungodly cold before imagining his skin on fire, then watching helplessly as the world around him fades to gray and he slides into oblivion.

Slowly threading our way up through the ice and rock bands, we scan the mountain with our headlamps. After fifteen minutes of slow progress, I spot something glinting in the snow off to my left. I try to shout, but the combination of bronchitis and the desiccated air I've been breathing has reduced my voice to a thin rasp. Whatever we think we see in the snow doesn't respond. False alarm. It's nothing more than a discarded oxygen cylinder from a previous expedition.

We continue upward, but I can't shake the thought that it was not a dropped headlamp but a climber that I saw falling. And what if that person was Jeff, whose whole purpose for being on this mountain is to film me. How will I live with that on my conscience? How will I tell his wife?

Then out of the night a headlamp feebly reaches out to us. The fallen climber.

"We've got to go out there and bring him back," I rasp to Norbu.

"No," he snaps, convinced the thin air has taken its toll on my senses. "Cannot go there. Must climb now. Not from our team. Not our responsibility."

Norbu shakes his head and points in the direction of the summit. "Your chance to climb mountain," he shouts. "May not come again." I cough up a green clump from my lungs and spit it out, cursing the viral infection still blooming inside me. The flickering of the distant headlamp continues in a series of desperate Morse code–like pulses.

"But this is a man's life. The climbers behind us are *jinjaput*," I say, using the Sherpa term for Westerners with no mountaineering ability who buy their way onto expeditions. "They cannot help him. It will be fifteen hours before anybody passes back this way again. He will die."

Norbu remains unmoved. Awkwardly wrestling my pack off my back, I turn to Tashi, our strongest climber, and ask if he feels comfortable picking his way out over the steep glacier and bringing back the fallen mountaineer. He agrees and disappears into the darkness. I turn to Norbu and ask him to take out his rope and assist Tashi.

Norbu is resistant. "It is for summit, this rope."

"Yes," I whisper, "but we need to use the rope for this person now." Reluctantly he pulls off his pack and retrieves the coiled nylon line. I cradle the pack in front me as he traverses over to Tashi.

To save my precious oxygen, I crank the canister valve shut. But when I pull off my goggles, I immediately feel my eyeballs turn sticky; in the bitter thirty-five-below-zero cold, the moisture covering my eyes has already started to freeze. After twenty minutes I realize this has been a terrible move. A lungful of air at this altitude contains only about a third of the oxygen found at sea level, and without the extra trickle of oxygen into my lungs, the feeling is draining from my limbs. I twist the valve back on to a 1.5-liter flow, which dribbles a quarter of a lungful of oxygen every minute. This is not like scuba diving.

Tashi and Norbu are flickering shapes on the landscape as they work on the stricken climber. Hoping to repel the deadly cold by keeping my body hydrated, I unzip my one-piece down suit and retrieve one of my water bottles. Only a few hours ago the bottles contained boiling water, but I'm horrified to discover that little of the water remains; the portion located away from my body has frozen into mealy slush. I take a quick sip, but even that nip nearly causes me to vomit; tolerances are razor-fine in these upper reaches of the mountain. I'm beginning to see that the term "Death Zone," used to describe that stretch of mountain above 25,000 feet, is no overdramatization.

With the wind, the temperature has been pushed down to minus-eighty. The stump of my leg has turned beyond cold and I'm gripped by the unshakable notion that I'm sharing my climbing suit with something dead. Given my relatively fragile anatomy, it's quite probable that I'm experiencing the first stages of frostbite—something amputees are particularly susceptible to. In an amputation, after the radial saw slices through a limb—through tissue, tendons, muscle, and bone—the surgeon merely ties off the scores of arteries and veins. The network of capillaries is charged with the task of rerouting the blood supply, and circulation never fully recovers.

The two Sherpas finally appear with the injured climber tottering on a short rope between them. I recognize him as the American physician who inspected my stump several weeks ago at Advanced Base Camp in the Western Cwm (pronounced "koom"). He can barely walk, and from the way he winces, then recoils with each breath, I can tell that several of his ribs must be broken. After plummeting nearly 250 feet, Tashi tells me, the doctor landed in a crevice filled with a soft patch of wind-packed snow. If he'd bounced over it, he would have rocketed all the way down to the Western Cwm five thousand feet below.

Norbu and Tashi turn the doctor over to some of his team members. I begin running some calculations in my head. The summit, I figure, could still take eight hours to reach and the descent back to Base Camp and relative safety will require an additional sixteen. The cyclone now brewing out over the Bay of Bengal is due to collide with the mountain in twelve to fifteen hours. I am prepared to fight my way off the mountain in deteriorating conditions, but I have to be off the Lhotse Face before the storm arrives. Though my window of opportunity has all but slammed shut, I know I've done the right thing. No summit is worth a human life—no matter how much training, planning, fund-raising, and effort have gone into reaching that summit.

By now, Jeff is more than an hour ahead of us. We continue on, but once again I feel like I'm bumbling. Whatever confidence and rhythm I'd regained after reattaching the crampon to my prosthesis has evaporated. I'm no longer climbing with any true focus or conviction. My foot is deathly cold, but it is my stump that has me concerned. Could the poor circulation, exacerbated by lack of oxygen at these extreme altitudes, cause my flesh to freeze? Despite two previous expeditions to Everest, I can't recall ever being colder. The lack of oxygen has caused my movements to become increasingly jerky and awkward. For more than fourteen hours I've been working in Everest's Death Zone, where the body begins to devour itself in a desperate effort to survive. The longer you stay up here, the sicker you get. At this altitude, your ability to perform is dictated more by your ability to function in an oxygen-depleted state than by fitness and strength. It's a bit like duct-taping a drinking straw into your mouth, clamping a clothespin on your nose, tossing a thirty-pound pack on your back, and trying to run up a set of bleachers. After five steps you run out of oxygen and have to stand there sucking for air. After another five bleachers you have to stop again. It doesn't matter if you're a superb specimen or a cripple. Everyone runs out of oxygen at about the same time.

No matter how hard I try to shake it, the cold burrows deeper into my body. As I proceed, I get hopelessly entangled in the headlamp's electrical cord, the tube from my oxygen tank and the backpack straps crisscrossing my upper body. Every few steps, my thick hood droops down over my goggles. I reach up to rearrange it, only to feel my headlamp pushing my goggles down over the oxygen mask.

By approximately 3 A.M. we've moved up through a vertical, ice-lined gorge that empties out onto a steep wall of horizontal lime-stone bands. We begin traversing upward, zigzagging across a series of ledges the width of a boot, but everything seems to be falling apart. The snow conditions have deteriorated; the powder is sugary and unconsolidated, providing no security as I struggle up over the rock bands. Nearly all my focus gets sucked away contemplating my horrible footing and the consequences of an error. In moun-taineering, they say, it's not the fall that kills you but the sudden stop. One wrong step, a single screw-up with my footing, or simply snagging a crampon point on a piece of clothing could instantly transform me into a human toboggan. If I'm unable to stop my momentum by rolling over and digging the blade of my axe into the snow or ice within the first ten feet, my chances for survival will be remote. Typically you start to slide. As you accelerate you bounce and slam down against the terrain. If your crampons snag the ice, you begin doing flips, bouncing higher and higher as you go down.

Gripping my ribs in pain, I am once again consumed by a cough-ing spasm that drops me to my knees. I gasp for breath, waiting until my racing metabolism calms down. Time to get going again. Because of the pitch and loose snow, I need to plunge the ferrule of my ice axe (the metal spike at the end of the handle) into the moun-tainside with each step, both for balance and in the event that I lose my footing. But each thrust comes up empty. The ferrule merely chatters against the layer of rock hidden under the eight-inch coat-ing of snow. Must be where the doctor took his tumble. It hits me that if I slip here, my chances of using the axe to prevent myself from launching into a deadly free fall are virtually nonexistent.

In a matter of minutes, my loss of confidence transforms me into a liability, both to myself and to my companions. With the terrain growing steeper and more technically challenging, I'm finally forced to admit that my responsibility isn't to push on but to turn around. I've already fought my way off this mountain once before, in 1989, when a lesser storm than the one forecasted for this evening dropped ten feet of snow on the Western Cwm. At the time, I was fit, rested, and nearly a decade younger. Even then, it required all my strength and then some to escape. I at last managed to pull myself down—after spending five days hunkered in a tent at 21,000 feet—but I had been reduced to a zombie. Now I'm going to try to beat a retreat, absolutely wrecked from having done forty hours of mountaineering? At some point, even this Welshman has to face reality.

I tell Norbu of my decision. "You have seen me climb," I explain, trying to push the words from my swollen throat. "You know I can climb strongly and with confidence. But I don't have confidence now. I have to go back down."

Norbu peers into my goggles, trying to determine if I'm kidding. When he reads my expression, he frowns. "No, we should climb," he says sorrowfully.

I shake my head. "I can't go on now. I'm climbing like a *jinjaput*. I must go back. One of you should continue on with Jeff. The others can come with me."

All three men move away and talk quietly, periodically glancing over at me. I sit down, gazing out at the glittering stars, which seem to hang impossibly close. I think of Cindy and Lizzie, and suddenly getting to the top of this mountain no longer seems a priority. I picture the old juniper tree back home in Arizona; several mornings each week, Lizzie climbs into my backpack and we hike up into the mountains to the "Treasure Tree" to place a stone or flower in its branches. Right now I long to be back there, with my daughter on my back. But that's on the other side of the world.

Norbu carefully moves across to me, pulls the nearly empty oxygen cylinder from my pack, and stuffs it into his rucksack. Tashi announces that he will go find Jeff. Wasting no time, we begin heading back down. Nothing more to do but try to stay focused on the wretched terrain. This phase of the climb is more tiring and treacherous than the ascent; roughly a third of all deaths that occur on Everest happen during the descent to Camp Four. With my prosthesis locked in one position, whenever I take a step only the heel makes contact with the mountain, meaning that only two crampon spikes are positioned to bite into the ice. On my left side, in contrast, all ten spikes are utilized. I can do nothing more than trust that the teeth land onto something frozen instead of teetering off the edge of a loose rock. Each step becomes a highly focused act, as I try to ignore the pain in my right knee joint, caused by my lack of a kneecap, my destroyed ligaments, and the tendons I hyperextended at the beginning of this climb.

After an hour of dogged down-climbing, a faint light washes over the eastern sky. One by one, somebody appears to be turning out the stars, and before I know it, the sky changes from a pitch black to a cobalt blue that bleeds down onto the snow. The colors intensify as the terrain eases. Before long, the sharp mountain faces of Lhotse and Nuptse have turned purple. I stop to gaze in wonder at the jagged ridge lines as they slice into the morning sky.

My tranquility doesn't last, however. In a flash, I realize that my chances of ever reaching this summit have faded. I've blown it, fallen short. I've failed. And to make matters worse, I didn't even reach a recognizable spot on the mountain, such as the South Summit. I just climbed up the summit pyramid a ways and then turned around.

Three years ago, with my climbing partner Greg Child, I fought my way up to within fifteen hundred feet of the summit before running out of gas. Greg continued on to the top without me. A few days later, while I was moping around Base Camp, he walked up to me and pressed a dark gray piece of stone into my hand.

"Whittaker," he said, "I picked this up on the summit. I want you to put it back where I got it from."

This stone, straight from Everest's peak, rests now in the pouch that hangs round my neck. Greg's challenge was one of the main reasons I even bothered coming back here. *Well, Greg, I haven't done it.*

For more than a thousand years, Tibetans have referred to Everest as *Chomolungma*—"goddess mother of the world." At this moment, I want to curse her, but can't find it in me. I want to curse my rotten luck, but that doesn't make much sense either. I can't afford to waste my energy feeling sorry for myself, but at the same time I can't deny my frustration. Even though I know I've made the right decision, the profound disappointment remains. Despite all the skepticism I encountered in planning this expedition, a huge number of people have hung their hopes on this dream of mine. We have a Webcast going out to 750 schools in the United States and Canada, and CBS is producing a television documentary about the expedition. I have not only failed to achieve my dream but also proved the skeptics right—and it feels worse to validate a naysayer than disappoint a supporter.

Another coughing spasm hits. My eyes water and I want to vomit. Removing my oxygen mask, I spit out a green string of phlegm.

Working my way down the mountain, I finally spot Camp Four in the distance. Moments later I'm unzipping the fly sheet of my tent. Expecting to find Tommy inside, I'm surprised as hell when Indra pokes his head out from beneath a pile of sleeping bags.

"Don't worry about it, Indra," I rasp, watching him scamper out the door and to the nearby Sherpa tent.

The sun's first rays are just beginning to illuminate my blue nylon home, launching the temperature inside the tent up to a balmy fifty degrees. I quickly strip off my boots and down suit, then pull off the carbon-fiber sleeve that attaches my prosthesis to my leg. My mind races. If this is indeed frostbite, doctors may be forced to cut away more leg. I press my fingers into the waxy, cold flesh, observing how the color returns as the capillaries refill with blood. Thankfully, my tissue lacks the hardness of frostbitten skin. Once, after spending several hours pulling capsized rafters out of forty-degree water in the Colorado River, my stump got almost this cold. Burying myself under the mound of sleeping bags, I decide to take my chances and catch two hours of sleep, then try to beat the storm and make it down to Camp Two.

Just before the fatigue overwhelms me and I drift off, I think of Tashi and Jeff a few thousand feet above me. "Climb fast, my friends," I mutter. "Climb fast."

CHAPTER 2
Fighting Gravity

This is where it all begins. Just after lunch in Kingston, Jamaica. My bare feet are dangling twenty feet above the concrete courtyard of the garrison house that my father, a captain in the Royal Welch Fusiliers, has been assigned to.

Just two days ago we received the news that, somewhere on the other side of the world, Edmund Hillary, a New Zealand beekeeper, and his climbing partner, Tenzing Norgay Sherpa, had become the first humans to dig their crampons into the ice-covered crown of Mount Everest. Word of the expedition's success on May 29 reached us the same day that our new monarch, Queen Elizabeth II, was crowned; June 2, 1953, was indeed a banner day for the British Empire. As we huddled around the family's wooden Philco radio, listening to the BBC Overseas Broadcast, we toasted the queen, waved the Union Jack, and kept a special place in our heart for that craggy New Zealand honey farmer.

This is the first that I, a boy just shy of his sixth birthday, have ever heard of Mount Everest, but now it's all I think about. Like every other patriotic Brit, my father eagerly followed the climbers' progress in the newspapers, and he's regaled me with stories of their heroic exploits. I imagine the two mountaineers inching their way up a snow-caked ridge to the most prized summit on the planet. Dad explained that if they fall, it will probably take several minutes before their bodies hit the ground. No room for error. They push themselves upward until finally they can go no further, because there is no place left to go; they've run out of mountain. So they stand there, surveying the earth below, the Union Jack crackling beside them in the dry, frozen wind. . . .

I'm supposed to be taking my afternoon nap, but I'm wide-awake thinking about the climbers. A commotion in the courtyard below has drawn me to the window, and I watch as some workmen struggle to carry a ceiling fan into the house. If I squint just so, it's easy to make believe they're the sturdy Sherpa porters my father told me about, lugging mountaineering gear and other supplies up to some high-altitude camp. As the workmen disappear into our house, I lean out the window, clutching my bedroom curtains like a climbing rope, dangling with my feet pressed against the blistering hot wall. I glance up into the lagoon blue sky, then drop my gaze down at the hard concrete below and feel my stomach flutter. The rest of my world seems to fade away. All that matters is my makeshift climbing rope and the placement of my feet against the house. No room for error here, either.

When the dry wooden curtain rod snaps under my weight, it sounds like a gunshot. The curtains I continue to clutch snag on a jumble of barbed wire wrapped around a pipe just beneath my window, and I hang there for an instant, watching the fabric slowly rip apart. From below, I hear the shrieks of my rotund nanny. When the curtains finally tear apart, I plummet earthward. There's another crack the moment I slam into the concrete, only this time it feels to be my femur. My loyal Sherpas rush to me, wrap me in the curtains, and start to carry me inside until my mother, fearing that I've broken my neck, shouts for them to stop. But this is not my concern at the moment; I'm preoccupied with how different and strangely comprehensible the world looked for that brief instant after I pushed myself away from the safety of the window ledge and dangled from my curtains.

Then everything goes black.

Lindisfarne College is the end of the line for me, as it is for nearly everybody who ends up here. (As the saying goes, if they don't accept your boy at Lindisfarne, you'd better have a doctor check for a pulse.) My academic ineptitude has had me tossed out of one boarding school after another over the past five years, so here I am at age fourteen, on a campus overlooking the tiny mining town of Ruabon in North Wales.

If nothing else, the school proves something of a climbing wonderland for teenage boys. Towers are fashioned from Cotswold stone, the roof is made from Welsh slate, and each floor is separated by a narrow balcony of stone twelve inches wide. On the tower corners, copping stones extend from the rooftop down to the ground. And while none of my classmates would consider himself a rock climber, most think nothing of scaling the walls in order to sneak a drag off a ciggy or to mount raids on an adjoining dorm room.

This particular Sunday in early June 1962, as we queue up for our march into town to attend church, clad in straw boaters and blazers, all of us watch with fascination as a massive lily-white tent is erected in preparation for parents weekend. Parker, Anderson, Samuels, and I take particular note, and by late afternoon we can no longer resist. A quick leg up sends Anderson onto the roof of the tent. Like a midshipman on the HMS *Victory*, he races up the canvas to the crow's nest, followed in short order by the rest of us. Soon we are scrambling to the peak and sliding back down the pitched roof. We've taken the precaution of scouting a getaway route into the labyrinth of rhododendron bushes behind the tent, but in the excitement we break the one cardinal rule of schoolboy survival: always post a lookout.

Our bravado increases. Eventually we're allowing gravity to launch us off the lip of the tent and into the air. If we aim our bodies correctly, a thick pile of burlap sacks cushions our fall. After a few such kamikaze descents, I find myself standing atop the canvas rooftop all by myself, my three compatriots staring up at me. I take a running start, but no sooner does my hell-for-leather plummet begin than, from somewhere inside the tent, I hear the bellow of an unmistakable voice. Petrified, I misjudge the placement of the cushioning sacks and slam into the hard ground with a heavy thud, knocking all the breath from my body. My friends have vanished. In their place stands Mr. Simpson, all six feet, six inches, and 230 pounds of him.

Known by the boys as "Carp," Simpson was a major in the Royal Artillery before coming to Lindisfarne. He now oversees the school's army cadet force, along with the wood shop, which is where he derived his nickname. On my list of nightmarish unpleasantries, the prospect of a beating from Carp ranks right up there with bubonic plague and decapitation. But such beatings are a reality here at school. Lindisfarne may have been named after the twelfth-century monastery credited with the rebirth of learning in Britain after the Dark Ages, but names can be deceiving: the place is a dismal throwback to institutions that flourished in the early nineteenth century.

"Whittaker, you and your friends will be outside my study by 5 P.M. today," Carp says, his eyes narrowing behind his National Health–issued black-rimmed spectacles. "Do you understand?"

"Yes, sir," I reply, my heart pounding. As soon as Carp leaves, a now somber group of boys emerges from the rhododendron bushes.

"What did he say?" asks Samuels, my Trinidadian friend.

"Carp wants us to be outside his study at five," I reply.

Samuels's face turns as white as the tent canvas. "Shit," he mumbles.

We immediately launch into negotiations. Our job is to figure out what Carp knows, or what he suspects, and hash out a compromise. In short, we need to determine whose turn it is to be the sacrificial lamb. Ordinarily this is easily resolved; in schoolboy subculture you gain respect in the eyes of your peers by saving the bacon of others. But this time it's different. This time we're dealing with Carp.

At ten to five, things are still deadlocked. Nobody wants to look the others in the eye. I'm getting nervous; Carp isn't the type to be kept waiting. Finally, Anderson, a stubby, freckle-faced boy with a mass of curly black hair, stands up.

"Come on, Whittaker," he mutters as he heads toward the main building. A fun-loving kid, perpetually in trouble for petty offenses, Anderson knows the routine better than any of us; in the past two years he's been beaten more than any other student at the school.

Anderson and I stand outside Carp's office, awaiting the inevitable. At British boarding schools, retribution is swift, but not too swift. The condemned are forced to stand and wait in silence, to ponder the folly of their deeds. At the moment, Carp is more than likely sipping his afternoon tea and listening to the cricket match on the radio.

Suddenly Anderson turns toward me. "I can't do it," he says softly.

"Knock it off," I whisper. "It's not like we have too many options right now."

Anderson just shakes his head pitifully. "I can't take another beating," he says, then turns away from me to stare back into the comforting blankness of the wall. His face looks ashen, all the color drained away. But what really gets me are the tears welling up in his eyes.

Neither of us utters another word; we just stare straight ahead, dreading our impending encounter with Carp. The door to the office opens. "Whittaker!" I walk slowly into the book-lined study to find Carp standing beside a chair, his massive hands wrapped around a bamboo rod. Carp isn't a sadist or vindictive man, he's just a cog in the wheel, and what's about to happen is the dominant reality in his world and mine.

Staring at the chair, which has been pushed to the middle of the room for the express purpose of my thrashing, I hear myself blurt out, "Anderson didn't do it, sir. You can't beat him."

Carp grins and remarks, "You don't say?" He begins flexing the rod between his hands. "Pray do continue."

I explain how the only thing Anderson is guilty of is being in the wrong place at the wrong time. "He's actually afraid of heights, sir," I stammer, going on to recount how Anderson tried to talk me out of climbing up the tent in the first place.

"So if that's the case," Carp growls, "what's he doing polishing the wall outside my study?"

"Well, sir, he had to own up or you wouldn't buy it," I reply, trying my best to hold his gaze. "I couldn't come to your office by myself."

"Whittaker, you argue a good game," Carp says, scratching his jaw. "I'll agree not to beat Anderson—if you agree to take his punishment."

I've just argued myself into a ridiculously tight corner. Common sense tells me I can't endure Anderson's punishment on top of mine, but if I don't accept Carp's terms, I'm either lying or lacking in moral fiber.

"Yes, of course, sir," I stammer, suddenly feeling sick to my stomach. I've never heard of anybody taking more than six strokes of the cane. Now I'm about to get twelve. I don't bother looking up, but I clearly hear the office door opening.

"Anderson," Carp booms, "Whittaker here has agreed to take your beating. And against my better judgment, I've agreed to let him. Now get out of here and think about this while you enjoy your supper." Carp kicks the door shut again and motions toward the chair. According to the dictates of caning etiquette, I bend over and grab the lowest rung of the chair with both hands. With the tip of the rod he touches my knees to check that my legs are straight. This ensures that the fabric of my pants will remain taut against my backside, guaranteeing I'll experience the true sting of each blow. To do otherwise, to accept a caning with rumpled trousers, wouldn't be honest.

Holding my breath, I wait for the blows to come. The rod makes a whistling sound as it cuts through the air toward its target. About twenty seconds later, it's all over. I stand up, my top front teeth embedded deep into my bottom lip. "Close the door on your way out, Whittaker," is all Carp says as I hear him lean the rod against the side of his desk. I don't dare look at him. "Yes, sir. Thank you, sir." My hand trembles as I reach for the brass doorknob.

Once outside, I'm relieved to find that Anderson is gone. And as a blaze of white heat erupts across my buttocks I walk stiff-legged to the bathroom, tears streaming down my face. After washing my face in the basin, I drop my trousers and survey the damage. Five livid welts stand out a quarter of an inch from my bottom. Suddenly it dawns on me that Simpson struck me only five times, not twelve. Even more peculiar, the beating lacked his trademark heavy-handedness.

By the time I reach the dining hall, the entire school appears to know of my fate. Anderson must have spread the word. The room grows quieter when I enter, and all the boys turn to look at me. But something in their gazes strikes me as different. The upperclassmen, who usually look at me with contempt, if they pay me any mind at all, give me nods of appreciation. Lloyd, our "head of house," meets me before I have a chance to sit. This hard-as-nails South African wreaks the same havoc on the rugby field as he does with the local girls. Normally he'd think nothing of swatting someone of my lowly stature. Like most of my cohorts, I'm in awe of him.

"That was a good thing you did today, Whittaker," he says. "Come on, you're sitting at the head table with the prefects and monitors. And get your head up, Whittaker. Put on a good show."

When we get to the table, he points to an empty chair. "Go on," he says, "sit down." I try not to wince as my raw, swollen rump makes contact with the flat wooden seat, but I don't do a very convincing job. Instantly I'm hit with a barrage of questions from the upperclassmen.

"Did Simpson give you a bad one? . . . How many strokes did you get? . . . Which cane did he use?" Once I've sated their curiosity, they return to their conversations and ignore me. But as the meal concludes, one of the prefects turns to me and says, "Whittaker, we're going down the Short Cut tonight. You can tag along if you like." I know better than to accept his invitation, but just his asking is salve on my wounds. I may not have arrived, but I've been noticed.

I spot Anderson down at the far end of the dining hall, sitting with Parker and Samuels. I want to join them but doubt I can stomach the pain of standing back up and sitting down again. When Parker sees me looking in their direction, he nudges Anderson, who immediately looks up at me. I can see that his eyes are bloodshot from the tears, but he smiles anyway.

By the winter of my final year at Lindisfarne, instead of having moved on to a university track in the Sixth Form, I've been relegated to Five B. Winding up a Five B at the age of seventeen is another way of saying that I'm destined to be a ditchdigger. Miraculously, however, I haven't been kicked out of Lindisfarne. Then again, this really says more about my ability on the rugby pitch than my wretched grades; my recent invitation to try out for the Welsh National Schoolboy Rugby Team has caused an intense buzz of excitement among the faculty and students.

On this gray December afternoon, I'm hunkered down in a desk in the middle of the gym. One hour, twenty minutes into my senior French final, I finally stop kidding myself. It's painfully clear I won't be attending a university after my time here is done. Of the eight courses I need to pass in order to be considered for college, I've managed to fail six. But this exam, which I'm taking for the second time, clinches it.

I've always disliked French. Of course, I probably shouldn't blame the language. My brain might have something to do with my linguistic troubles. I'm dyslexic. If it's possible to scramble the letters in a word or hopelessly mangle a number, I always manage to find a way to do it. My I.Q. is a respectable 120, my memory, superb. But in that gap between seeing a word written on a chalkboard or in a book and processing it inside my brain's switchboard, something goes horribly haywire. A full disconnect. All the letters get reshuffled, and I might as well be staring at hieroglyphics. It takes me months to read the same book that my classmates can breeze through in a week. Because of my wretched spelling, all my essays are automatically marked down 30 percent, leaving only a thin margin for factual error if I'm to pass. Unfortunately, I inevitably end up a few points on the wrong side of that margin.

Sitting here in the gymnasium, staring at this hopeless exam, I'm transported back to the last parents weekend, held a few months before. The speaker that weekend, the Bishop of Manchester, was an extremely charismatic man and a riveting orator, and his message, that the measure of a person's maturity is the number of deep experiences he's had in his life, made an instant connection with me. As the bishop spoke, I forged a connection between his words and those of the American poet William Wantling, whose writings I'd recently discovered. Wantling wrote:

> at the market-place
> we sell many things
> including love & courage
> but these you must bring
> with you
> & pay for when you leave

On the one hand, the bishop was telling me that the only way to live life is through direct, hands-on experience. On the other, Wantling seemed to be saying that this journey can be guided only by the qualities of love and courage.

Now, with an hour left in my French exam, these two philosophies take on added significance for me. My time at Lindisfarne is nearing an end, and, despite how I once loathed this place, I realize I'm going to miss it sorely. The school is familiar and stable, peopled with friends. I understand the rules and have welded intense relationships here. More important, I've even begun to define just who Tom Whittaker is. Unlike my older brother, Giles, whose agile mind and scientific bent have him following in the family footsteps to the Royal Military Academy, I have no clear path to pursue. I'm about to be tossed into the world with little more than a talent for rugby.

But to hell with a destination, I tell myself, at least I've got these two philosophies to guide me in the days ahead.

I close the test booklet and lay down my pencil. The proctor sees my movements and eyes me suspiciously.

"Whittaker, you finished so early?"

"Yes, sir," I reply, standing up and handing him my uncompleted exam. "I'm just going to have to give France a wide berth."

Fresh out of Lindisfarne, and much to the distress of my parents, I move home to work construction and play rugby for the City of York. I also fall hopelessly in love with a twenty-one-year-old peroxide blonde named Samantha, the type of young woman who becomes a traffic hazard when she dons a miniskirt. She's studying to become a teacher and shares a house with four devoutly Christian roommates. On Wednesday nights, she and her housemates visit with the elderly at government-run geriatric hospitals. Afterward, they reward their good deeds with a few pints at one of the many nearby pubs. Always eager to spend time with Samantha—not to mention "sup" a couple of ales—I tag along on the group's missions of mercy.

The hospitals we visit always reek of disinfectant; they're completely desperate places with white-haired skeletons lying on thin horse-hair mattresses perched atop metal-framed beds. Everything about these institutions is ship-shape and clean, but warmth and joy are sorely lacking—that is, until Samantha and her pals sweep in. For two hours, they transform the dreary place with their chatter, laughter, and generous hearts. To avoid getting caught up in their energy proves impossible, and it doesn't take long before my initial awkwardness vanishes and I'm sitting beside a sagging mattress with a bony hand clasped in mine, dreaming about Samantha and thankful that my rugby mates can't see me now.

Joyce looks like all the rest—sunken eyes, tissue paper skin, hopelessly alone. Nevertheless, lying there on that old mattress, trapped in a strange purgatory between life and death, she seems somehow different. As soon as I sit down she grabs my thick hand and squeezes it.

"What are you doing here?" she demands.

"I—I came with my girlfriend and some of her housemates," I stammer. "You see, on Wednesday nights we sit—"

"No, not here," she interrupts, waving her thin arms around in the air as though chasing away invisible flies. "But *here*. Here in *life*. What are you doing while you're here alive?"

I shrug, tell her about the motorcycle my brother, Giles, and I are rebuilding, how I'm playing rugby for York, and even how I'm filling out an application to attend night school at a technical college.

She rolls her eyes. "Then what? Then what are you going to do?"

"No plans, really," I admit.

She frowns, begins violently coughing, then starts gasping for air. Her grip grows tighter on my wrist with each spasm. All I can do is sit here, watching. She finally whispers, "Look around this room, boy, and tell me what you see."

"Elderly women," I reply, wondering if maybe it's time I go sit at another bed.

"Bollocks!" she snaps. "What you see is a bunch of dying old women, a roomful of them, all filled with regrets, sorrows, and missed opportunities. All of them want their lives back so badly it makes them cry." She pauses, then adds, "Or haven't you been listening to what they tell you?"

I feel dizzy, wobbly, like someone just cleated me in the side of my head. She begins coughing again. When she finally stops and catches her breath, she glares at me.

"Don't mortgage your soul, boy," she says. "Feed it well. Stuff it full of nourishment until it explodes. Live your days, so when it comes time to leave here, you don't end up feeling like these old women."

From somewhere behind me, Samantha walks up and gently taps me on the shoulder.

"We're waiting for you," she smiles. "Downstairs, by the front door."

"Be right down," I tell her.

Joyce and I sit together quietly, holding hands, for a few moments longer. Something tells me I won't be seeing her the next time I come for a visit.

"Fix that motorcycle, boy," she says when I finally get up to leave. "And if you do come back here next week, think of me when you sit and talk to whoever they've stuck in this lousy bed."

That night, after I return home from the pub, I see a want ad from *The Daily Telegraph*. It seems Warriston School, a small boarding school in the lowlands of Scotland, is searching for a sports coach. On a whim, I apply. My athletic accomplishments speak for themselves, but I lie about my age to get the job. Three weeks later, I'm racing up the A1 to Scotch Corner, squinting into the wind, squeezing the throttle of my freshly repaired motorcycle.

When I receive the letter at Warriston, I immediately recognize the handwriting. Yet this envelope is not nearly as thick as the ones I'm accustomed to receiving, and it lacks the usual hint of perfume. A sense of foreboding settles over me, so I stash the letter in my pocket to read later.

Back in the comfort of my room, I pull the single sheet of paper out of the envelope, and as I read, a lump forms in my throat.

I suppose it's called a "Dear John." The words are loving and kind, but the message is hopelessly final: this is how things will be, and there's nothing I can do to fight it.

But fight it I will. I rush to my motorcycle and head off into the cold October night toward York. Hurtling down the winding Scottish roads, I think of Joyce in that geriatric home. Overwhelmed by anguish and self-pity, so far away from Samantha, I blurt out, "Why the hell did she tell me to fix the motorcycle?!" But slowly I begin to see that I know even less about affairs of the heart than I do about the conjugation of French verbs. I've gone charging off on my motorcycle to throw myself at Samantha's feet and proclaim my undying love, but I realize that this is the foolish impulse of a jilted lover. I turn my motorcycle around and head back to Warriston.

And Warriston is indeed my place now. The school's headmaster, Brian Larmour, treats the students and faculty as family, and I am one of the big brothers who help mentor the thirty-eight boys. One night, over a game of snooker and a glass of single malt whisky, this exceptional man told me that I had a gift and that with the right combination of work experience and academic qualifications I could get into a British teachers training college. This is something I had never considered—after all, at Lindisfarne they had me pegged as a ditchdigger—but he convinced me that, with guts and tenacity, it could be done.

By the time I pull my motorcycle back into the school's drive, I know that Joyce was right. I won't get over this heartbreak right away, but I understand that Joyce and Brian Larmour have conspired together to give me something more important: the courage to dream and the fortitude to pursue those dreams.

Within two years I'm working as a sports hall attendant at the University of Kent, coaching squash and trampoline. When my boss, John Poppelwell, asks me how many General Certificates in Education I hold, I tell him that I have five at the ordinary level.

He frowns. John and I both know that I need eight at the ordinary level and three at the advanced level to be considered for university entry. At this rate I will be thirty before I get accepted. "Well," he says, "I'm lunching with Miss Hinks, the principal of Nonington College. She's got more whiskers on her chin than you or I do, and she runs the place like a prewar girls boarding school."

Just as I'm wondering what all this had to do with my dismal academic qualifications, he says, "The Department of Education is adopting a co-ed policy and is forcing her to open the doors to men or close up shop. She's been slow to comply in the past, so this year she's been told she has to double the amount of men at Nonington. I could put your name forward. Are you interested?"

"Rather!" I say enthusiastically.

"There are a couple of drawbacks, though."

"Such as?" I ask warily.

"Well, for one, even though it's a specialist P.E. college, Hinks detests team sports, so you'll spend as much time flitting around a dance studio as you will on a sports field."

"And the second drawback?"

He looks over his spectacles at me and grins. "There'll be about seven women to every man."

Graduating from Nonington College proved easier than getting hired as a teacher. I made the mistake of crossing Miss Hinks, and after my final examinations she ordered that all my papers be turned in to her. When it became apparent that I was too strong a candidate to flunk, she took another approach. She attached a scathing reference to the transcripts that went out to all potential employers.

I tried desperately to land a job as a P.E. teacher in Great Britain's public school system, but Miss Hinks's "recommendation" did the trick: she ruined my chances of ever getting a job in my chosen profession. Out of money and desperate for work, I finally gave in to the old principal and sought out another job.

I guess I wasn't too discriminating about what line of work I should head into. Which is why I now find myself stark naked on the deck of a North Sea oil rig with my hands wrapped around the throat of a Spanish maintenance worker. It all seems perfectly logical. Forty-five minutes ago I finished my twelve-hour shift as a rig diver, and I've been trying to grab some sleep before descending into the frigid water once again. But the maintenance worker apparently had no plans to let me sleep. Soon after I dozed off, he took his high-speed electric grinder to the rust outside my tiny metal trailer, jolting me from my sleep. I explained my delicate situation and convinced him to work elsewhere, but no sooner had I fallen back to sleep than he was back at it again. It seems he needed more convincing. . . .

After I relax my grip on the man's throat, he crawls away cautiously, leaving me alone and naked. I sit down on the deck, listen to the waves crash against the rig, and close my eyes.

Look at you, Whittaker. You've really lost it this time. Gone completely over the edge.

How did I end up out here in the middle of the North Sea, hundreds of miles off the coast of Norway? It isn't a bad job, really, and the money is certainly better than anything I've ever earned before. But this definitely isn't how I pictured my life playing out.

Being stationed out at sea for a month at a time feels like an Alcatraz prison sentence. We work like zombies, shivering in icy waters we share with conger eels and battling against the powerful swells. Most of the time, however, all I think about is how long I have until the next shore leave.

On my downtime, I hop a high-speed launch back to civilization, where I habitually overstay my welcome with my friend Tony Bradborne. Tony, a six-foot-seven former British Special Forces soldier, works as an instructor at Brathay Hall, an outdoor pursuits center tucked away in the Lake District village of Ambleside. In recent months he's introduced me to climbing, caving, and orienteering. It proves a stark contrast to my lonely life at sea.

It hit me my first day out on the crags. In truth, I can't even recall where the crag was located or the name of the climb. But as I was way up there in the clouds, looking down on a glaciated valley, raw exhilaration flooded my body, more primal and satisfying than anything I ever felt playing rugby or cricket. It wasn't just the aesthetics of moving over rock, propelling myself by using just my hands and feet. No, somehow I stumbled upon a new way of experiencing life. By the time I reached the belay ledge, the sun had fallen away and I could see night fast approaching. I leaned against the rock and rested, absorbing the sights and sounds around me. For the first time in my life, I felt like an integral part of the world I live in, not just a witness to it.

Now, every day I climb, I feel myself exploding with life; every time I ride back to the rig, contemplating another straight month of work out at sea, an unshakable depression sets in. Sitting here naked on the rig's deck, I see it: I'm dying. My life is dribbling down a black hole. Simply because I can earn some money on this wretched rig, I'm living a life I detest. As with all amateur sports, there's no cash to be made learning outdoor pursuits, but right now this is what I want to do. It's time for a change.

When I realize the Spaniard isn't coming back with reinforcements, I stand up, walk back to my trailer, and get dressed. Then I go looking for my boss to tell him the news.

"There's a transport coming the day after tomorrow and I'm going to be on it," I explain.

"How so?" he asks.

"I'm quitting."

"Do that," he tells me, "and I promise you that you'll never work in this industry again."

"You can't begin to know how badly I hope you're right."

Two days later, I'm bouncing over the rough water on a high-speed transport, choking on diesel fumes. I'm heading home. Looking up at the rig, I spot the Spaniard, who pretends he doesn't see me.

"Thanks, mate," I shout in his direction, but my voice gets lost in the din of the engines.

CHAPTER 3
"Up or Off!"

"You sure that's it, Whittaker?" My buddy Sam stares worriedly up at a formidable mass of overhanging rock.

"Closest thing I've seen to Tony's description," I reply, rubbing my hands together to keep warm.

After quitting the rig, I launched headlong into climbing. The first thing Tony did was take me to the local climbing store in Ambleside and load me up with gear—a pair of fifty-meter ropes, rock boots, a climbing harness, a helmet, carabiners, and several aluminum wedges threaded on nylon cord. For the past few weeks we've done nothing but climb, the rocks growing steeper with every ascent, the handholds smaller and harder to locate. Although I possess all the tools to excel at climbing—I'm tall, rangy, and strong, with good athletic ability—I've flailed my way through these early ascents. Despite the frustrations, however, the lure of climbing is unmistakable.

On this afternoon, Tony has pointed Sam and me toward a climb called Slip Knot on the White Ghyll crag. Sam and I are both novices, and Tony mentioned that this intermediate route would be a good introduction to the V.S.—Very Severe—grade. But now that we're up on the mountain, I wonder if Tony might have led us astray.

Another climber trudges past. "Excuse me," I say, "but you wouldn't happen to be carrying a guidebook, would you?"

"Let me guess, you forgot yours," he says, eyeing our sparkling new gear, then shaking his head to reveal his disdain for the two rookies standing before him.

"No," I smile. "Ran out of brass before I got to the book section. We're looking for Slip Knot. This it?"

He nods slowly, then fishes a tattered guidebook out from his pack. "Why do I suddenly feel like an accessory to a suicide?" he asks, opening the book to the entry we need. "There it is, hotshot. Memorize it well. Gets a bit tricky just after the first pitch."

My worries disappear when I study the write-up; the book lays out the climb exactly as Tony described it to me yesterday. "Thanks, mate," I tell the veteran, stumped as to why he thinks the route is so problematic. After watching Sam fly up the first pitch, I'm still wondering what all the fuss is about.

As soon as I pull myself up on the ledge next to him, Sam scratches his head and asks, "Any idea which way we go from here?" Scanning the wall above and around us, I can't remember if the guidebook said to go left or right. Sam reads the uncertainty on my face.

"You dyslexic moron!" he shouts, only half kidding. "Hmm," I mumble, turning to inspect the bulging outcrop nearest me. "I thought the book said to go right, but that looks a bit . . . well, ridiculous." I pull myself up onto that wall to get a better look, and after a few moments of inspection I decide that can't be the route. "Must be out left," I announce.

Sam eyes the wall once again, then smiles. "Go on," he says. "Ladies first."

"Well, why not?" As I begin moving out onto the rock, I'm not quite sure where I'm going to locate a crack to insert any of the center-drilled aluminum wedges hanging from my sling. And I don't even want to think about what will happen if I take a tumble without any protection. Moving off the ledge, I see what Tony meant when he said that the second pitch has "a fine sense of position"—the sense of exposure is mind-numbing. *Well, it's no good looking down there; your future is up,* I tell myself.

"You OK up there?" Sam asks.

"Just savoring my splendid sense of position," I lie.

The rock seems to suck the warmth out of my hands as a few, straggling snowflakes swirl around my body. It's slow going, but I'm making progress. I'd feel much better if I could safeguard my progress by locating a crack to place one of my wedges, but there's nothing doing. Suddenly my climbing helmet clunks into a bulge of rock directly above me.

"Where'd that come from?" I mutter, craning my neck to inspect the massive obstacle. A violent gust blasts up the rock, and I wedge my boots into the crag, hanging on with all my strength. Panic creeps up my body. My right leg begins shaking uncontrollably, the heel jiggling up and down. Sewing machine leg, curse of the neophyte.

Now twenty feet above Sam, if I take a "screamer" from here, I'll fall twice that far before the rope goes taut—provided it goes taut at all. Everything rests on Sam's ability to stop my descent using his own weight, a fact I try not to dwell on, considering that Sam is a bag of bones. He's 145 pounds, while I weigh 190 pounds in my cotton socks. God only knows how many hundreds of pounds gravity will add on my forty-foot free fall.

Should have stuck to rugby, Whittaker.

My sewing machine leg starts up again. Realizing that my overgripping of the rock is causing me to lose what little energy I have remaining, I force myself to relax all but the most essential muscles.

Down-climbing looks impossible, and since I can't continue past the overhang, going left appears to be my only option. The rock is smooth, and the wind slams my body about, threatening to fling me into space. I've never pushed myself like this before. After a couple of tenuous moves, I arrive at the bulging rib and find some marginal holds, but there's still no place for me to insert any protection. Just six feet of rock to go, but every move I make takes me further out on a limb.

Once again I'm panicking. I flatten myself against the buttress and begin trembling.

"Go on, fall off," I hear someone shout from below. Another group of climbers has stopped to take in the unfolding drama of my climb, and one of them is encouraging me to rely on the rope that stretches back to Sam. Closing my eyes, I drive the spectators out of my mind and visualize what needs to be done. *Just six bloody feet of rock, Whittaker.*

Each move, I tell myself, must be precise and smooth. I must keep three points of contact on the rock, so only one of my hands or feet can leave the surface at any given instant. Reaching up with my right hand, I insert my fingertips into a small indented hold; with my right foot I step over to a tiny sloping nubbin. As soon as I stand on it, I'm balanced awkwardly. *Moved your wrong foot, didn't you, Whittaker?!* I've forgotten to locate a hold for my left foot, which now dangles uselessly in space.

My mouth goes dry and I can feel my nerves short-circuit once again. There's only one option—somehow I have to switch my feet on the tiny hold that bears all my weight. But how to execute such a maneuver. While jumping upward, I slip my right foot off the hold and replace it with my left. Damn awkward, but it works.

Finally in proper position, I'm able to pull myself up the ledge with two additional moves.

Once on the puddle-filled rock, I collapse. It takes several minutes for me to gain enough composure to arrange a belay and bring Sam up.

"Jesus, that looked hideous," he says upon reaching me. "You OK?"

"Not quite sure," I whisper.

On the way back down, I don't say much. When we finally arrive at the hotel at the base of the crag, I head straight into the climbers' bar, desperate for a pint of ale to treat my frayed nerves. Strange, up until about an hour ago, I never realized the commitment required of a climber. I'm questioning why I was attracted to climbing in the first place; it's hardly the fun I imagined. Working as a diver on North Sea oil rigs never seemed this dangerous. The bloke with the guidebook was right: this is suicide for me. Never have I been so petrified about anything. For once, I've found a physical endeavor for which I'm positively unsuited.

Spotting a bulletin board with advertisements for tents, backpacks, and other climbing gear, I decide to rid myself of all the equipment Tony and I bought just a few weeks ago. As I calculate how much my new climbing gear will fetch, Sam arrives at the table with two new pints. "Hey, Whittaker," he says, "I just found out what happened. We started off climbing Slip Knot, but you ended up taking us up a whole other route. Much tougher climb."

Sam is nonchalant about the whole matter, but his words jolt me. "So I noticed," is all I can offer in response. But as I look back at the bulletin board, I think to myself, *Maybe I'll hang onto my gear for just a bit longer.*

That miserable afternoon on Slip Knot sticks with me. I can't shake the fear, but I also can't shake the climbing bug. As much as I tell myself I should give up the game, I find myself back out on the rocks. I take epic spills, get scared, and often end up on routes hopelessly over my head—but I keep climbing.

Eighteen months after my Slip Knot adventure, Tony and I are looking for a climb to tackle when he suggests we try our luck on Kipling's Groove. Tony knows that I climbed that a couple of months back, but what he doesn't know is that I took a nasty tumble. Fortunately my partner that day, "Mucker" Brown, arrested my fall, but I'm not eager to head back out there.

"Already done it," I remind Tony.

"I know, but I haven't," he replies, throwing on his backpack and lumbering up the trail. "So let's go."

I pay out the rope as he leads the first pitch, moving effort-lessly along the traverse. Tony is a brilliant climber—wiry, strong, and blessed with a long reach. He's my mentor on the hill, and not simply because of his physical gifts: his mental fortitude allows him to take on any situation he faces on the rocks, no matter how difficult.

I follow Tony up the route, only to hear him say nonchalantly, "You're leading this next pitch."

"What are you talking about, Tony?" I stammer, as he shoves the climbing gear into my hands and motions for me to rack the equipment. "I've already led this pitch with Mucker Brown."

"I know," he says. "I've wanted to climb this for a long time, but I'm not bloody leading it."

I can't believe what I'm hearing. But at the same time, I'm not about to show my fear before the unflappable Tony Bradborne. So, after clipping a second carabiner into the long sling looped over my shoulder, I begin climbing up the vertical crack. When I reach an aging piton hammered into the rock, I clip one of my carabiners through the eye of the peg and attach the other end of the sling to my climbing rope. Nervously, I begin a slow, difficult traverse to the right, bypassing the shelf that caused my fall the first time around.

Reaching the narrow ledge, I struggle to "mantle" by perform-ing a push-up with both hands flat on the ledge. With both arms locked and my nose pressed against the rock wall in front of me, I inch my foot up until I can place it on the ledge beside my hands. "Well, the easy part's done," I say to myself. Though I'm on the verge of losing my balance and plummeting backwards, I have to move one of my hands. Very carefully I take my right hand off the ledge and blindly feel around for a hold that will allow me to maintain balance while I force myself into a standing position on the ledge. While I desperately grope about, I feel the strength draining from my left arm.

"Tony, watch me!" I shout. "I may be joining you!"

The best thing I can find is a small side-cut hold. It's now or never. Inch by inch I straighten my right leg until I am in a standing position. "God, I hate climbing!" I exclaim as I stand plastered against the rock, looking back across twenty feet of wall to the weary piton. If I fall off here I will be back down with Tony. And if the peg fails—well, who knows what will happen?

"So, Whittaker, you're well scared," I tell myself. "But let's think climbing rather than falling." I have one sketchy move and then I'm on easier terrain. After working out the sequence, I move up onto the thin holds. The world goes silent. Blinking the sweat out of my eyes, I reach up to get a good hold with my left hand. Two more moves and I place one last piece of protection into a crack, clip in my rope, and howl with joy.

"God, I love climbing!" I yell, sending two startled sheep running across the fell.

Tony follows my lead and joins me at the top, whereupon he announces quite matter-of-factly, "Good lead, youth. I never could have led that." He stares at me after saying this, peers right into my eyes. "And I absolutely mean it."

Maybe, just maybe, I'm a better rock climber than I've been giving myself credit for.

In 1973, thanks to Tony's teaching on the rocks and my training as a P.E. teacher, I land a position as an outdoor pursuits instructor at Hollowford Training Centre in Derbyshire, England. Taking over where Tony left off, Hollowford colleague Guy "Guido" Lee decides I'm a worthy project. A rock jock since the age of sixteen, he has climbed some of the toughest routes in the British Isles. The more time I spend with him, the more I learn that courage has nothing to do with being fearless and everything to do with learning how to overcome fear by facing it.

I've come to understand the many shapes fear can take, what it looks like, how paralyzing it can be. Most important, I learn how to deal with being frightened, to develop techniques for shrinking my fear to the size of a walnut in the pit of my stomach, freeing up the energy it sucks out of me and channeling that energy back into solving the problem.

I also realize I've been climbing for the grade rather than for the sheer joy and exhilaration it brings me. My ego has demanded that I tackle routes beyond my skill level because I've been in competition with Sam, Tony, Mucker Brown, and everyone else. I've wanted to prove that I'm worthy of their respect, but that, I see, is not the reason I should be climbing.

By the summer of 1975, I'm ready for the Alps. This will be my proving ground. In June I pull into Chamonix, France, with Guido and another Hollowford instructor, Derek Kingsland, who between them have a dozen Alpine seasons under their belts. I've been climbing for four years now, but this is a wholly different experience. In Britain the ethics of climbing are everything—it is not whether you ascend a route but *how* you ascend that route. In contrast, here in the Alps the sport revolves around raw speed. The reason is simple: spend too much time working out moves and you'll end up dead. Every August an average of seventy mountaineers perish in the Western Alps, and two-thirds of those deaths are weather-related. The cruel reality is that, because of the manic swings in the weather, you always climb looking over your shoulder. So, whereas in the U.K. it is considered rather unsporting to rely on pitons, Alpine climbers routinely pound protection into the rock if they think it will get them up quicker.

As soon as I get out on the peaks, I discover that my metabolism is strangely suited to this extreme environment. The altitude—which ranges from 12,000 to 15,000 feet—doesn't seem to affect my stamina, and the headaches, fatigue, and shortness of breath that plague Derek and Guido are less severe problems for me. Lower down, both these men climb circles around me, but up here in the thin air I have a distinct advantage.

Though it's just my first season in the Alps, to my surprise I'm accepted by the bright young stars on the U.K. climbing scene, including the Burgess twins, with their chiseled movie star faces. One night in July, when the twins arrive back in camp after having added another "British first ascent" to their resumé, we decide to celebrate at the Bar National, which is owned by a local legend named Maurice. The Burgess twins are as accomplished at drinking as they are at climbing, and by the time we uncork our third bottle from Maurice's wine cellar, I'm contemplating doing a solo climb of the northeast spur on the Chardonnet. One of the area's shorter routes at some fifteen hundred feet, it seems well within my technical climbing abilities. After some discussion the brothers deem it a worthy undertaking—bold but not suicidal. When Maurice's daughter goes to fetch our fourth bottle, I bid my countrymen adieu.

"Just after midnight, Whittaker," one of the twins points out. "Turning in a mite early, aren't we?"

"Gotta be up in about three hours," I reply. The two hard-living brothers roll their eyes. For the Burgess twins, there's nothing the least bit unpleasant about climbing on three hours' sleep.

When daylight breaks over the camp, my aching head has dampened whatever enthusiasm I had for soloing the Chardonnet, so I decide to push my climb back a day. After a leisurely morning I throw my bivouac ("bivy") gear and a headlamp in my pack and hitchhike to La Tour to catch the last tram up to the mountain hut. As I jump off the packed car, I realize that if I'd followed the schedule I so tipsily established back at Bar National, I'd have finished my climb by now and would be en route to camp. Instead, because I don't have the money to pay the hut fee, I crawl into my sleeping bag near the front door and drift off to sleep.

Just before sunrise the next morning, the sound of crampon spikes on metal steps startles me awake. I follow a string of yellowish headlamps across the glacier and peer up at the eight hundred feet of rock and ice lying between me and the ridge. Inside my belly I feel the anxiety sprouting roots. That's when I start my running dialogue, my internal pep talk:

Nothing wrong with being scared, Whittaker, but do you truly want to do this thing?

Yes, but I don't want to die trying.

So what can go wrong?

I could screw up, or the rock or ice could break off.

But you know what rock or ice looks like when it's dodgy, don't you?

Of course.

Well, then, stay alert and you'll keep the objective hazard to a minimum. This will also ensure that you don't make any mistakes.

Using this question-and-answer technique, I'm like a balloon pilot dumping sandbags out of his basket: I'm lightening myself for the journey ahead. Every anxiety successfully resolved frees me up to climb.

I make good progress up the steep rock and ice, and once I hit the ridge, I see, looming in the distance, the final headwall, which looks to be a sheer face of shimmering white. I'm traveling quickly and efficiently, unfettered by rope, relying solely on my own judgment.

At the end of the ridge, however, my mouth drops open and I feel the anxiety growing in my gut. To reach the headwall I have to climb what's known as a "bomb-bay" couloir, a three-sided chute that falls away more than a thousand feet to the glacier below. My heart pounds.

Not this again, Whittaker. Think climbing, not falling. Think up, not down.

I take a deep breath, sink my axe into the bluish ice of the couloir, and step out and kick the front points of my steel crampons straight into the wall, up to the hilt. My heart seems to have worked its way up my throat. Suspended above a bottomless chute by just my crampons and ice axe, I wonder why the hell I thought solo climbing to be such a worthy pursuit. *Should have stuck to rugby*, a voice inside my head chides.

But it's time to commit. Prying my axe out from the ice, I concentrate on the exact spot I need to hit and drive the tip home above my shoulder. It goes in with a reassuring thud. I repeat the process, keeping my wrist firm. Next I pull my crampon out from the wall and plunge it back in about twenty inches higher, followed by the next boot. *Thud, thud, kick, kick, thud, thud, kick, kick.*

The progress is steady as I make my way up the headwall. But my concentration is shattered when a four-inch-thick chunk of ice the diameter of a dinner plate whistles past my head.

"*Attention! Attention!*" I shout at the three climbers above me, then immediately flatten myself against the wall as two more frozen projectiles whiz past. Within a few minutes I join the belayed climbers. Their leader, it becomes clear, is in way over his head, and I volunteer to extricate the Frenchmen from their mess. After anchoring the leader to the wall with one of my precious "just-in-case" ice screws, I take one of the double ropes from the second man on his rope team and clip it into my harness. Now I'm attached to the leader with one of his ropes and he's tied to his belayer with the other.

Just below the summit I create an anchor in the wall with my last "just-in-case" ice screw. Once I've brought up the Frenchman, I tell him I'll collect my ice screws and carabiners when the four of us meet up at the refuge hut. Without so much as a word of thanks, he waves me off and goes to work trying to belay his partners.

"And pleased to meet you, too," I shout, then strike off along a razor-thin ridge that has been transformed to mush by the afternoon sun. For several steps I straddle the two sides with my boots, but my bravado wilts and I crawl all the way to the spot where the guidebook insists a fixed rope should be hanging.

I should have checked the publishing date of the book: the rope is nowhere to be found. Either I wait for the rope the inept

Frenchmen brought with them or attempt to descend the ice wall without any protection. I don't have much time to make up my mind, since the hour for rock falls approaches.

It will be at least an hour before the French team arrives, so I decide to go it alone. But just as I'm about to lower myself over the icy lip, two Italian alpinists cross the ridge to where I stand and graciously offer to let me use their rope to rappel down. For the remainder of the afternoon I watch as these two forty-something shoe factory workers, who live for their weekend climbs, maneuver effortlessly through the icy terrain. Although we can barely communicate, I learn volumes about the reverence these two men have for the terrain and the compassion they hold for their fellow climbers. The contrast to the Frenchmen is striking.

Back at the hut, I catch a glimpse of the French climbers, but when they spot me they duck back into the crowded lodge and disappear from view. Guess I'll write off the ice screws.

Finally I make it back to Chamonix, thanks to a lift from my Italian partners. When I get to my tent I see that all my gear is gone. Makes sense. Based on the schedule the Burgess twins and I worked out, I'm now officially twenty-four hours overdue. The weather has been serene, so that can't account for my tardiness.

No, there's only one explanation: I have to be dead. And so, it goes without saying, I won't be needing my gear any longer. Climbing is a tight-budgeted world, so the longer gear sits without an owner, the more likely it is that someone will walk off with it.

I head off to the Bar National to show my face around and prove that rumors of my demise have been greatly exaggerated. Just as I figured, my friends act as though they've seen a ghost. "Hey, look, everybody, it's Whittaker," I hear someone shout.

"In the flesh, mates," I grin. "Alive and quite well." As I begin to recount my adventures, I know all my gear will be safely back in my tent by morning.

The summer only gets better when my old buddy Tony joins us in Chamonix. It's great to be climbing again with the man who introduced me to the game. Tony and I hit some difficult routes, but I'm still eager to tackle the Courtes, which is considered something of a test piece—and is rather ambitious for my first season. One evening in August, as my eight-week sojourn in the Alps is drawing to a close, I meet a man named Larry, a charismatic American climber with seven seasons in the Alps under his belt who has been well received among the British climbing elite. He has learned that I hope to attempt the Swiss Route on the Courtes, and he tells me he wants to join me. For the first time, my plan to tackle the Courtes as a rookie doesn't seem so foolish: I've got a ringer in Larry. Tempering my excitement is the realization that I have to tell Tony I'm dumping him for another partner—one I've just met. I break the news to him, and though Tony accepts my decision stoically, I feel despicable for abandoning my friend and climbing mentor. Just a few hours later, however, Tony arrives back at our camp looking quite a bit more chipper than when I last left him.

"Whittaker," he says, "I've found someone who's going to partner me on the Courtes. Mind if we tag along?"

The next morning the four of us catch a bus to Argentières and start the grueling five-hour plod into one of the most stunning mountain cirques in the Western Alps. By 3 A.M. we've washed down our muesli with tea, stuffed our bivy gear into our packs, and headed over the glacier to the foot of the climb. Ascending the steep valley wall, we arrive at the *bergschrund*, a gaping crevasse where the glacier has torn itself away from the Courtes' North Face. After nearly a half hour of searching for a spot where we can cross, Larry graciously concedes the honors to me.

I cautiously peek over the lip of the "schrund" to get some sense of the distance I'll need to leap across. Because I desperately want to justify Larry's confidence in me, I pretend as though jumping across this five-foot-wide abyss is no big deal. Before I can change my mind, I throw my body out into the darkness of the chasm. As soon as my crampons rip into the frozen wall, I fling the curved steel tips of my two axes wildly into the ice. To my relief, I stick—but the faint beam of my headlamp reveals that I have to climb twelve feet of dauntingly steep ice capped by an overhang.

"What do you think, youth?" Tony shouts, his voice sounding strangely comforting. I realize how happy I am that he came along. Now I have two reasons not to falter.

"Walker Spur: up or off!" I grunt, offering the phrase that has become something of a mantra for Tony and me. We first heard it from a Japanese mountaineer who told us he was about to solo the difficult Walker Spur; when the climber saw I was incredulous that he would attempt this route on his own, he gave that matter-of-fact explanation. "Walker Spur: up or off!" is now the expression we call on when we face a challenge out on our climbs.

After a couple of minutes of wild flailing, I chop through the overhanging lip, pull myself up, and flop onto the ice flow like a walrus.

Chipping a platform into the gently sloping slab is easy, and I place a couple of ice screws into the glacier to bring the crew over. Tony is the first one to come up.

"Good lead," he says as he belays his partner. I'm relieved that he's decided to put my selfish behavior behind him.

When Larry's turn comes to make the crossing, I'm shocked at what I see: he makes three flailing attempts before finally gaining the stance.

"Not much of an ice climber," Larry apologizes. "Thank God you are. I'm more of a rock man. I just really wanted to do this route."

I can't believe what I'm hearing. Back at "Bar Nash" Larry exuded cool and confidence. Tony pretends to be tinkering with some equipment, but I detect a smug "you've-made-your-bed-now-sleep-in-it" expression on his face.

I take the lead, and as dawn breaks I'm being belayed from the bottom of the Narrows—three hundred feet of 70-degree granite slabs crisscrossed by slender veins of ice. On this steep, exposed, and technically demanding terrain, sometimes the front points of my crampons are embedded deep into the ice, while at other times I'm balanced on the tips from tiny horizontal rock ledges. Often I'm able to locate only a half inch of ice into which I drive my axe, and I have to pray that it holds.

Two hours into this tenuous climbing, a block of granite the size of a tombstone whizzes past my head, plummeting into the glacier a thousand feet below. When I reach the lip of the Narrows, I learn where the rock came from. As the day has worn on, the weather has become sultry, and the sun is now melting large obelisks of granite out of the ice and sending them toppling down the face. Frighteningly, we're still 250 feet below this hazard; we're horribly exposed. To safeguard the others, I climb as swiftly as possible, periodically stopping as a large rock breaks loose and hurtles down past me. Within forty minutes I'm above the rocks, and Larry soon joins me. When I look down I see Tony belaying his partner from the last ice screw I placed.

And that's when it happens. A chunk of granite more than a foot thick and several feet long is freed from the ice and careens straight toward Tony.

"Tony!" I scream. "Look out! Rock!"

If the rock hits Tony, it won't just kill him, it will probably rip his body and the ice screw away from the tiny ledge, no doubt also dragging his partner to his death.

As the rock thunders toward him, Tony dives up onto the ice screw in a crouch, four feet of slack rope lying between him and the mountain. At the last possible moment he heaves his body up and off the mountain.

My eyes shut instinctively. When I open them again, Tony lies limp at the end of his belay rope, suspended by the single ice screw. My throat goes tight and I feel as if I'm going to vomit. If Tony had been my climbing partner, he'd have been above the granite projectiles by now.

With slow, cautious movements, Tony pulls himself into a sitting position.

"Whittaker," he calls up casually, "happen to have a change of underwear in your pack?"

Relieved that he's alive, I begin laughing. "Not that I don't need," I shout.

On the descent I let the other three go well ahead of me, as I'm physically and emotionally exhausted and more than a little embarrassed over my shoddy treatment of Tony. I certainly managed to get my precious climb in, but in the process I also dumped the guy who introduced me to climbing, who rescued me from my miserable life on the rig.

When I finally arrive at the hut at the mouth of the valley, Tony looks worried.

"Something strange is going on inside," he insists.

I poke my head through the door in time to see the bear-like owner force a group of customers to vacate a table.

"What did they do to deserve that?" I ask.

"It's not what they did," Tony whispers. "It's what we did."

A moment later, the owner produces a freshly laundered tablecloth and sets up a feast at the table—bottles of red wine, bowls of soup, several baguettes, plates of green beans and potatoes. With great flourish he waves over two sturdy-looking helicopter *gendarmes*, the ones who patrol the mountain passes.

"What the hell are you talking about?" I ask Tony. "What did we do?"

"Not so loud," Tony says, waving to the *gendarmes*, who have just spotted us. "When I got here, those two blokes asked me what route we'd just done and how long it had taken. But my

French is even more feeble than yours, and I thought they asked how many of us were in our climbing party."

"So what's the big deal?"

"So I told them *four*. That's all I said, '*Quatre*.' The next thing I know they're patting me on the back, whistling and shouting for the *patron*. Listen, they think we climbed the North Face of the Courtes in four hours."

"But Tony, that's . . . that's . . ."

"A bloody record," he says faintly. "No one's come close to pulling off the Swiss Route in four hours."

The *gendarmes* are now motioning us over to the table.

"How long'd it take us anyhow?" I ask as we walk slowly to the table. Our two high-altitude constables stand and toast us, saying something in French that sounds terribly grand.

"Nine hours," Tony whispers.

We eat a hearty supper, then watch the *gendarmes* fly off in their helicopter. After dinner we decide that as long as we don't register the climb with the French guides, nothing more will come of it.

But when we arrive back in Chamonix the next afternoon, caked in sweat and dust from the trail, we find that word of our supposed feat has spread quickly through the climbing community. A celebrated French climbing guide has put out word that he wants to meet the daring young Brit who led the charge up the North Face of the Courtes in four hours. Maybe the time has come for me to get out of Chamonix.

Not long afterward, however, we learn that a Frenchman has soloed the Swiss Route on the Courtes in three and a half hours. Just after that, a Brit knocks it off in two and a half. Strange, but if we didn't know better, Tony and I would swear that our bold four-hour climb set into play an international alpine speed trial on the Courtes.

CHAPTER 4
Lots of Pluck

My Christmas trip to the Matterhorn gets off to a wretched start. Maybe it's an omen, but then again I've never been particularly adept at noticing such things. I tend to blow right by the signposts.

It seems Tom Hurley has forgotten his passport. No real surprise there, but since he's an hour late meeting us, our driver, my friend Ken, insists we have no time to retrieve the travel documents. We've got to catch the last ferry across the English Channel to Calais.

Ken, already seething at Tom, drives like the clappers to make the ferry just in time. British immigration officials are hardly thrilled that Tom is missing his passport, but they let him on the boat. The big question is what French immigration will do.

As we roll off the ferry in Calais, three lines of vehicles, mainly heavy trucks, creep toward the customs and immigration checkpoint.

"Here goes your shortest trip to the continent ever," Ken mumbles.

"Let me just stow away in your trunk," Tom pleads for the umpteenth time.

"I told you, forget about it!" snaps Ken. "If they catch you, we're all screwed. And we can kiss the climb goodbye."

Tom leans his massive head against the window and looks outside. Gazing out at the twelve-foot-high chain link fence, he suddenly opens the car door and proclaims, "Meet you wankers on the other side." Before we know it he's disappeared in the line of huge trucks ahead of us. Apparently the floodlights and barbed wire weren't enough of a deterrent.

"Next time we see him," Ken ruminates, "he'll probably have a Doberman pinscher muckeled onto his arse." The vision seems to cheer Ken up for the first time since we picked Tom up at the service café on the M6 expressway. As we move between two trucks, I catch a glimpse of a shadowy figure scaling the fence. He pulls himself over in a single powerful jerk and slips back into the shadows.

Fifteen minutes later we find Tom standing casually under a street lamp. "One international border down, one to go," he laughs. "But damn it's cold out there."

Ken looks furious, but Tom is oblivious to our driver's mounting irritation. This partnership is shaping up to be a disaster.

When we reach the crossing into Switzerland, we find soldiers with machine guns patrolling the checkpoint. Tom talks us into stuffing him into a bivy sack, tossing him on the car's roof rack, and piling more bags on top of him. Ken watches his pristine roof sag under the load. When the guards wave us into the Switzerland, he steps on the gas, flying down the highway through the white, frigid landscape.

"Pretty cold out there," I say after a few minutes. "Probably ought to pull over and get Tom off the roof."

"Screw him," Ken announces. "Let him stay up there for a while."

I decide not to push the issue any further, but soon Tom is desperately banging on the roof. We can hear his muffled pleas for help, but Ken just cranks up the volume on the radio. I try calculating the windchill based on our speed, but the number I keep coming up with seems too horrible to ponder.

After ten more minutes Ken stops the car and I drag a frozen, corpse-like Tom off the roof. He doesn't utter a word, probably because he can't stop his teeth from chattering.

Arriving in Zermatt four hours later, we track down the mayor, an alpine buff, who confirms what we already suspected: the weather stinks. Two climbers have already been avalanched off the Matterhorn's North Face, which we are about to climb. But, he says, for the next two days the weather might cooperate.

The next day, we catch a chairlift as far as it will go up the mountain, then post-hole through calf-deep snow. By nightfall we reach the Hornli Hut, a hotel that is closed for the winter. The mayor told us that we'd find an unlocked basement window, but he obviously never bothered notifying the hotel owners of the arrangements—we find all the windows bolted tight. Tom eventually pries open a window with his ice axe and we escape the cold, building a fire in the ancient potbellied stove.

At 3 A.M., after just five hours of sleep, we head out across an enormous snowfield by the light of our headlamps. After crossing the *bergschrund*, a deep fissure between the glacier and the icy North Face of the Matterhorn, we face the daunting task ahead. Unroped, each of us packing thirty pounds of bivouac and climbing gear, we begin our steady diagonal ascent up the mountain's face, climbing through a maze of black ice and unconsolidated snow. By the time dawn begins to pale the winter sky, we've reached the top of the initial ice field, some fifteen hundred feet above the *bergschrund*. The mountain rears up before us into a watery sky with no clear line of ascent, just a jumble of frozen rock, ice, and snow. We reckon that just under nine hours of daylight remain, and today will either make or break our climb.

With Ken in the lead, we forge our way up the mountain. After about four hundred feet, I take over. The terrain varies between snow-covered rock and black ice that our crampons and ice tools can barely scratch. Much of the ice, in fact, is frozen so hard that we're forced to avoid it rather than use it as a fast, convenient way up the face. By noon we're totally enveloped in cloud, with no reference points to head for. I've climbed through Scottish winters and tackled ice routes in the Alps during the summer, but those experiences have done nothing to prepare me for these wretched conditions.

While leading one of the pitches, I kick my left boot into the ice as I have a thousand times before and feel something give way. Looking down, I'm horrified to see that I've bent one of the two steel crampon points projecting from the front of my boot.

"Never heard of that happening before," says Tom, trying to sound optimistic.

"Now you have," I grumble as I'm being pelted with rock-hard pellets of ice and snow that are blowing off the mountain's face. The headache that has raged between my ears since I left the Hornli Hut now feels as though someone parked a lorry on my skull.

By dusk we're desperately searching for a place to dig in for the long night ahead. It is 5 P.M., and we use our last remaining strength to chip out a tiny ledge in the ice for our bivy sacks. After locating an ice-filled crack, we pound two pitons into the rock and use them to anchor us to the mountain.

As we crawl into our bags, our feet dangling over the three thousand feet of mountainside we've just climbed, Tom informs us, "The trick is not to drop a boot down the face." Of more concern to me, however, is preparing for the frigid thirteen-hour night that's about to engulf us. Gazing down at the lights of Zermatt, five thousand feet beneath us, I suddenly remember the date.

"Merry Christmas, boys," I announce, reaching carefully into my sleeping bag for the little package my brother, Giles, handed me before I left Edinburgh a lifetime ago. I discover an airline bottle of Lagavulin single malt Scotch whisky and a slice of Christmas cake. We each cram a piece into our dry mouths, then pass around the bottle.

"Sixteen years to brew," I mumble, by way of a toast, "and two seconds to drink."

No sooner have the thimble-sized shots of alcohol slid down our throats than the winds commence to howl and the snowfall becomes heavier. As the winter storm engulfs us, completely obscuring the comforting lights of Zermatt, I realize that sleep is not an option this evening.

I duck down inside my bag as spindrift avalanches roar down the mountain, pounding my fragile little cocoon. Unlike full-on avalanches, these scaled-down versions aren't lethal, but the snow, which pours over me for several minutes at a time, invades my bag and burns my exposed skin like scalding water. Worse, the snow collects behind me, constantly straining to wedge me off my precarious perch. Throughout the night I push myself against the rock face, fighting the cold and straining to keep out the onrushing snow. I pull my bivy sack over my head to protect myself from the snow and the frigid air. The storm's violent blasts of wind suck the air out of my protective cocoon through the tiny makeshift breathing hole, then instantly reinflate it with an ear-shattering bang. If my bivy sack tears apart, I've no one to blame but myself, since I stitched it together on my girlfriend's sewing machine.

When morning finally comes, the mountain is plastered with fresh snow. Because we're not used to the altitude, we have had no respite from our headaches. We watch as clouds billow up from the valley below and envelop us.

"Ruddy abysmal," announces Tom, his sense of humor long since depleted. In the present whiteout conditions, none of us can spot any landmarks to shoot for, and the wind makes all attempts at communication between climber and belayer futile.

Tom leads our unconvincing charge up the face, but after two brutal hours the futility of our quest becomes apparent. The blasts of wind haven't let up, and my nerves are shot to hell. We have to make our way back to the Hornli Hut to get off this mountain, but there's no way we can descend along the ground we've covered. Even if we could down-climb, the huge North Face is now covered in so much loose snow that it would take at least two full days. With only six pitons and very few places to use them, rappelling the route is not an option. Our only chance of making it off the mountain is by gaining the ridge. Of course, this new undertaking proves equally difficult. With belay anchors ranging from poor to nonexistent, traversing sideways over this terrain is nerve-wracking and incredibly slow-going—in all likelihood it takes just as long as it would have to make the summit. Nine miserable hours after we emerged from our sleeping bags and recommenced the climb, the last remaining light slinks off over the horizon and curls up for the night. Our world goes black. With no stars overhead, the faint beams of our headlamps become our only guide.

Continuing along in the driving snow and biting wind, we at last reach the ridge, a welcome parking lot where we dig down into the soft snow, crawl into our bivy sacks, and drop off into a deep, dreamless sleep. Sometime in the night the storm dies off, and we awaken to see the sun shining down on our battered, motley crew—the first rays we have glimpsed on this entire, ill-fated expedition. We take our time, soaking up the warmth, eating muesli and drinking tea.

With the break in the weather, we decide to shoot for the summit once again. But Ken, having already climbed the Matterhorn in the summer, tells Tom and me to go ahead without him. "I'll wait for you here," he says.

All the snow that has fallen in the past thirty hours has completely obscured the trail. As Tom and I head off, we can't even determine whether we should remain on the ridge or traverse over onto the East Face. Ultimately choosing to stay on the ridge, we plod along, often struggling through waist-deep powder. After an hour and a half an armada of clouds blows in, and we both know that another storm can't be far away. Once the white curtain falls, we'll have little chance of locating Ken again. No time for summits: it's time to get the hell off this mountain. We head back down the ridge and find Ken.

Ken, Tom, and I tromp down the mountain, relieved that we're finally putting an end to this awful trip. But due to the whiteout and the fresh snow blanketing the terrain, nothing looks familiar to Ken. The ridge becomes impassable, so we zig onto the mountain's East Face, where we encounter moderate terrain. After twenty minutes of encouraging progress, we arrive at the first in a series of overhangs. To "suss" out the best route, Ken leads the way down a snow-covered slab.

As he begins down-climbing, however, his crampon snags the gaiter on his other leg. Ken pitches violently forward and begins somersaulting like a load of clothes in a dryer. He's tumbling down a slab straight toward the lip of another overhang, and Tom and I can do nothing but watch. Moments before launching into a deadly free fall, Ken manages to spread his boots out wide, bury his ice axe in the snow, and grind to a miraculous stop with only four feet to spare.

Tom and I look at one another, trying to register the near disaster we've just witnessed. But I turn away, afraid Tom can read in my eyes what shot through my brain during our partner's fall: "There go half our ropes!" Instead of thinking, "Oh, shit! Ken's going to die!" I was concerned only because he was about to leave Tom and me stranded.

I'm tired of what this mountain is doing to me. Yesterday, after seven hours traversing that snow-covered wall, I resigned myself to the fact that I was going to die and performed my basic mountaineering functions barely conscious of what I was doing. Convinced that I was already a dead man, I feared nothing—dead men do not fear death. Yet, miraculously, we made the ridge and earned a reprieve; I could feel life flooding back into my deadened soul. Now to see that hope nearly wrenched from me is unbearable. I can feel tears leaking out from my eyes as Tom and I churn down the slope to reach Ken.

"Damn, you had me worried," I tell Ken as we dust him off. "Thought you had the car keys in your pocket." He and Tom both laugh. We have no choice but to continue on, so the three of us start our descent once again as the clouds boil up to meet us.

Traveling from one overhang to the next, we are down to just four pitons when the East Face begins to tip up in an alarming fashion. The weather continues to worsen, and the wind blasts straight up into our faces, making it increasingly difficult to get our ropes down the rappels. As the hours dribble by, we slowly zigzag down gullies and traverse out onto little slabs.

Then we reach an impasse. With no other options, we begin clearing the snow off the hump of a boulder covered with ice. Using our axes to chip a groove around its back, we create a channel into which we can lay the rope. I watch as Tom eases his belly over the lip of the overhang and descends out of view, and as Ken follows suit. When I finally make my way down the rope I find my companions perched on a tiny ledge 120 feet below. In the swirling clouds it's impossible to tell how much further we've left to go.

With a crazy smile, Tom holds up a piton. "Our last one," he laughs. We grope about our tiny ledge for something—anything—to hammer it into. But when Tom pounds the piton into the ice-filled crack of a boulder precariously situated on the lip of the drop, I can only stare in disbelief. This rock, about the size of a beanbag chair, inspires no confidence as an anchor, particularly because the crack appears to run completely through it. Nevertheless, Tom threads one end of our rope through the piton and tosses it down the cliff.

"Rope!" he shouts.

"Who the hell do you think is down there?" I ask.

"You can never be too careful," he reminds me. "OK, Whittaker, off you go."

I take another look at the sketchy anchor and just shake my head. "You must be shitting me! I'm not rappelling off that."

He merely shrugs. "OK, give me the rope. I'll go," he says, reaching for the rope clutched in my hands. Instinctively, I snatch it away.

"No, I'll go." In a split second I've processed the situation. If the piton pulls, whoever is attached to the rope will be the lucky one.

He merely plummets into space; everything will be taken care of in the blink of an eye. It's the two other bastards left behind on this slab who'll become the real victims—no place to bivouac, no way to climb back up, and rescue out of the question, since no one will even think of looking for us on the East Face.

To my surprise, the piton doesn't blast out of the rock as I rappel over the edge of the cliff and down to a steep snow bank. Now all that separates me from the glacier is 150 feet of terrain that is steep—sloping away from me at 55 degrees—but manageable.

"We're almost home," I shout up at Tom and Ken, praying that the piton continues to hold for them. As a precaution I slam my ice axe into the snow and situate myself so that if the peg does pull I'll have the other end of the rope.

They both descend safely. We collect our ropes and cautiously make our way down to the massive field of white.

Once on the glacier we walk on firm, flat snow for the first time in what seems like an eternity. It squeaks beneath our crampons, making the most beautiful sound imaginable. My heart beats calmly now, and in my mind, the three of us are basking in the heat thrown off by that old potbellied stove in the basement of the Hornli Hut.

Then I spot the fracture lines in the snow. Maybe they've been here all along and I just refused to see them in my joy at reaching the glacier. Whatever the case, accompanying our every step is a hollow thud rather than a comforting squeak. No doubt about it: we're walking on top of an eggshell of wind-packed snow, perhaps only a few feet thick. Thousands of tons of snow with a void underneath—and all that supports it is the adhesion of one crystal of snow to the next.

The settling snow could go juddering away at any moment, shooting us down a quarter mile of 30-degree slope, then straight off the edge of an eight-hundred-foot cliff. Here we are, survivors by a miracle, or two, only a bloody half mile from the safety of the Hornli Hut, and the snow about to drop us into eternity.

Every step now is like advancing in a minefield. Each new foothold hurls up a sickening fear that crunching snow is the sound of the ledge about to shear off. We "think ourselves light" and move forward, slowly and fearfully, advancing across the precipice; then gradually pick up the pace, afraid to linger too long. By the final few hundred yards, our frayed nerves are driving our accelerators, and we're moving as fast as men in our condition can travel. Ahead of us is the Hornli Hut. Finally, breathing hard, we leave that terrible snowfield and climb the ridge to the hotel. As Tom jimmies open the hotel's basement window, I scan the glacier behind us, waiting for the high mountain avalanche to come crashing down. After Tom gets the window open and we dive into the basement, we pull off our gear, none of us speaking. Desperate for warmth—and to unfreeze the crampon that clings so fiercely to the sole of my boot—I try to start a fire in the stove, but the air in the metal chimney pipe is too cold to get a good draw. Using whatever I find handy, I soak the kindling in white gas from our portable stove, drop a match on it, and . . . *BOOM!*

The fuel-soaked wood explodes as though fired from a cannon. In the blast my icicle-covered beard and down jacket begin burning.

Tom and Ken sit on the floor and watch the flailing madman trying to beat out the flames with his gloved hands. After what we've been through, they're far too tired to lend any assistance. "Whittaker, don't bloody hog the fire all to yourself," laughs Tom. "Extinguish yourself and tend to the stove. It's cold in here, youth. In case you haven't noticed."

Back at the Whittaker family home in Ash, a sleepy little hamlet in Hampshire, I sit in the garage with my father, Warren, plucking a large white turkey. Recently retired from the military, Warren has become secretary of the Army Rifle Association. In keeping with his character he's turned the twenty-hour-a-week position into a fifty-hour-a-week job, setting new standards for marksmanship through better training, more practice, and more exacting ammunition standards. Talking to Warren is a difficult undertaking, due mainly to a lack of practice. Most of my upbringing took place in boarding schools, and when I was home, my mother shouldered most of the burden.

But right now conversing with him—or with anyone—is particularly difficult for one simple reason: my mouth looks like an exploded sausage. To save time and assure security on the Matterhorn, I often clenched carabiners, ice screws, and pitons between my teeth. In the frigid conditions on the mountain the metal would inevitably stick to my lips or tongue, and with no other options available to me, I'd just rip the hardware out of my mouth, taking small divots of tissue with it.

As painful as talking is—and as painful as plucking the turkey is, with fingertips deeply cracked by the cold of a Swiss winter—I'm savoring this moment. Tethered to the Matterhorn's North Face, with my tiny square of Christmas cake, I realized how important my family is to me, and in that desolate moment when death seemed not just a possibility but the sure result, I saw that I would die without having ever let them know it.

Having been given a reprieve from death, I will not waste another opportunity to express myself to my family. As fate would have it, the Royal Mail and my uncle Roger conspired to help me.

Every Christmas Uncle Roger sends us a turkey. This year, however, he was late getting it off, and the postal service was even later delivering it. The bird didn't arrive until two days after Christmas—perfectly coinciding with my and my brother's arrival at the family home. Christmas is in full swing at the Whittakers', albeit on New Year's Eve.

Since Warren was raised on a North Wales hill farm, he does most of the plucking while I do most of the talking. Just as the bird is about to run out of feathers, I unload everything that's been kicking around in my heart since I hung there tethered to a hillside above Zermatt. I tell him how much he and Mum mean to me, how I love them, and how wretched I'd feel if I were to die without their knowing this.

Warren doesn't say much at first, just pulls the few remaining feathers from the bird and watches them drop into the box that sits between us. But when he starts asking questions, I know in my gut that he respects what I do and who I've become. After all, ever since he followed Edmund Hillary's Everest expedition, he's been an armchair mountaineer. And something about the look in his eyes tells me that, although we haven't had much of a past, we're on the verge of having a future.

Tom Hurley dies a few winters after our Matterhorn expedition. While attempting a winter ascent of the Droites, one peak over from the Courtes, he apparently took his climbing harness off or didn't cinch it up tight enough; all rescuers found was his rope and harness lying in the snow.

The news hits me harder than I would have expected. I climbed with Tom only that one time, and I met him perhaps another half dozen times. Still, he won my admiration on our Matterhorn expedition. Sure, he caused some petty frustrations at the trip's outset, but in the midst of that wretched experience he took charge and led every inch of the harrowing traverse. I never would have come so close to the summit without his decisive and courageous leadership, and I'm sure that even Ken believes, as I do, that we wouldn't have made it off that mountain without him.

Though I didn't know Tom well, I always considered him a kindred spirit, someone who helped me understand the kind of person I hoped to become. He did what he did—kayak white-water, climb difficult ice and rock, build and race motorcycles, whatever—because of his exuberant love for life, not because he was trying to impress others.

Try as I might, I've never understood how a human life should be judged. If it is in terms of financial wealth or charitable works, then Hurley's life was an abject failure. But if it is by the sense of loss others experience at a person's death and the warmth in their heart they feel whenever they remember that person, then Tom's life was a resounding success.

I've never quite been able to figure out where people like Tom Hurley go when their time here runs out. But, whatever his address in the cosmos might be, I still feel his presence at times, especially on those rare occasions when I find myself covered in flames. I imagine he's sitting back, laughing hard at the whole, ludicrous scene—and not even thinking about lending a hand.

CHAPTER 5
Living the Dream

Deep inside the Trou du Glaz, I struggle to drag my equipment bags so that the cave exploration I've been invited on can continue. I'm roughly two Empire State Buildings beneath the earth's surface, in a network of tunnels more than twenty miles long.

In June 1976 I graduated with an advanced degree in Adventure Education from Moray House College in Edinburgh, Scotland. And while it's true that most people who secure this prestigious qualification wouldn't immediately head to the subterranean caverns of France, the Trou du Glaz is simply part of my carefully laid-out plan. As I see it, I'm long on professional qualifications and short on hands-on "salty" experience. So, instead of going to work and spending years trying to fit in all the adventures I need to give me credibility, I've opted to dedicate a block of time to getting my hands blistered, cramming in as much activity as possible—caving in France, sailing the Atlantic, kayaking the Colorado River through the Grand Canyon, climbing big walls in Yosemite Valley, mountaineering in the Tetons, ascending frozen waterfalls in the Canadian Rockies, and summiting Mount McKinley in Alaska. If I survive, I should return home with the type of outdoor pursuits resumé that will open doors.

Here, in one of the Trou du Glaz's tortuous limestone passages, I stumble in the darkness as the tiny flame on the front of my calcium-carbide headlamp sputters and burps. I've been traveling for nearly five hours, and the carbide is almost spent—as am I. My haul bags are heavy and hopelessly awkward. Finally I thrash my way out to the top of a vertical shaft that drops into blackness. A rope is suspended from three bolts drilled into the wall.

"Piece of cake," I tell myself. When I peer over the edge of the pitch I glimpse two lights flickering down below. Like me, my companions are hauling equipment down into the lower reaches of this 2,600-foot-deep cavern.

Before transferring onto the rope and descending, I must first properly situate the two gear bags I've been pulling through this narrow rock tube. I wedge my body against the wall and drag the first bag next to me. The second refuses to budge, but if I tug on the rope too hard, the bag could suddenly pop free and drag me straight down into the chasm. I brace myself by pressing my legs against the wall and then tug with all my might.

Craccckkkkkk. The sound is like a rifle shot as a chunk of limestone behind my shoulders breaks free from the wall. All that prevents the rock from plummeting down the pitch onto my two companions is the pressure of my body trapping it against the passage wall.

Did my climbing partners hear the noise? Was it loud enough to alert them to the danger looming above their heads? Try as I might to keep it in place, the rock is slipping.

"Rock! Move now!" I shout, realizing that, like the limestone block I'm straining to hold, I'm on the verge of tumbling down the blackened shaft. If I let go of the rock, I'll save myself, but my teammates will probably be killed. I've got to hang on a few moments longer. Once again, I scream down to my companions, but there's no reply.

Then it happens. The rock shoots out and plunges on a deadly free fall, and the force sends my body lurching against the rock wall at the head of the pitch. When my helmet slams into the rock wall, my headlamp dies out and I'm swallowed in darkness. As I lose balance and tumble outward, I lunge for the fixed line that protects the traverse. I feel my hands make contact, but I've managed to grab the line from the jammed gear bag instead of the fixed rope.

Hanging in space, desperately clutching the rope, I scream, "Rock! Rock! Rock!" as the twenty-pound chunk of limestone careens toward my companions at 120 miles per hour.

The faint lights of their headlamps disappear, and next I hear yelled obscenities explode upward from the depths. Well, at least I can tell they're both alive—they must have ducked into a passageway to avoid the rock. But the damn ingrates have no idea who's hanging about above them.

Sweat trickles into my eyes and the rope cuts into my hands. This bloody gear bag, it seems, has saved my hide. After catching my breath, I pull myself back into the cramped passageway. Lying there listening to the wild thumping of my heart, I want to get the hell out of this cave. I'm an experienced spelunker who has spent hundreds of hours guiding underground, but never have I had this feeling of dread. In the past the sheer isolation has bothered me— all alone, suspended somewhere in the bowels of the earth, engulfed in darkness—but this experience is different. Though I'm a skeptic when it comes to the mystical or supernatural, I can sense there's something wrong about this cavern. It's as if there's a malevolent presence down here, and it's hunting my companions and me.

Of course, I have a job to finish, so I click on my auxiliary light and get to work. But there's one thing I know: I've spent enough time wandering beneath the earth's surface—it's time for me to get on with my plan and seek my fortunes on the high seas and in the vast wilderness of North America.

Yosemite is what I've been aiming for all along. For four years I've been dreaming about this hallowed land of smooth granite and enormous walls, this mythic testing ground for the body and soul.

It's the summer of 1977, and over the past several months I've followed a circuitous path to get here. After leaving the caves of France, I hitchhiked through Spain to Gibraltar, where I hopped a ketch across the Atlantic. Once in the States I hitchhiked to

Chicago and began working construction in the bitter cold winter months. A few months on the job gave me enough cash to head out to Vail, where I beat myself up on the slopes and managed to blow through most of my money. From there, Yosemite beckoned.

But now that the piton has snapped, I'm starting to think that Yosemite was perhaps not my best plan. This is the eleventh pitch, more than a thousand feet up the face of the Chouinard-Herbert route, directly under the Afro-Cuban Flakes, the major roof on the Sentinel.

Just a moment ago I was hanging on rock, on the last step of my nylon five-rung ladder (known as an etrier), and now I'm accelerating earthward, tangled in my climbing rope. The sensation of free fall is sickening, bewildering. *What the hell's going on? How did I screw up?*

The rope finally yanks tight and arrests my plunge, and I swing lazily over a dizzying panorama of meadows, woodlands, and the Merced River some 2,500 feet below. My partner, a young Brit named Chris Gore, holds on with grim determination. He was 120 feet below me, but now we can practically touch. The force of 220 pounds of free-falling climber and gear has jerked my 135-pound belayer three feet above his belay bolts. Chris has been making a name for himself on the British climbing scene, but, fresh off the Greyhound bus, he's on his first Big Wall in Yosemite. He's never had so much air between him and the deck. And it shows: his face has turned as white as the knuckles on his belay hand.

"You OK?" he asks, obviously shaken by my sudden reappearance.

"I will be," I reply, "just as long as you don't relax your grip on that rope." I go to work untangling myself from the ropes that have twisted tight around my right arm and left leg—and that have given me serious rope burn. Chris lowers me the last few feet to his level, then grabs my leg and pulls me toward the wall. I clip myself into a sling that I placed on my way up, and Chris sinks back down into his belay seat.

"What happened up there?" he asks, looking much happier.

"This," I reply, holding up the head of the broken piton still attached to my etrier. "Must have been welded so far into the crack that I couldn't spot the break."

Climbing on fixed pieces is a common practice. In return for speed and convenience, however, you sacrifice the peace of mind that comes from placing your own hardware into the rock. On this route I was clipping my etrier into the network of weathered pitons (affectionately known as "old rusties") that jut out from the rock face. This sort of climbing is a bit like Russian roulette, ultimately, and I got the chamber with the bullet in it.

No time to dwell on such matters, however. Time to press on. Jamming my hands into the vertical crack in the rock's face and using the friction of my smooth-soled shoes, I free climb upward, back to the part of the route where I took my plunge. Here I have to switch over from free climbing to aid climbing using my etriers. I reach the spot where I left an etrier swinging in the wind, and with both feet balanced on the top rung, I reach upward to attach my other "et" through the eye of the piton above. In this round of Russian roulette, the chamber is empty, and in just three pitches Chris and I arrive at the top.

As the sun disappears over the horizon, we head toward the gully that will take us back to the valley floor, several thousand feet below. While we cut through the meadows I ask Chris about a certain section we ended up climbing after we inadvertently got off route. "Sure felt serious," I offer. "How would you rate it?"

"I'd put it around 5.11b," Chris says casually, no doubt used to negotiating rock of that dizzying difficulty.

All I can do is smile. It's been a good day on the crags.

Greg Child and Charlie Rowe give me my chance on El Capitan. When I first arrived in the valley in May, a climb of this length, severity, and technical difficulty was so far above my capabilities that it wasn't even on my wish list. But in the intervening three months I have been honing my skills with rock climbers from the upper echelons of the sport. As my capabilities expand, so do my dreams and aspirations.

I eagerly await the expedition, but not just because it's a chance to climb the Nose route on "El Cap": I also know that this will be my last climb in Yosemite. I'm running out of time on my tourist visa and have almost no cash in my pocket. Because of an arbitrary date stamped in my passport, I must strike out for Canada in a matter of days, but I yearn to stick around Yosemite. I've been here just a few months, but it feels more like a few years. To hell with the notion that time flies when you're busy. That's what happens if you're stuck in a routine, predictable existence; the years end up whipping by in a blur. Once you depart from the tried and tested, once you truly begin packing as much experience into each day as it'll hold, time grows outrageously fat.

Before the climb, Charlie and Greg fix ropes up to Sickle Ledge and then return to camp to collect our gear. After a last supper we head down to the base of El Capitan and bivy beneath the mind-bogglingly high granite wall above us. Thankfully, no bears discover us during the night. The next morning, we use mechanical ascenders, known as jumars, to haul our way up the fixed ropes, and by nightfall, sixteen pitches later, we devour our supper on the El Cap Tower, some two thousand feet above our starting point.

The rope burn I sustained a week ago on the Sentinel has come back to haunt me. The inside of my right elbow is a festering mess. Each morning I awaken tied into my sleeping bag, with my toes dangling above the valley floor, and I have to straighten my arm to break the adhesions that have formed during the night. This, of course, merely causes a half dozen new fissures that bleed freely.

For the next three days we battle not just the rock face but also the hot August sun. Several hours after sunrise on our final day spent clinging to the rock, I'm nearly crazy with thirst. Despite the blistering heat, I haven't broken a sweat in two days. We now regret our decision to abandon a gallon of water that was making our haul sack too heavy. I slip a stone into my mouth and suck on it, hoping I will draw some moisture out. Five minutes later I spit it out, bone dry.

When we finally top out and stand on the summit, having climbed more than three thousand vertical feet of granite, I'm gripped by the desire to do something symbolic. I pull off my rock boots, tie the laces together, and hang them in the branches of a nearby tree, an offering to the climbing gods. Since this is my last climb in the valley, it's only fitting that they should stay.

Wracked by thirst, we hurry across the cliff top to a spot where another climb known as Tangerine Trip tops out. Greg stashed a gallon of water here nearly two months ago. Stringy green organisms hang suspended in the liquid, causing my teammates to decline. But I am too thirsty to be put off, and when I bring the bottle to my lips, it tastes like gooey ambrosia. To my amazement, before I can remove the jug from my cracked lips, sweat blinds my eyes.

That evening, I walk with my girlfriend, nicknamed "Smelly," down to Rickson's Pinnacle, where the cool air snakes up the Merced River. As we lie here staring up at the stars in the night sky, I know that when I set off for Canada in the morning, I'll again be leaving her behind. This only makes leaving the valley that much harder. Smelly has stuck with me through some rough, tempestuous times. She was waiting for me when I got back from the oil rigs, and she came and met me in the States after I left on my adventures through France, Spain, and Gibraltar. No matter what direction life seems to pull us or what the distractions are, we always end up back together. So, although I feel the pain of our pending separation, I fight the tears and simply make plans to meet up with her in a few weeks.

Three nights later, I'm shivering in the doorway of a mission in Gastown, the old quarter of Vancouver, British Columbia, longing

to be back in Yosemite. The cold rain pelts down on me mock-
ingly. If the mission has run out of cots, it's going to be a long, wet
night. An Ian Tyson folk song blares out of a crowded bar across
the alley, and the lyrics plunge like a harpoon into my heart.

> *Four strong winds that blow lonely,*
> *Seven seas that run high,*
> *All these things that don't change,*
> *Come what may.*
> *But our good times are all gone,*
> *And I'm bound for moving on.*
> *I'll look for you if I'm ever back this way.*

After two days searching for employment without so much as a
nibble, I remember that Outward Bound runs two schools in
Canada and line up a phone interview. I land the job as an instructor and hop on a Greyhound bus to Keremeos, British Columbia.

Created in the United Kingdom during World War II, Outward
Bound originated as a result of the heavy losses that German
U-boats were inflicting on the British merchant fleet. Young, fit
sailors were dying while the "old dogs" often survived the attacks.
Lawrence Holt, owner of the Blue Funnel shipping line, asked his
friend Kurt Hahn to solve the problem, and Hahn, a German Jew
and renowned educator who had sought political asylum in
Britain, realized that what the youth needed was a training course
to toughen them physically and psychologically. Hahn designed
a program that used the wilderness as a backdrop to give the
sailors the tools necessary for survival. In his program, groups of
eight to ten strangers confront a variety of unnerving situations
that require teamwork, resourcefulness, courage, communication, and trust. The experience more often than not profoundly
transforms individuals, but much depends on the instructor, who
ensures the physical and emotional safety of the participants.

As soon as I begin working as an instructor, I realize that landing the job has been something of a coup. Just as my rock climbing ability improved dramatically during my summer at Yosemite, my skiing, winter mountaineering, and kayaking skills take a quantum leap in my tenure at the Canadian Outward Bound Mountain School. I'm surrounded by wild-eyed Canadian boys and expatriate Brits who are cutting their teeth on giant mountain peaks, frozen waterfalls, and rapid-filled rivers. "First ascents and redefining the possible" is the order of the day, and the cement that holds us together is made from laughter and mutual respect.

This joyous atmosphere, it turns out, is exactly what my spirits need. At this point I learn that even Smelly—who's hung with me throughout the previous seven years, who followed me to the States and then came north and met me in Canada—cannot put up with this lifestyle forever. She's told me that her affections are split between me and another—a man with a job, a car, and American citizenship. Smelly wants to live permanently in the States, and he offers an airline ticket and marriage. All I have is a blue rucksack with a Union Jack sewn on the front and a burning dream to make a major contribution to the outdoor pursuits profession. I've done stupid things in my life, hurt people's feelings, and regretted my words and actions, but until this point I've never experienced something that I couldn't somehow turn around. After she accepts the offer of the plane ticket and the wedding ring, however, I have long winter nights spent in igloos, snow caves, and back-country cabins to think about how I lost Smelly.

I thank God for the conviviality of the Outward Bound boys. Little by little, my open wound begins to heal.

In May of 1978, I return from an early season ascent of Mount McKinley convinced that my true strength as a mountaineer lies in the world's high mountains. Although my rock and ice climbing skills—both essential components of the so-called super alpine game—are solid, I'll never emerge as enough of a standout at these elements to attract international recognition. But, as I first observed in the Alps, my metabolism is extremely well-suited to high altitudes, so when I climb hard technical faces tucked away in remote mountain ranges where the effects of altitude are inescapable, I feel as though I've just begun to tap my potential.

When I arrive back in Keremeos, I run into an old friend from Wales, Bill March. The last time I saw March was two years ago, when he was assessing me for my Mountain Instructor's Certificate. Now he's in Canada directing an outdoor pursuits program at the University of Calgary. Over breakfast, he tells me about an outdoor program in Pocatello, Idaho, offering a graduate assistantship.

"Same place I spent a year getting my master's degree," March says, chewing a mouthful of eggs. "They pay your tuition and give you three hundred bucks a month. Not a lot, but I'm sure you've lived on less." When he sees that my eyes are beginning to glaze over, he adds, "On one side of Pocatello, you have the Grand Tetons, and on the other, City of Rocks and the white-water rivers are amazing."

Just before he drives back to Calgary, he graciously offers to write me a recommendation to "H" Hilbert, the program director at Idaho State University. A note from a respected climber like Bill March will open just about any door in the outdoor pursuits discipline—especially when it's to a trusted friend.

After he leaves, I wonder what the hell I'm thinking. This dyslexic and former academic underachiever has already defied the odds once by getting accepted to Nonington College of Physical Education, a wing college of the prestigious University of London, to train as a teacher. When I got admitted to Moray House College, it was largely due to my promise in adventure education. But a master's degree? It's pure lunacy. Still, H offers me the position, so I'm off to Pocatello.

Once at Idaho State (ISU), I cram just about every scrap of knowledge on the topic of outdoor education I can into my skull, and a year later, in the summer of 1979, I emerge as the proud owner of a Master of Arts in Student Personnel with an emphasis in outdoor programming in higher education. What's more, in Pocatello I've made close friends and fallen in love with a beautiful woman. And I've climbed extensively—in the Tetons, at City of Rocks, in Yosemite, in Boulder, Colorado, and around Salt Lake City. By now I've completed more than twenty "first ascents" on rock and ice, and kayaked more than five hundred miles down the Payette, Salmon, Snake, and Colorado Rivers. Though I can't say for certain what the future holds, I know I've found my calling.

After getting my degree, I head to Sun Valley, a choice destination for any outdoorsman—a place that also offers plenty of chances for me to earn some cash on the side. For the past few weeks I've worked as a carpenter, learning the trade fast, and as soon as ski season kicks in I'm assured a job in a surf-and-turf restaurant. The manager insists that if I'm not making $100 a night in tips, he'll fire me.

On this, the night after Thanksgiving, 1979, as I drive a borrowed VW bus back to Sun Valley from Pocatello, I reflect on the festive holiday I just spent with friends and look forward to the long winter on the slopes that awaits me. In the darkness of night, however, the two-lane Arco Highway that stretches between the tiny town of Blackfoot and Sun Valley begins to feel rather lonely, especially as Johnny Paycheck moans over the radio. I have the heater cranked to keep out the November chill, and dry wisps of spindrift snow dance across the road in front of me. On both sides, a moonscape of lava and petrified rock wanders off and takes up with the star-speckled horizon. But it's just a couple of hours until I get back to Sun Valley.

A few miles outside of Blackfoot, a herd of cattle straggles across the highway. I stop for a moment as the cows wander slowly in front of me, then grow impatient, gently nudging the van's bumper through the bovine roadblock. For the next few minutes, I flash my brights at oncoming vehicles to give them a heads-up about the potential hazard.

Then, way off across the Arco Desert, I see a pair of headlights. Almost immediately, I'm wondering whether to flash the approaching car. *Nah, by now the cows have no doubt cleared the road—don't want to do anything to disorient the driver in conditions like these.* But as the headlights grow larger and brighter, a strange uneasiness worms inside me, forcing goose bumps to sprout on my arms and the back of my neck. I can't pinpoint where it's coming from, but something tells me the approaching vehicle is locked on a collision course with my bus. Call it a premonition, but I've never been more sure about anything in my life.

I scan the roadside for someplace to pull over, but the highway has no shoulder, merely a wasteland of twisted and deformed lava rock. I have to plot out my options, but what options do I have? A voice from somewhere within my head urges me to head into the lane of the other vehicle to avoid the impending crash, but my rational mind wants none of that.

"Get a grip, Whittaker," I mumble, watching the headlights grow brighter, then tapping the brake and slowing to a crawl. "This ain't Hollywood. Real life doesn't work like that."

The vehicle speeds closer, the lights grow brighter. My universe slows, as moments tick by frame after frame. Just as that little voice predicted, the headlights drift lazily into my lane. Gripping the steering wheel with all my strength, I force my body back into the seat and brace for the impact.

CHAPTER 6
The Accident

When our two vehicles collide, my steering wheel slams into my chest, forcing the air in my lungs to explode from my mouth. Milk crates from the back of the microbus rocket past my head and crash through the windshield. In the moment of impact I glimpse the frightened face of a woman just before she disappears sideways toward the empty passenger seat and beneath the dashboard. Then my world fades to black.

When my eyelids open, a still hangs over the highway, and all is dim, the world appearing as it did when I worked deep in the ocean as a rig diver. Suddenly, my body convulses and my chest cavity expands, filling my empty lungs with the chilly night air— it's the involuntary impulse of an organism clinging to life. The searing pain of that first breath is excruciating, almost unbearable. *Does a newborn child experience this same agony with its first breath?* I shake the thought from my mind and focus on the present.

A few feet away, one of the other car's headlights oscillates on its wires, eerily resembling an eyeball dangling from its socket. It casts a yellow, hypnotic glow on the asphalt. The hot engines of our two vehicles emit a curious clicking noise as they cool in the frigid night air. The smell of radiator fluid, motor oil, and gasoline fills my nostrils. I'm hanging out of the space that the windshield once inhabited; fortunately the milk crates crashed through it a fraction of a second before my face did. Flopping over my head is the tiger lily I purchased to thank Susan Peterson for lending me her vehicle.

"Oh, God, no," I mutter. "Look at Susan's bus."

A pickup appears, slowly inching past the wreckage. With all my strength I lift myself up to wave at the driver, but he punches the accelerator and speeds away. No doubt he's hightailing it into Blackfoot to alert the authorities.

A low, muffled groan ekes out of the darkness and I instantly forget about Susan's mangled car and my own desperate situation. I struggle to pull myself back onto the driver's seat.

"You OK?" I shout out into the night. All I hear in reply is another groan. "Hello? Can you hear me?" I call out once again. The only sound that comes this time is the ticking of the cooling engines.

You've got to get to this girl, Whittaker.

Looking down at my legs, I notice that the pressure created by what must be a broken right femur has ripped apart my new Levi cords. Damn, just bought them this afternoon.

All right, Whittaker, you may have a broken leg, but you can still get out and give this girl some assistance. Do something.

I grab my left leg behind the knee and wriggle it free from where the dashboard and front seat have pinned it. After several minutes, I manage to extricate it. My foot dangles like a lifeless piece of meat at the end of my leg. I flop it out through the windshield.

Two broken legs. You're not going anywhere.

If I can't do anything to assist the woman, I've got to prevent my situation from getting worse. I have to be very careful. If my broken femur severs my femoral artery, I'll bleed to death in minutes. By wriggling into the space between the backseat and the roof of the vehicle I'm able to place my right thigh in traction and minimize the danger. For the next ten minutes I force myself to concentrate harder than I ever have before.

"You're in a pickle, Whittaker," I say aloud. "But you were in a pickle on Slip Knot and the Matterhorn. What about the time you wrapped your kayak around that rock on the South Fork of the Salmon and freed yourself by tearing it apart with a broken hand? You got out of those situations by making your mind work when it was overwhelmed and wanted to quit. And you forced yourself to act no matter how bloody scared it made you.

You've got to think things through as best you can and decide on a course of action."

I listen carefully to every word that comes out of my mouth. It's the only way not to lose my place and wander off. Things seem to be getting pretty jumbled in my mind now. I force myself to remember my mountain rescue training and soon I'm reciting a section from a textbook I once read. "The victim is stabilized, sedated, and transported to emergency care. Further assessment is carried out and, if stable, the victim will be taken to X-ray, then be prepped for surgery."

My mind ponders the scenario that will soon unfold. No use kidding myself: I'm a prime candidate for the surgeon's knife.

"Decisions are going to be made according to medical procedure, none of which will take into account who I am or what I do," I tell myself. "The doctors won't consult me before doing it."

"So what's the solution, damn it?" As when I was at the foot of the Chardonnet, the question-and-answer session helps me cut through the anxiety and focus on a course of action.

"The only solution I can see," I proceed, "is to speak to the surgeon, tell him why I came to America, tell him who Tom Whittaker is. Convince him to work for me, not by the book. Try and have him agree to get a second opinion before he does anything hasty, or send me someplace where they can do a better job." My leg begins to twist with spasms and my perch gets increasingly difficult to maintain. "You're gonna need all your mental faculties, old sport. That means no sedation, no drugs. You're gonna have to tough this one out."

Eventually another truck rumbles up, only this one stops. A young man with dark hair introduces himself as a local rancher and peers at the carnage through my driver's side window.

"Jesus," he mutters, "what do you need me to do?"

"Got a couple of busted legs and I need to keep the right one in traction," I inform him. "I'm starting to fade. Can you get in the back and help me support my upper body?" He looks a little uncertain but climbs inside and gives it a go, leaning his shoulder up against my back, easing the strain on my stomach muscles and arms. We sit in silence as we wait for an ambulance to arrive—I'm fresh out of chitchat.

Twenty minutes later, sirens wail and lights flash. Firemen go to work cutting through the van with compressed air tools and prying it apart to free my leg.

"Gotta be careful here," one of them shouts. "His foot is hanging on by threads. If we drop this section wrong, it's gonna take his foot."

After nearly an hour in the cold I've begun shivering uncontrollably. From my training in first aid and working on mountain rescues, I know this to be an indication of two things—shock and hypothermia. My spasming muscles cause the splintered ends of my broken bones to grind together, which sends excruciating jolts of pain through my nervous system. Using what's left of my will, I force myself to bring the shaking under control.

"Every cloud has a silver lining, Whittaker," I remind myself. "Injuries like this must be worth at least a half million dollars." In my head I start using the cash to purchase several acres of lakeside property in McCall, Idaho. After all, I've got to concentrate on something else, something besides the pain. I imagine building a house from scratch there among McCall's ponderosa pines. At some point in my delusion, I decide to remodel the place, rip out some walls, and install lots of glass out front, even a redwood deck. Whenever a medic tries talking to me, the structure collapses, the image dissolves, and I have to start over.

After nearly two hours, the firemen manage to extricate me from the twisted steel of the van and paramedics take over, wedging an ice-cold metal gurney beneath me and pulling me out. I try to make sense of the paramedics' grim expressions as they drape a blanket over me, whisk the gurney to an ambulance, and place me inside. Without even bothering to switch on the overhead light, they put an IV in my arm and prepare to inject a syringe into the tube.

"Wait," I stammer. "What's that?"

"Something to help the pain," one of them responds.

"No," I whisper. "I need to speak with the surgeons first. Then you can pump that stuff in me."

"Come on, big fella," he says patronizingly. "This will make it all feel better."

"No. This isn't about feeling better. This is about the rest of my life. I can handle the pain. I know what I'm doing. You give me that shot and the game's over. I go to sleep and whatever happens, happens."

"Look, I'm not gonna bullshit you," he says, frowning. "Your legs are messed up, badly messed up. This will just take the edge off."

Shaking my head, I eye the needle poised in his hand, unsure of whether he's going to sedate me despite my protests.

"I need my faculties," I explain, noticing that hypothermia or shock has begun clouding my ability to speak. The words come slowly. "I need to tell the doctors who I am, how I came to the U.S. to become a brand-name climber. You know, feet are definitely part of the job description when you're a mountaineer."

"OK," he says, backing slowly out of the compartment. "You make the call." Just as he's about to shut the door, he sticks his head back in to add, "Good luck."

The ambulance doesn't move, however, and I just lie there in the freezing cold, hanging on to the moment by a thread so thin I wonder if it has already snapped.

Breathe, breathe, breathe Shit, I've landed in purgatory. I try to drift back to McCall. Time for the green shag rug and pink flamingo lawn ornaments.

Thirty minutes later, the door swings opens. "We at the hospital?" I ask.

"The power is out back here," a voice informs me. "Can't get any heat or light. We're gonna move you to the other ambulance."

Back out into the night I go, past the crumpled heaps of metal and into the other vehicle. It's much warmer inside, but just as dark. In the bunk beside me I see the form of the woman who was driving the other car. I can barely make out her features in the darkness. When she sees me, she lets out a low moan. *Why in the hell would they throw us together in the same ambulance?*

"I'm so sorry," she sobs. "I—I knew I shouldn't have been driving tonight. The road . . . I could barely see. I'm sorry."

Despite the pain flooding every square inch of my body, my heart goes out to her. "It's OK," I hear myself tell her. "You didn't mean for this to happen. It was an accident."

The ambulance lurches forward. Nearly three hours after the collision, we're finally under way. Through the back window I watch as the tow trucks and wreckage shrink and then vanish in the night. The woman still sobs. Too tired to continue renovating my dream home, I decide to take my mind off my legs by attempting to cheer her up.

"Don't worry about this," I sigh, speaking softly toward the faint shadow beside me. "All my life I've known that disabled people could benefit from outdoor pursuits. But I've been too busy to act on it. Maybe this is what I needed to get going."

What a bunch of rubbish, a voice inside my head scolds. Nevertheless, my words quiet her and soon I hear her measured breathing.

An hour later, after changing ambulances again in the town of Blackfoot, I arrive at the Pocatello Regional Medical Center. Inside the emergency room a nurse gives me the work order to sign, but I refuse—I'll put pen to it only after I've spoken to the surgeon. Again I go through the hassle of denying pain medication, and I can tell I'm pissing people off.

A nurse slices off my corduroy pants and then prepares to cut the sleeves of my Polar jacket. There's a lot of Tom Whittaker tied up in this garment, which has accompanied me from the oil rigs to the Matterhorn to frozen waterfalls in the Canadian Rockies.

"Just a minute," I say. "Do I have any upper body injuries?"

"Not that I'm aware of," he replies.

"Tell you what," I explain, slowly. "You run those shears up the sleeves of this jacket and when I get out of this mess I'll come looking for you."

"Really?" he says, with an amused grin.

"Too right," I reply. "And I know exactly what you look like and where to find you."

Another nurse asks if I won't reconsider taking something for the pain, but I give her my spiel about needing to talk to the surgeon. She whisks me off to X-ray and preps me for the surgery to follow. More waiting.

"The surgeon will be here soon," a nurse informs me.

I remember how I felt while fighting my way up through the thin air and heavy snow to the summit of Mount McKinley, North America's highest peak. *You were on your own then, Whittaker. And there was nothing more significant than the top of a mountain at stake.* Every ounce of energy I can muster goes into maintaining my focus, not letting the pain pull me away from my goal. *Just bite the bullet a little bit longer.* I think back to my ill-fated trip up the Matterhorn and a handful of other climbs where it looked like the end, where it would have been far, far easier just to lie down and become part of the mountain. *There's only another couple of hundred feet to go, Whittaker.* If I can just push on for a bit longer, a whole new set of options will open up. I'm sure of it.

A man in green scrubs approaches my bedside. "You the surgeon?" I ask

"No," he says, "I'm the nurse in attendance." He busies himself taking my vitals and replacing my IV drip.

"You happen to know what the prognosis is?"

"Well, I've seen the X-rays," he says, "and you have some very severe crush injuries and multiple breaks to your lower legs. Both your knees have also taken quite a beating. Dr. Bacon won't make any decisions 'til he's had you sedated and he can do a detailed inspection. The bones are really only part of the picture. The state of the tissue and the robustness of your health have a lot to do with it."

He pauses and seems to check to make sure I can handle what he's telling me. "The first time around," he continues, "he'll only do what he feels is absolutely necessary. Then, in a few days, he'll get you back in and finish up."

"This Bacon, what's he like?" I inquire.

"Bacon?" he laughs, pausing again to properly word his reply. "There's not a soul in the hospital who's not afraid of him. But he's really a likable old codger and a damn good surgeon. Definitely no-nonsense, with the bedside manner of a badger. He likes you, though, because you won't take meds or sign 'til you see him. Strange, everyone here thought it'd make him hopping mad."

"So what's going to happen first time round?" I ask.

"Like I said, that's up to Bacon and what he learns." I can sense the nurse is feeling uncomfortable, but I have no choice except to push him—there's too much at stake here. "Put yourself in my place," I tell him. "I gotta know what's up before Bacon gets here. Don't say anything unless you think he won't do it."

He looks confused.

"It works like this," I say. "Do you think he'll amputate my wiener?"

He laughs and shakes his head. "No."

"I'm pretty sure I'll lose my right foot. Do you agree?"

He doesn't reply.

"You're a natural," I tell him. "You've got the hang of the game already." Just as he's about to leave, I say, "One more question." He pauses, then turns around and faces me. "And you have to be honest," I command. My stomach begins churning, but I have to ask the one question I dread.

"Do you think I'll lose my left foot?"

He doesn't move. *Say something, damn you.* His breathing even appears to have stopped. *Say they won't, you pillock!* I lift my head. My heart is beseeching him to respond. But all he does is look into my eyes, then spin on his heels and dart out of the ward.

His departure falls like an axe on my dreams. Emotionally and psychologically, I was prepared to lose one of my feet, but the nurse's silence brings on the panic that I've managed to keep at bay all this time.

And then, like an apparition, he's there beside my bed. We look at one another for a moment, then he says, not unkindly, "I hear you've been refusing to take sedation because you want to talk to me. So what is it you want to say?"

Up until this moment I knew exactly what I needed to tell the doctor, but now, as I confront the flesh-and-blood man, my brain turns to mush. It's as if I'm back in Carp's office, preparing to get caned. In my frayed mental state, I have no clue where to begin. Something about Bacon tells me he's not the type to take kindly to my making demands of him, and diplomacy has never been my strongest suit. I need to buy some time.

"I don't know who you are," I say.

"Dr. Gilbert Bacon, at your service," he says with a stiff bow.

My mind is foggy, but I force myself to focus. The sensation is not unlike what I've experienced on cloudy days out on the hill: I can be enshrouded in fog, but suddenly I get a glimpse of my surroundings that is more vivid than anything I might see on a sunny day.

"I'm sorry," I say. "I'm pretty whacked out right now and the last thing I want to do is piss you off before you pick up a scalpel." I watch his expression soften as I look through a keyhole in the clouds that have formed around my mind. Nice to see I haven't lost my touch at making people laugh. "My dear old mum always says that when it comes to diplomacy, I'm like a bull in a china shop: what I don't break, I shit on."

He fights back a smile. *Don't waste time, Whittaker.*

"So I'll cut to the chase. My name's Tom Whittaker. I spent last year as a graduate assistant at the Outdoor Program at ISU, here in town; I played rugby and worked as a mountain guide. I came to the States to become a world-class mountaineer. I've worked in mountain rescue for five years and I'm used to dealing with trauma. So what's the prognosis, Doc?"

"Won't know what the prognosis is until you're sedated and I've thoroughly investigated the situation," he replies.

"But based on my X-rays and chart, you must have an idea," I insist.

He frowns. "I don't work on ideas, only facts. And as I said, I don't have all the information and this is not the place for conjecture."

I can feel I'm losing him, so I try to lighten things again. "Well, for a rugby player and mountain guide, feet are kind of necessary. I guess I'm a little nervous about losing my livelihood and recreation all in one fell swoop."

He nods his head. "So what else?" he asks kindly.

"I've been hanging on now for more than four hours to talk to you. Now that you're here, I'm kind of nervous."

"Go on," he says. The clouds close in again, but I search intently for the light, forcing myself to think lucidly.

"Well, this is it," I reply. "First, that you won't make the decision to amputate on your own, that you'll get another opinion. Second, that if you both think that I can be better served elsewhere, you'll send me on down the line."

"Very well. I can agree to those terms. Anything else?"

I shake my head. I was sure there was a third thing, but I can't remember it now.

"Now, will you put your John Hancock on my work order?" he asks, holding out a pen and clipboard. I scrawl my signature, and as the clouds engulf me I hear his voice again: "You've got guts, Whittaker, and I admire that. I know you're scared. You'd be a fool if you weren't. But rest assured that whatever the outcome, I'll do the best I can for you."

"I know you will, Doc," I mumble as tears form in my eyes. It would appear I'm all out of stoicism. I sense I'm lucky to have Bacon as my surgeon; with another doctor my lower legs would probably be bagged and off to the hospital incinerator already.

"Ninety-nine, ninety-eight, ninety-seven, ninety. . ." The bright light in my eyes goes dim and I feel warm. The pain melts away and I'm falling, falling, into blackness. . . .

When I finally awaken, I raise my head from the pillow and peer downward to see fresh sutures angling across both knees and down the front of both legs. At the bottom of my right leg, where my foot was, is an ooze-drenched bandage. But that's not what holds my gaze. I'm staring at my left leg, gloriously intact. Splayed out are the most beautiful swollen, purple toes I've ever seen, which are connected to a swollen yellow-purple-black thing that I know to be my foot. A wave of relief surges though me. "Thank God," I murmur.

Performing what is known as a Syme's amputation, Dr. Bacon has cut through my calcaneus and tibia, drilled into each of these bones, inserted two stainless steel rods through the holes, and clamped the bones together. This has squeezed the cut portions of the bone together, fusing the joint and in essence transforming my limb into a peg leg. Apparently the good doctor listened to my pleas, because, I learn, I'll be able to put weight on the stump I now have. If he had performed the standard amputation, I would have lost much more of my lower leg, since he would have cut about six inches below the knee.

For the next seven days I float in and out of consciousness, fighting to stay alive. I lose so much blood that the citizens of Pocatello organize a blood drive to keep me fully stocked. I have multiple fractures in both lower legs and my right femur is broken in two places. Bone marrow leaks into my bloodstream, sending potentially lethal globules of fat on a collision course with my heart and brain. On five separate occasions I experience "life crises," but each time I somehow manage to escape alive.

While I'm drifting off in this never-never land of unconsciousness, I'm often looking down on myself from above, watching as my body lies face down in a warm pool of water. I can see my hands gripping the railing, struggling to keep me from slipping down under the water.

"Just let go of the rail, Whittaker," a soft, lulling voice whispers. "You won't feel any more fatigue or pain. Just open your hands and relax." Instinctively I understand that once I let go of the railing, returning won't be an option. Existence, as I've come to know it, will cease, but it all seems so wonderfully pleasant, so easy. One afternoon I sense the presence of my parents standing beside my bed. They must have flown over from England to be with their mangled son. Although I'm unable to speak or even open my eyes, I can hear every word they're saying.

"Perhaps, for his sake, it's better if he doesn't pull through," my mother whispers. "What kind of a life is he going to have now? He's already lived three lifetimes." My father sighs softly.

As I listen to them talk, I realize, for the first time in my life, that my parents have actually followed the path I've been wandering, and they even sound proud of my accomplishments. They've been with me every step of the way, but never said much about it. Realizing that I've never been alone, that they haven't written me off as some thrill-seeking vagabond, causes my grip on the railing to tighten. I ignore the sweet, gentle voice that calls to me. Whatever pain, whatever problems I'll have to face by coming back will, I finally decide, be worth it. My fingers squeeze the railing, and although I can't pull myself out of that pool, not yet, I know now that, on the strength of my mother's love and my father's admiration, I will indeed get out.

On November 30, 1979, seven days after I was admitted, they wheel me out of the intensive care unit, but I have a difficult time seeing this as a positive sign. I lie in bed and flip through channels on the television, vainly trying to find some way to pass the time until the nurse arrives to dump morphine into my arm. Pain scorches my body as though I've been doused in kerosene and lit. I click the TV off. No use trying to hide from it; it always finds me.

A week later, Dr. Bacon enters the room and goes about the grim business of inspecting my stump. Not one for idle chatter, he informs me that it isn't responding the way he had hoped. The flap of skin and the fatty pad he attached to the front of my exposed leg bone simply aren't bonding as they should. If the condition continues to deteriorate, he'll be forced to choose between one of two options. First, he could remove the plates holding the shattered tibia of my right leg together and bend the limb sideways; cut a flap of flesh from the calf of my left leg; take off the heel pad that has been stitched to the bottom of my leg; then sew the flap of calf tissue over my stump. But, Bacon says, he's uncertain how durable this would be.

So then he tells me the second option. "We may be better off just starting over and performing a standard amputation by cutting six inches below the knee," he says casually. He marks my chart at the end of the bed and wanders off to finish his rounds.

This is not exactly the news I wanted to hear. When the nurse finally arrives with morphine, I'm a mess.

"What's the matter with you?" she asks. After recounting Bacon's words, I awkwardly wipe my face clean.

"You better get a grip on yourself," she snaps. "That kind of self-pitying attitude isn't going to do you any good."

But she doesn't leave me much time to dwell on her words, as the narcotic almost immediately takes hold and the familiar veil of warm fuzziness descends between my eyeballs and brain. As the taste of metal comes into my throat and nasal passages, I drift away.

Nights are the roughest time, suffocating and compressing. I often shake like some machine running on broken bearings. I could control my shivering that night in the VW bus, but this is different—no matter how much I focus, I'm unable to calm myself.

One night, as perspiration pours down my face and body, I can no longer take the convulsions and I desperately ring the buzzer for the night nurse. When she arrives she hands me two green tablets and pours me a plastic cup of water.

"You're covered in sweat," she says, wiping a towel across my brow and over my body.

"I can't stop this shaking," I tell her. "I feel like I'm about to tear myself apart."

"You're not shaking now. Just try and rest."

"Not shaking?!" I blurt out, looking at my body vibrating madly beneath the sheets. "How can you say that? Just look at me!"

She nods, smiles wearily, then replies, "No, you're not shaking. You're just scared, that's all." She presses the plastic cup into my hand. "Just swallow your pills and everything will be OK."

I do as she says and soon feel my eyelids closing, but the next night the shaking returns. When I'm alone in the darkness, with no distractions, staring at the shadows cast on the ceiling by the street-lamp outside my window, the anxiety overwhelms me. Crowding my thoughts are the fears of what will happen with my stump and knees, not to mention with my escalating medical bills. But there's a deeper fear that I suppose the nurse recognized. As I lie awake at night, I dwell on what has become of all that I worked for, of the identity I've forged over the years. And as I realize that everything has been snatched away, I begin to shake uncontrollably.

When Jimmy Lane, a friend from ISU, sidles into my room, he's grinning from ear to ear. But as soon as he looks down at my stump and my horribly swollen left foot, he turns white. Clearly, nobody warned him of my sorry condition.

"Daaaamn," he says, his Tennessee drawl stretching out the word. Jimmy storms out of the room and down the hallway. As soon as I hear the shouting, I crane my neck to see him grab a nurse by the lapel and lift her over a desk so that their two noses are only inches inch apart. Jimmy seems to be taking this much harder than she had predicted.

"You think that's funny?!" he yells. "When someone comes to visit their friend and they ask you how he's doing, you damn sho' don't say, 'Oh, you'll see when you get in there.'" I fear what Jimmy, a massive man who is a star on the ISU football team, can do to this little nurse. But he just lowers her down to the floor and says, "Don't you ever do that again . . . ma'am."

When he walks back into the room, tears are running down his face.

"Look, Jimmy, you're gonna have to quit that," I tell him, feeling something bubbling up inside of me that I've desperately been trying to suppress. "You're going to make a baby out of me."

He nods. "I'll be back later," he says.

The next day, two women from my Counselor Ed. classes stop by to visit. Something about them, about that moment, causes the bubble to rise back up to the surface. I tell them about Jimmy Lane and how I hadn't wanted to show any emotion in front of him. They tell me that it's OK to cry, that with them I'm safe. I've been trying to ignore reality, but I just can't any longer. So I begin to weep, deep choking gasps of loneliness and fear. And they both weep with me, holding my hands in theirs.

I'm thirty-one years old and over the past ten days I've traveled from youth to middle age, from being a remarkable physical specimen to a bedridden wreck. There couldn't be a clearer sign that one stage of my life has ended and another begun—and this new stage is one I detest.

That evening, the on-duty nurse comes into my room. "Tom, there's a David Lovejoy on the phone," she says. "I told him you were resting, but he insists he speak with you." Since Jimmy Lane's little talk with the nurse, the standard care around here has improved remarkably.

"Go ahead," I tell her, "put him through." Lovejoy is a tough ex-Marine who recently moved to Maine either to finish up his studies at Orono or to be closer to his mother's walk-in refrigerator—it depends who you talk to. Over the past year I became something of a climbing mentor to Dave, as we took on frozen waterfalls in the Wasatch and Teton mountain ranges and climbed rock in Idaho, Utah, Wyoming, California, and Colorado. He's become a talented climber himself, but more important, we've forged a bond, one based on total honesty and trust. I've shown him what I know about climbing, but he has given back to me, showing me how to transform every climb into a joyful celebration of life.

Right now, I need to speak with him more than any other person on the planet. I'm smiling even before I talk into the phone. "David, old bean!" I shout, giving our standard greeting.

"Don't 'old bean' me, old bean," he says cheerfully. As the words begin flowing, so do the tears and the laughter. God, how good it feels to laugh. For the past ten days, I've told myself that I've been handling everything admirably, apart from coming unglued at night and needing rescuing by those angels who float through the corridors in nurses' uniforms. But until this moment, I've been suppressing everything, not just the tears but the laughter as well. And with the laughter comes the realization that somewhere within this pile of broken bones and sutures, Tom Whittaker's spirit remains intact.

Before we hang up, Dave announces that he's decided to take his final exams early, hitchhike out to Pocatello, and nurse me back to health. It's exactly the news I need to hear. If, in my fragile state, I can survive Dave Lovejoy as a nurse, nothing can kill me. That night I tumble into a deep and restful sleep.

CHAPTER 7
Climbing the Steps

The night Linda appears in my room, I can't sleep. I'm alive, but so weak that all I do is stare out the window at the barren branches of a cottonwood. My stump still refuses to heal properly; the all-important granular tissue on the heel pad has finally appeared, but so has gangrene.

"Do I know you?" I ask when I see Linda. With her olive skin, she appears to be Hispanic. Though she looks to be only in her twenties, something about her makes this nurse seem older.

"No, you don't know me," she replies, "but I've seen you before. You were sleeping. You're the talk of the town, you know. There have been a couple of pieces about you in the paper. Seems you made quite an impact when you were here coaching the rugby team and doing all your outdoor stuff. I've been praying for you and God asked me to come here."

"Really?" I say with a shrug, before turning back to watch the tree branches.

"Why are these dressings so dirty?" she inquires softly.

"Why are you here?" I ask, feeling anger and frustration welling up in my chest.

"I feel drawn to you," she says. "When I read about you and heard them talking in the canteen, I came up to see you and started praying for you. Last night God told me that if I didn't nurse you, you'd lose your stump."

"Bully for you," I reply. But something about this young woman—perhaps it's her kind brown eyes, or how nicely she fills out her starched white nurse's uniform—stops me from lapsing into further sarcasm.

"When was this dressing last changed?" she asks.

"A few days ago."

"A few *days*?" she says incredulously. "Why isn't it changed more often?"

"You tell me—you're the nurse," I reply, immediately regretting using the harsh tone that has become so customary for me.

She shakes her head solemnly, touches the gauze, and asks, "May I have a look?"

I nod, and she deftly unwraps the dressing to reveal the festering tissue. She gives no indication that the gruesome object at the bottom of my leg and the stench coming off it are anything but normal.

"This is what I was expecting," she says. "Your stump doesn't look good. You know that it needs to be cleaned and dressed at least once a day, right?"

Soon she's going to work on my stump, cutting away the gangrenous tissue with scissors and scalpel. As she works, she tells me of her Eskimo heritage, how she traveled here from Alaska so that her two children can spend time with her husband's parents, and how she has taken a nursing job to raise the cash for the trip back. I revel in her nurturing touch, the care, the tenderness.

I don't care how ludicrous her story sounds about God sending her here to tend to my stump. All I know is that I need Linda. She's my last hope, as everyone else in this place has practically written me off. I'm weakened, drained, gaunt, barely fighting to keep my spirit.

"Who on earth gave you the authority to do this?" I ask while she dresses my stump in clean bandages.

"I have my own authority," she replies, smiling angelically.

"But Dr. Bacon will hang you from a meat hook if he catches you doing this."

"How's he going to find out? Besides, I'm not afraid of Dr. Bacon."

Exhausted, I shut my eyes, and when I open them, she's sitting beside me on the bed. "I'll be back tomorrow to change the dressing," she says, patting my arm. After she disappears into the hallway, I return to gazing at the tree branches, counting my breaths until the liquid poppies arrive.

Just before Christmas I move from the hospital to a second-floor room in ISU's student union. The food-service providers even throw in a free meal ticket for the cafeteria. Their largess couldn't have arrived at a better time. Ever since I graduated from ISU a few months ago I've had no health insurance, and it's going to take a team of accountants working overtime to add up my medical bill. Worse, my student visa is about to expire. But I'll be damned if I'm going back to England strapped to a gurney. I may be shy a foot and have two horribly damaged knees, but the next time I return home I'm going to walk off the plane, not be carried.

Bill March and his wife, Karen, arrive from Canada. Not one for the stuffy confines of a room, Bill bundles me up and takes me for a spin through ice-rutted streets. He comes by almost daily, and I sense that he feels in some way responsible for this wretched turn of events, as if he set it all in motion by steering me toward Pocatello. Dave Lovejoy arrives from back east. The powerful antibiotics have wreaked havoc on my intestines, and when he shows up I'm battling constipation. The big moment finally arrives, but I'm so weak that he has to lug me into the bathroom, where he gets his first taste of the joys of nursing an invalid.

Fortunately Dave has some help, from my beautiful, raven-haired girlfriend, Mary Romano. She has moved into the adjoining bed in my student union room, and I seem to open my eyes only when she is around. Though Mary is still an undergraduate, Dr. Bacon trusts her to administer my meds. Three times a day she must search my bony rump for an elusive square-inch of virgin real estate that will accept her needle. The doses are so large that the pain from one shot has not subsided before it is time for my next.

I feel trapped in my small room, and the dark thoughts intensify. In between visits from friends, I sit alone with both legs sticking straight out in front of me in my wheelchair. I begin to wonder if I really want to deal with the pain and uncertainty of my day-to-day existence—no visa, no money, and no ability to earn a living. And what about all my grand dreams of being a professional mountaineer, a prominent figure in the outdoor pursuits profession? What use are they to me now?

Slowly I slip into anger and self-pity. My body has always defined me, and now all I can do is sit in its wrecked remains, scared, hopeless, and alone. Thoughts of suicide begin darting in and out of my head. I ponder the different scenarios. I don't own a gun, so shooting myself isn't really an option. Besides, blowing my brains out seems like such a messy way to exit, especially for the poor wretch who has to mop everything up. If I could get my hands on some sleeping pills, that might be an attractive possibility. But pills pose problems of their own. What if someone finds me half dead on the floor and manages to save me? That way, I survive, but then I'm three-parts brain-dead. If done properly, suicide takes time—something I don't have with friends continually dropping by. If only I had a quiet, dignified way to end it all. I grow depressed over not having an easy way out and even more guilt-ridden and depressed that I'm looking for one in the first place.

In January 1980, shortly before I'm due back at the hospital for more dreaded surgery on my stump, some mountaineering buddies stop by my room. In an effort to lighten everyone's mood, I tell the group that before two years is up I'll climb Yosemite's Outer Limits. First climbed in 1971 by Jim Bridwell, it earned a reputation as one of the toughest free climbs in North America. Just a few months before my accident I successfully tackled the route, and now I realize that by heading back up I would force everyone to stop treating me like I'm all washed up. But as soon as the words have left my lips, I see my visitors' eyes dart down to what's left of my legs and looks of embarrassment spread across their faces. Here

I am trying to lift everyone's mood, trying to prove that I'm still alive, and all I've managed to do is make things worse.

"Whittaker, you're gonna be out of here in no time," one of my buddies says. And with that, the conversation shifts and my insane pronouncement is forgotten, written off as nothing more than the desperate ramblings of a crippled Welshman.

After my visitors leave, however, I start thinking again about what I said. Sharing my dreams with as many people as will listen has always kept a fire lit beneath my backside; after all, I know if I don't follow through on my grand declarations of purpose, I'll come across as a mere windbag. But judging from my friends' reaction and my fragile state, I decide to rethink my strategy. I've begun learning that, with the best of intentions, society doesn't feel particularly comfortable allowing the disabled to dream. After all, why get your hopes up if you're only going to fall on your face? It's the first lesson for a man without a foot.

So for the time being I'll keep my dreams to myself—but I'll be damned if I'm going to let them die. I reach for a pen and the notebook I've taken to using as a diary. I have to see if this dream looks as crazy on paper as it sounded to my friends. So I make this diary entry, looking ahead nearly two years:

> *September 25, 1981: Today I climbed Outer Limits (5.10c), Cookie Cliff, Yosemite Valley. Not a remarkable event in itself except that I did it with an artificial foot, which makes the climb a full grade harder. Seeing as I've only led four 5.11 pitches in my life, this means I am now climbing at the all-time limit of my abilities. And to all those of you who said it couldn't be done: You ain't seen nothing yet!*

That winter I'm back at the hospital. Dr. Bacon wants to "revise" the structural irregularities at the end of my stump so that one day it will better fit a prosthesis. I understand that "revise" is a euphemism; Bacon plans to slice through the tissue, peel it back, and grind away the bone. "On a pain continuum from one to ten," he tells me, "bone surgery is a solid eight. This will be the toughest procedure you've been through yet." Gilbert Bacon is not one to exaggerate, which is why I feel a titch uneasy.

When I wheel into a suite with two beds, I see my new roommate staring down at his knee, looking as if he's about two minutes from a trip to the gallows.

"When's the funeral?" I ask.

"What?" he asks, frowning. "What're you talking about? I'm here for knee surgery." He turns his gaze back to his knee. "Why are you here?" Apparently he hasn't registered my missing parts.

"Having a bit of trouble with my toes," I tell him, straight-faced. He glances over in my direction but almost immediately looks back down at his swollen knee. Then it hits him, and he does a double take.

"Stupid mistake, really," I explain. "Came in to be circumcised and somehow the carts got mixed up and—presto. When I woke up . . ." I lift my leg in the air. "Quite apologetic, they were. They said if I came back, they'd graft some new ones on." I can tell I've got his full attention now. "Say, maybe you're the guy they told me about!"

"Beg your pardon?" he says, looking puzzled.

"You know—the one who's donating the foot."

When he finally realizes I'm pulling his chain, he grins broadly. I instantly feel better, too, since getting him to take his mind off the impending surgery helps me do the same. For the rest of the afternoon we have a great time—well, at least as far as hospital stays go. His name is Larry Zajanc, and he works for the U.S. Forest Service; it turns out we've met each other before. After spending hours harassing nurses, swapping jokes, and jawing about our adventures in the wilderness, we both fall asleep laughing.

When I wake up, I'm in the post-op recovery room. The pain reaches down inside me and pulls me out of my dreamless, anesthetized bliss. Even before I'm fully conscious I can hear myself screaming. Never in my life have I felt anything more hellishly consuming. My entire life I have been taught to deal with adversity in a stoical, stiff-upper-lip manner; the British are masters at absorbing huge quantities of punishment. Whenever I've faced severe pain in the past, I've retreated into my mind and pretended that I'm an agent holding vital information my captors desperately need; if I give in to the pain and divulge the secret, scores of lives will be lost. As crazy as it sounds, this game has always made pain more bearable. But this . . . this pain is different.

I've come unglued, thrashing about trying to escape the agony at the end of my stump. The eyes of the nurse standing above me widen.

"I can't take it!" I yell at her. "You've gotta get me something."

In an instant, Bacon arrives in the room. "Get ten milligrams of morphine in this patient!" he shouts.

"But that could kill him," the nurse protests.

"Granted," he snaps. "But if we don't, the shock will. *Ten milligrams—now!*"

I watch the needle slide into my arm and taste the drug's metallic flavor in my throat. The pain relinquishes its grip on my stump, but I know it will be back.

The next time I wake up, Larry is sitting in a wheelchair in my room, his knee wrapped in a massive wad of gauze. He looks worried again, only this time I sense he's worried about me.

"How did it go?" he asks, and all I can manage is a wave. "That's the spirit. You hang in there, bud. I'll be back." I shut my eyes again and fall back into a deep sleep. My days become a blur of morphine and exhaustion. I'm totally dependent on the drug— I need it and would be lost without it. As I've grown accustomed to the glorious mind-numbing detachment it brings, I spend most of my time and energy thinking about how to hold on until my next installment of opiates. Two hours becomes far too long to wait. I'm soon watching the wall clock intently, knowing exactly how many minutes must pass until my next fix, trying not to curse the slow sweep of the second hand.

I've also learned how to maximize the experience once the morphine enters my bloodstream. I allow myself only twenty minutes to surf the cottony buzz, then force myself to fall asleep. That way, when my stump feels like it's been through a wood chipper and I'm jolted awake, only forty-five minutes of pain must be endured before my next shot. When that doesn't work, I revert back to my spy scenario. "You crack, Whittaker, and hundreds of lives will be lost," I mumble to myself like a mantra, over and over again. The greater the discomfort, the stronger my will to crush it.

When a staph infection begins devouring the flesh on my right leg, I'm placed in an isolation ward. The doctors fear that the infection will spread into the bone, but after nearly two weeks of pitched battles, I emerge with my stump intact. The doctors have begun weaning me off the morphine, but they pump me full of bush-league substitutes that do little to extinguish the pain and do nothing for my habit. Physically, I'm withering away; I've dropped more than fifty pounds since the accident. I'm a pathetic bag of bones.

After I get out of the hospital in mid-February I move back into the student union guest room before finding an old decaying house that has been converted into apartments. But my meager savings don't go far, so I have to drum up new housing options—and fast. I find an empty place in the basement of the same building. I soon find out why it is vacant; every time it rains or thaws, the apartment floods. Still, to prevent the building from decaying too rapidly, the absentee landlord keeps the central heating turned on, so I move in—or I suppose I should say I start squatting.

My new home shows all the signs of having been long ago abandoned—broken windows, a front door knocked off its hinges, and a floor covered with swampy mulch from the leaves that have accumulated over the years. Jimmy Lane and Dave Lovejoy help me shovel off my floor and set up the place with furniture from Goodwill. Soon 614 East Halliday becomes home. After the first rainstorm, however, I watch my mattress swell as it soaks up the six inches of standing water on my floor.

To give me respite from my plight, Dave and Jimmy delight in taking my heavy steel wheelchair over rock-strewn mountain paths. With these two brutes leading the way, wheelchairs get broken, and broken often. Wheels fall off, support rods snap, bolts rattle themselves loose. Almost once a week we end up at Medical Mart, where Dave or Jimmy shouts, "Got another subpar chair for y'all." The sales staff always looks at us in disbelief, then begrudgingly takes the broken apparatus from us and wheels out another chair.

After about a half dozen of these visits, I realize it's probably no accident that this fifty-four-pound chair keeps breaking on me. It must be the universe's subtle way of telling me I'm not going to get very far sitting on my arse.

Dave and Jimmy also get me out of the house by taking me to the Green Triangle, our favorite watering hole. Finding seats should be difficult in this always-bustling tavern, but my two buddies love the challenge. They dive straight into the crowd, carving their way through the patrons to locate a table—usually the best table in the establishment, even if someone's already sitting there.

One typical evening, as Dave wheels me through the crowd, I hear Jimmy talking to the patrons who surround what we've come to think of as our table.

"Hate to trouble you folks," he tells the group, "but our friend here will be requiring this table for the evening."

One of the occupants begins to raise a voice in protest but stops himself. Jimmy's strong-arm tactics—not to mention his and Dave's imposing presences—convince the group of drinkers that resisting might prove unhealthy. If there is a perk to having your foot amputated, perhaps this is it. Once the table clears, we move in and begin ordering pitchers.

Because my legs project straight out in front of me, anyone trying to maneuver around me in the packed tavern is in for a bit of work. At one point I look up to see a cowboy trying to squeeze past.

"Excuse me, gimp," he says as he contorts his body to move around my chair. He vanishes into the sea of bodies.

"What's a gimp?" I ask my drinking companions.

"It's a term for . . . you know, a cripple," comes the reply. I swallow hard. The cowboy's words make me feel like I just took a knee to the gut. Suddenly I want to be away from here. But both Dave and Jimmy look like they're having too much fun to want to push a gimp home through the snow, so I just sit there and nurse my beer until closing time.

One of the shortcomings of capitalism, at least from this pauper's viewpoint, is that once your finances are exhausted, medical services tend to dry up at an alarming rate. My initial physical therapy proved excellent. But once my lawyer and kayaking buddy, Bruce Bistline, began settling bills for cents on the dollar, the hospital nixed my therapy. So, one morning in March, I track down my friend Phil Lucky, an athletic trainer at ISU, and ask him if he could put together a regimen to help me get my strength back. He announces that he can do better than that.

"We'll get you in the weight room for afternoon workouts with the wrestling team," he explains. "And I'll come in with you and put you through your paces."

"Whatever you say, Phil," I reply, not completely sure why he feels it's so important that I work out with a bunch of grapplers. But as soon as I roll myself into the weight room and get going on the conditioning program he's worked up for me, I understand why he has me pumping iron with all these ox-sized wrestlers. Their strength and intensity spur me on as I try to develop my now puny arms, chest, and back. And whenever I lie on a machine wanting to give up because I feel so weak, one of the team members always ends up picking me up like a rag doll and carrying me across the gym to my next station.

The three-day-a-week torture sessions begin paying off. After a month I'm out of the wheelchair and hobbling around on crutches, trying to toughen up the tender tip of my stump to the point where it can support my weight. A month after that, I've built up enough endurance and strength in my leg muscles and tendons to attempt what a few months ago I would have thought impossible—climbing and descending the bleachers at the university's indoor stadium, known as the Mini Dome.

After stashing my crutches beneath a seat, I peer up the countless concrete steps and begin my wobbly plod upward toward the rafters. I've fashioned a makeshift prosthesis from an Ace bandage and several layers of sliced-up flip-flop sandals, and if nothing else, it feels as though I'm building callous on the bottom of my stump. My raspy grunts echo feebly through the dusty air. By the time I limp over the top step, my heart pounds madly, I'm wheezing, and the scar tissue on the end of my leg throbs. Because of the screwed-up circulation, the blood is pooling in my stump. But I'm miles away from the pain. I've made it.

As I gaze down at the empty football field, which is hemmed in on all sides by concrete, it occurs to me that this view is more beautiful than anything I've glimpsed from the peaks I've stood atop. I feel like I'm standing on top of the world.

I've come to see that on that November night when I lay in the smoking, crumpled remains of my friend Susan's VW bus, Tom Whittaker's life ended and something new was born from the wreckage. And now I'm forced to admit that it was high time for the old Tom Whittaker to die. Perhaps my first inkling that something was amiss came when Smelly left. At the time, she was maturing and had a new set of needs while all I could do was continue with my gladiatorial contests against the environment. I wasn't a bad person, just an inconsequential one. The problem with the old Tom Whittaker was simply that he was having too damn much fun, hell-bent on continuing his adventures. Focus and self-absorption are almost essential for a climber to excel. Yet I practiced self-indulgence with the fervor of a zealot. As an army brat, I had a new home every two or three years. Community and any sense of permanency never existed in my life, particularly because going off to boarding school at the age of eight drove a wedge between me and my family. So, when I finished school, I became a tumbleweed, rolling wherever the wind blew me.

Suddenly, as I survey the green AstroTurf below me, I'm humbled as I think about how the people of Pocatello, Idaho, have made possible the emergence of this new Tom Whittaker. Day after day, the college community and townspeople donated their time and energy to getting me back on my foot. One woman raised money by crocheting shawls and selling them. The town held bake sales and dances for me. People I've never met helped pay my medical bills. The big walls of Yosemite Valley, the huge rapids of the Colorado River, and the frozen summit of Mount McKinley may have attracted me to America, but the people of Pocatello have made me want to stay.

Now, sitting here in the Mini Dome, feeling the throbbing in my stump fade away, I realize that I must somehow pay these people back. I gingerly retrace my steps back to my tiny apartment. That night I write a letter to the *Idaho State Journal*, thanking everyone in this town for seeing something in me that I never knew existed.

CHAPTER 8
"You're Not the Same Person"

Paying back the citizens of Pocatello begins here at St. Anthony's Hospital. Thanks to my master's program's strong emphasis on counseling, plus my new insight into disabilities, I've convinced hospital administrators to let me put together a group-counseling program for recent amputees. In theory we meet and discuss the issues and conflicts we face in our lives. But I'm just a volunteer at the hospital and don't carry any weight. Just as the sessions are picking up some momentum, nurses inevitably wheel away our members to various appointments with doctors, physical therapists, and the like. Too often I find myself alone in the room with a bedpan and a potted geranium.

After one session I spot a longhaired kid ripping down a hospital hallway in a wheelchair. He appears locked on a collision course with a flight of stairs. But, just seconds away from being launched into space, he clamps onto the wheels, heaves his body backwards, and uses his huge arms to jerk the chair back into a perfect wheelie. He vanishes—*bump, bump, bump*—down the stairs.

"Who was *that*?" I ask an old man walking nearby.

"That? That's a damn shame," he replies, shaking his head. "Name's John Howie. Local high school football star—'til he messed up, drove drunk. Damn shame, that's what it is."

Several times over the next few weeks I see Howie flying down the halls with his blond hair flapping behind him, a crazed grin plastered across his face. One afternoon he spots me sitting alone in a recently emptied room. I'm staring at the floor, angry and frustrated that my group has again been whisked away to other engagements.

"Hey, professor, you let class out early today?" he asks. I look up to see him rocking back and forth in the doorway on his back two wheels. Suddenly I feel like I'm staring at a kindred spirit.

"Mario Andretti," I say. "I don't believe we've been properly introduced."

We fall into that easy talk of two tired old soldiers home from the front, griping about our injuries but trying not to dwell on them. For the past ten months Howie has been paralyzed from the nipples down. Metal rods have been inserted along his spine to stabilize his back and prevent further injury. Once a powerful, gifted athlete who dreamed of playing football for ISU, these days he is confined to a wheelchair and needs to use a catheter and leg bag for his urine and suppositories to evacuate his bowels. Despite his wretched physical condition, Howie exudes confidence and spirit.

He admits to me that the only reason he's at the hospital is because a judge ordered him to perform community service for his drunk-driving accident. "This place gives me the creeps," he chuckles, popping his rig back up onto two wheels and spinning it around to leave. Just as he's about out the door, I blurt out, "Hey, Mario, you wanna go kayaking sometime?" The idea has been lurking in the back of my head since I first saw him shoot down the stairs in his wheelchair.

Howie stops, pivots back toward me, and snaps, "How's that?"

"Kayaking," I reply. "As in something you do in a boat on a river or lake with a paddle."

He grins and nods. "Sure, professor, next time I'm out jogging, I'll drop by your house and we can walk down to the river and go kayaking." He laughs, then adds, "Hell, let's go skydiving too."

But I'm not laughing. "This is no joke," I tell him. "You don't need your legs. You can use your upper body. We can rig up a boat to keep you stable."

He mulls over my proposition for a moment, then says, "Sounds cool, but I've never kayaked before."

"So what?" I respond. "If you're game to learn, I'll teach you."

The next day I stump over to see Dale Perkins, a tireless local prosthetist, to discuss my idea. As I explain my vision of a modified kayak seat with an elongated back, he sketches some crude drawings on a scrap of paper. By the time I leave, he's lost in concentration, hunched over his desk fine-tuning my rough idea into a polished, functional design.

When Howie and I arrive back at Dale's office, he leads us into his lab, where we see just how much energy he's poured into the design. We pull the seat out of the beaten-up fiberglass kayak I requisitioned, then line Howie's wheelchair cushion with plaster of Paris to create a precise mold of his thighs, buttocks, and torso.

A week later, Howie and I head to the university's swimming pool, where he lowers himself down into the kayak's cockpit and cinches a thick Velcro strap around his massive chest. The customized high-backed seat fits him like a glove. The design works better than I could have ever hoped and Howie is having the time of his life.

During our third session he attempts an Eskimo roll, a necessary maneuver for whitewater paddlers. He leans to his right, flipping the fiberglass boat over, then—while upside down in the water—reaches up and sweeps the flat blade across the water's surface while twisting his torso and dipping his head. I watch Howie and the boat roll up, hover on the edge of balance, and flop back underwater.

Two dozen attempts later, Howie is so close to nailing the roll that it hurts to watch. A few more tries and he'll have it, but by this point both of us are tired and cold. It'll have to wait until next time. We head straight for the warmth of the showers, neither of us speaking a word. After cranking the hot water on high, I help pull his neoprene wetsuit off and stumble into the locker room for some shampoo. When I return, Howie is lying face-down on the floor, sobbing. In a flash, I've gone from feeling great to feeling reprehensible. *Damn you, Whittaker. When are you going to finally wise up and understand that what's good for you isn't good for someone else? You've been messing with things you don't understand.*

Not knowing quite what to do, I join him on the tiled floor but say nothing. What a strange image we must make—two naked men lying on the floor, shrouded in steam, one of us a virtual skeleton with an Ace bandage in place of a foot, the other, who weeps uncontrollably, with a muscular upper body and useless, atrophied legs.

When Howie sits up and wipes his eyes with the back of his hand, I start to mumble an apology, but he cuts me off with a wave of his hand.

"Since I screwed up," he says, "I've woken up every morning as the most bitter, miserable person on the planet. At night when I dream, I'm running with a football tucked under my arm. I'm faking, taking hits and bouncing off. But then the alarm goes off and my legs don't move and it feels like I'm lying in bed with a corpse. I have to force myself to put on my game face and I don't take it off 'til I flop back in bed at night." He pauses, and then a smile creeps across his face. "This morning, for the first time since I messed up, I've had a reason to get out of bed. I just wanted you to know that."

The two of us sit there on the wet tile floor, the only sound the roar of the showers. I can feel my heart pounding, and I squeeze my eyelids together to keep the tears from pouring out.

"You'll get that roll, John Boy," I finally say. "Next time, I guarantee it."

"A one-footed man selling shoes. Damn, I love it!"

Ted Hunt, my new boss, is roaring with laughter. Until this moment, landing a job as a salesman at Hudson's Shoe Store a few months after losing my foot hasn't struck me as odd. I suppose existence, at least as far as it pertains to me, has always been fraught with ridiculous ironies. Ted is a respected member of the business community, but he also has a penchant for hunting, muscle cars, and raising hell. For some reason he took a shine to me when we met last year, so now he's offered me this part-time position.

As jobs go, peddling footwear is on par with scraping barnacles off of oil rigs in the North Sea, but I need the cash—and at least it doesn't involve my getting hypothermic halfway into my shift. It also gives me the flexibility to continue my work at the hospital. Each day after my four-hour shift ends, I head over to St. Anthony's for the group-counseling sessions.

But sitting within the four walls of a hospital room and getting folks to talk about all the nightmares and hopes welling up inside them has begun feeling ludicrously inadequate. I'm sure the sessions are useful to a degree, but each time we call it quits for the day, I'm reminded of the frailty of words. Voicing fear and anger and working through denial, guilt, and self-pity are important parts of climbing back on your feet, but this can take you only so far. Truly getting on with your life requires more than words. There's got to be a better way, I've decided.

So, each day at the store, my thoughts have been turning to a paddling trip. Prior to my accident, descending the seventeen-mile Murtaugh section of the Snake River ranked high on my paddling wish list. To date, no one has ever descended the river, which is filled with nasty hydraulics and big drops and is hemmed in by five-hundred-foot canyon walls of gray basalt. Whenever my kayaking buddies drop by for a visit, the conversation eventually leads back to the plans to run the river when the snow pack begins to melt in the late spring. From the outset I've been included in the plan.

One night, Bruce Bistline, the attorney who helped me after the accident by handling my claim against the other driver's insurance, drops by to play chess. An excellent kayaker, Bruce is one of the leaders of the planned expedition. Just after we've settled into our game, he abruptly tells me, "It's like this, Whittaker:

we had a meeting last night and . . . we decided the Murtaugh is going to be hairy enough without adding you to the mix."

I look up from the chessboard, feeling like I've just been sucker punched by my mum—never even saw it coming. "What are you saying?" Of course I know damn well what he's saying, but I never imagined I'd hear it from him, of all people. He must have picked the short straw.

Bruce's brown eyes drop awkwardly back to the chessboard. "We can't take responsibility for you," he says quietly.

"Nobody's asking anyone to take responsibility for me."

Bruce looks like he'd rather be anywhere else but here. He takes a deep breath and adds, "Whittaker, you gotta realize you're not the same person you were before the accident."

When he finally walks out into the night, I remain seated at my rickety kitchen table and try to make sense of what I just heard. For the first time in my adult life, a decision has been made for me behind closed doors and I can't do anything about it. Since my cohorts didn't bother to invite me to their meeting, I wasn't even involved in the process. How do you distinguish between taking responsibility *for* people and taking responsibility *away from* them?

For the disabled, I realize, this scenario must repeat itself countless times every day. The way I see it, I can either accept this state of affairs or turn the whole damn paradigm upside down.

The next day I get the perfect opportunity: Paul Hookum, a chum from my days at the Canadian Outward Bound Mountain School, tells me he and his girlfriend, Barb, are headed my way for a kayaking trip. Within a few days the three of us are in Boise to check out the South Fork of the Payette River. None of us knows anything about the Payette, so to get the best information possible, I telephone Rob Lesser, a legendary kayaker who lives in town—but someone I've never met.

"You don't know me," I tell him, "but I'm a Brit who's interested in paddling the Payette and I'm wondering if you could tell me where the put-ins and take-outs are on the river."

"When you planning to run it?"

"We're driving up there today and hope to do the gorge tomorrow."

"Right," Rob replies. "If you don't mind company, I'll show you exactly where the put-ins and take-outs are."

"I don't have a problem with that, but I should warn you, I recently had a foot amputated and I'm still on crutches."

"How's that going to affect your boating?"

"I wish I knew, but I don't," I reply, ready to hear him gracefully back out of his offer.

"What were you paddling before your accident?"

"I was a pretty steady Class V boater," I say, indicating that I could tackle some of the toughest rapids out there.

"Nothing harder than Class IV on the gorge section of the South Fork. And there's only one section where you'll be forced to portage." Rob continues his tutorial, telling me exactly where to park in order to start the run and what to look for in the river to know when I've come to the end. When he finishes, I thank him for his time, convinced that he's passively withdrawn his offer to accompany me.

Just as I'm about to hang up the phone, he says, "I'll meet you at the Banks Café around 8:30 A.M."

"Uhhh . . . yeah," I stammer. "The Banks Café. So how'll I know you?"

"You can't miss me. I'll be the one with chiseled good looks."

"This is the put-in," Rob tells us.

Paul, Barb, and I look down at the churning brown water of the Deadwood, one of the tributaries that feeds into the South Fork. The four of us head down to the bank over slippery, snow-covered rocks. I struggle to keep upright, feeling like I've quaffed one pint too many. The metal pins in my legs seem to pull the chilly April air deep into my bones, and the neoprene wetsuit that once fit me so snugly now hangs off my body like the skin of an old elephant. But I'm almost giddy thinking about how, for the first time in five months, I won't be held back by my legs.

Stashing my crutches in the hull behind the seat, I blow up my buoyancy bags. I've removed the foot braces, which allows me to position my battered limbs inside but doesn't do anything for my stability within the boat. It'll be like trying to ski with all the buckles on my boots unsnapped. Slipping into his sleek, new Perception Mirage, Rob glances at my boat and shouts, "Good God, Whittaker, what is that thing?!"

"Definitely not state of the art," I reply, patting my battered, duct tape–covered craft. "But for twenty-five dollars I couldn't say no."

It takes me longer to get back up to speed than I hoped, but I manage to stay inside the boat in the early going. Barb and Paul, in contrast, go in the water so often that, as soon as we complete the first stretch, they announce that they're going off to locate the much-touted hot spring near our campground. Rob and I continue downstream, with Rob hanging just behind me in case I get in trouble—and this for someone he met only a few hours ago.

As the gorge grows steeper and narrows, the whitewater becomes almost continuous, topped with waves as high as Rob has ever seen them. Fortunately the paddling is only of moderate difficulty, but in the distance we can hear the thunder of Big Falls, a nasty, bone-crunching stretch that we definitely don't want to paddle. We run our boats into the rocky bank on river left. I stiffly push myself out of the cockpit and retrieve my crutches, while Rob hoists his kayak onto his shoulder and starts off on the quarter-mile hoof that will get us around the massive falls.

"Be back for you in a few minutes," he grunts, disappearing up the bank and along the trail.

My stump feels numb, but after a few moments I'm able to knead some life back into it. I hobble to the front of the boat, clip my tow line through the bow loop, tie the other end around my waist, and begin pulling my sixty-five-pound kayak over the rocks. My crutches never wind up where they're supposed to—I'm either lurching forward or being jerked backward—and every few steps I'm forced to stop and extricate the boat's nose from the rocks. After just seventy-five feet I'm blinded by sweat. Rob laughs when he sees me. "What the hell are you doing?"

" 'Every little bit helps,' said the little old lady as she peed in the sea!" I reply.

Rob unclips the line, slings the boat onto his shoulder, and heads down the trail, then returns to help steady me for the rest of the portage.

I arrive at our next put-in to find that there are no sloping banks from which to ease our boats into the river. Instead we have to seal-launch off a ledge eight feet above the water. "You first," Rob says, pushing me into space. My boat plunges nose-first into the swirling liquid, and as I disappear beneath the surface I wonder if I'm about to collide with one of the logs I've spotted in the current. Thankfully the swirling pool is devoid of solid objects, and a split second later my stern explodes out of the water. I'm on my way.

Over the next hour I feel my body getting reacquainted with itself. Muscles I haven't used since last September, when I paddled the Colorado River through the Grand Canyon, twitch with life. I'm exhilarated by surfing the standing waves, by negotiating the many drops. In this more difficult section Rob takes the lead. Further downstream he surfs a boisterous standing wave over a large rock, but the violently surging water flips his boat. As he sets up for his roll, my boat washes on top of his upturned hull and the two craft do-si-do in the swirling current. Unable to remove myself, I see Rob looking up at me from just beneath the river's surface, his face turning purple, his eyes bulging out from the lack of oxygen. I can do nothing but marvel at his lung capacity.

Chiseled good looks—hah! I think.

When I finally get my craft off his, Rob roars out of the water on a roll. His face regains its normal color and he shouts, "After all I've done for you, Whittaker, you try to drown me!" But I detect a smile.

"Laugh at my kayak again, Lesser, and I'll have your rear end bronzed and sold as a bike stand," I reply, realizing I've made a friend for life.

We decide to call it a day at Little Falls. Barb and Paul have caught up to us and jump down to help lug the boats up the trail to the car. I can't remember ever feeling so alive—or so drained. As I pull off my sodden clothing, I reflect that this was to be the weekend that I joined Bruce and the boys on the Murtaugh.

That night, after Rob heads back to Boise, Paul, Barb, and I relax in the springs and enjoy a few beers. Looking up at the moon, which shines down like a searchlight, I suddenly ask, "You know that big rapid we took a look at on the way up here?"

"You mean Staircase?" queries Paul.

"Yeah, Staircase. Sure seems a shame to come all the way out here and not add it to the mix."

"Not for me it doesn't," laughs Barb.

"Go for it, Whittaker," Paul says, "but you'll be the only one on the river."

I can't blame them for begging off. For much of the year Staircase is a Class IV rapid. But with all this snowmelt, Rob told me, it's a Class V, which makes it a serious undertaking. The initial drop is violent with some large hydraulics, or holes. The water then collides against a cliff that juts out from the left bank, and as the river widens and grows shallow, a profusion of rocks and holes chokes the river.

The next morning, a cold drizzle, on the verge of turning to snow, falls from the gray sky.

"You don't have to do this," Paul tells me after we've packed the car.

"If I hadn't been run over a few months ago, you'd be right," I reply. "But as it is, I've got some questions that need answering."

My traveling mates glance at each other, then turn their eyes toward me, looking as glum as the weather.

"Hey, come on, you guys," I say, trying to sound upbeat. "This isn't a death wish—it's a life wish. That's why I'm starting up at the abandoned bridge. I'll have an hour's worth of boating to decide if Staircase is a calculated risk or sheer stupidity."

Paul and Barb reluctantly help me slide my kayak into the river. As the current tugs me along, I ponder my friends' reaction to my Staircase mission. It's as though they were saying: *Whittaker's been through a hell of a lot—certainly would be a tragedy if something else happens to him, especially on our watch.* Annoyed, I tighten my grip on the paddle's shaft. I realize they have the best of intentions, but having other people worry about me is hard to stomach, particularly because it feeds my self-doubt. What I really need is to have people push me forward into new experiences, not try talking me out of them.

As soon as I come around a blind right-hand bend, a rapid appears in front of me. Sitting up and grabbing my paddle, I scramble to avoid a wave that explodes off the front of a guard rock the size of a small car. I hang hard on a downstream brace and maneuver into the foamy water behind the rock, where I try to blink the water out of my eyes.

Whittaker, if that's how you handle a boat, then your pals are right to be concerned. You're not even close to Staircase yet. If you don't want people to feel sorry for you, earn their respect. Show them what you've got.

Wiggling myself down into the seat, I resume my paddling and pass safely through the obstacles below. After forty-five minutes I come to Staircase, so I pop my spray deck, retrieve my crutches, and head up the bank for a look.

My pulse races when I look down at this complex rapid. Water pulses over the two huge boulders that lie like brontosauruses at the entrance to the rapid. Further down, several other large boulders have created a nasty stretch of exploding waves and holes. One particular hole catches my attention: if I come out of my boat here, my body will be caught in the ugly hydraulic and sent slamming to the river's rocky bed. But what I am really nervous about is the cliff that juts out into the river. Two hundred tons of water per second crashes into this wall at roughly fourteen miles per hour, forming a cushion of water that surges between five and seven feet high. The colliding water recirculates upstream in a ferocious eddy along the left bank. The lower section of the route looks just as ugly, as it is littered with jagged rocks that construction crews pushed into the river when they blasted the road.

After looking at the whole rapid, I plan a route down the initial drop. I'll deal with the lower section when I get to it. The question is, will I still be in my boat when I get there? If I come out of my kayak, it's going to mean a nasty swim at least, and possibly broken bones or loss of life. More than likely I'll be forced against the cliff face. But will the cushion of water rushing against the wall push me away and float me downstream, or will I be plastered up against the cliff? I involuntarily shiver as this ugly scenario dredges up thoughts of the last river trip I took before my accident. The second day on the South Fork of the Salmon River, my boat broached sideways on a rock. As I tried to maneuver it forward, the kayak flipped upstream and the deck collapsed, pinning my legs inside. While I struggled to keep my face above water, the boat settled deeper and deeper into the river. Envisioning exactly what I had to do, I calmed myself and filled my lungs with air one last time before surrendering myself to the river. Then I plunged my numb hands into the gash where the rock had shattered the fiberglass hull and systematically tore the boat apart. A flotation bag burst out of the torn hull and the back of the boat filled with water, dragging itself backward off the rock. As the boat bounced along the riverbed I could glimpse the surface but couldn't reach it. Intense pain tore across my chest; I was running out of air. Frantic, I wondered, *Why the hell hasn't the buoyancy in my life jacket kicked in?* Then I saw that the front of my spray skirt was snagged on the boat. Yanking it free, I rocketed upward, back toward life.

Paul's voice interrupts my reverie: "What's up, Whittaker?" He and Barb have hiked down to the overlook after spotting me from the highway.

"Just wondering what the chances of a pin might be against that cliff," I reply, pointing toward the vertical granite wall in the distance.

"You sure you're up for doing this?" asks Barb, sounding more than a tad bit concerned.

"Never been more unsure of anything in my life," I tell her, forcing a laugh. I stump back along the bank as I locate and memorize the rocks that will determine crucial maneuvers in the rapid. Despite my trepidation, I know that if I were truly embarking on a suicidal run, deep down I'd know it and I wouldn't put my boat back into the river. So often—whether looking up at a mountain, staring into the mouth of a cavern, or examining Class V rapids— I've been put off, intimidated, only to find once I've begun that the task isn't so daunting.

This, I realize, is no different from those other occasions: navigating Staircase is as much about overcoming my fear as it is about handling the turbulence of the river.

"I think I'll give it a whirl," I yell up to Barb and Paul.

To create a soft bulkhead for my foot and stump to push against, I borrow my friends' life jackets and stuff them into the bow of my kayak. I rewrap the Ace bandage around my stump to be certain that it doesn't come unraveled if I go into the drink.

When Paul takes my crutches, I tell him, "See you at the beach on the far side of the North Fork."

After stretching the neoprene skirt around the lip on the cockpit to create a watertight seal between myself and the craft, I make sure the nylon "panic strap" is visible; in the event I dump, all I have to do is pull the ripcord and I'll eject from the boat. Then I move out into the current.

My paddle feels ten pounds heavier, and my hands feel like they belong to someone else. I glance over my right shoulder for my landmark but can't find it. Usually a river pools up before dropping into a maelstrom, but there's no respite here. *Shit, why is it that nothing ever looks the same from the water as it does from the bank?*

Ahead of me looms a huge rock over which the river's brown water surges, and behind that is an ugly, boat-devouring hole. I know that awaiting me after these two hazards is a triangle of flat water, a rest stop where I can slow things down in order to line up my next move. As the river picks up momentum, I accelerate sideways into the rapid, my bow pointed at the hole.

"Now!" I grunt to myself, punching the nose of the kayak forward. It rises over the mound of water and the first third of the boat slams sideways into the outer edge of the hole as the current whips my stern downstream. For a moment I'm facing the bank, and I flash Paul and Barb a grin and get a thumbs-up in return.

Holding the craft behind the hole, I spot the parcel of water I want to catch; it rockets alongside the closest of the two brontosaurus-like boulders I saw from the overlook. If I hit the tongue—that point where the two currents merge—at precisely the correct angle and speed, I can exit behind the giant rock. But as I make my run, a twelve-foot ponderosa pine trunk appears directly in my path. I work my paddle feverishly and miss the log, but everything else goes to hell and I slam into the boulder. Bad move. I stall out and get dragged backwards along the side of the rock. Caught between the ripping current and the eddy line, I struggle to keep the kayak upright. With a thud the stern of the kayak slams into the cliff wall, jerking my body backwards and submerging the bow. Seeing my worst-case scenario play itself out, I flip over and hang upside down beneath the water's surface.

This is definitely not the place to get sucked out of my cockpit, so I wedge my stump and foot together in the boat, forcing my knees upward into the thigh braces. The violent underwater current tears at my paddle; the force of the water crosses my arms, and I have to release my right hand and regrip the shaft to retain the paddle. My eyes are wide open, but in the murky snowmelt I can't get my bearings. *Am I still against the cliff or have I washed clear?* Instinct tells me to roll upright, but experience commands me to hang on, to stay under. The cold squeezes my head.

Count to ten, Whittaker, then give her everything you've got. One, two, three—slow it down, mate. Four, five, six—that's it. Seven, eight, nine . . . ten! I'm out of here.

I lean forward and extend the paddle up to the surface. Crunching my stomach muscles and pulling with my knees, I bring my body along the side of my deck and reach my hands up to the sky. I'm about to unload all I've got into an Eskimo roll when I'm up and wobbling backwards, around the edge of the cliff, in exactly the direction I want to go.

"Thank you, God," I mumble, not entirely irreverently. Perhaps I should crack the Bible that nurse Linda left me before she headed back to Alaska. But before I can do that, I still have to get through the next set of rapids. . . .

By the time it's over, I'm shivering uncontrollably and my heart is thumping wildly. My stump has slammed into the boat's insides so many times that I wonder if some of the liquid now soaking the bandage is blood. But I can hear Paul honking his horn from the highway, and I know I've survived. *Forget about your missing parts, Whittaker. It's what's inside that counts. That may have been a miserable excuse of a run on Staircase, but your boat was in the river, not on the roof of your car.*

As I spin my kayak around to gaze back at the portion of river I just survived, I silently thank Mother Nature for being my salvation. Outdoor pursuits defined the old Tom Whittaker, preventing him from becoming the ditchdigger that everyone had thought he'd be. And now the outdoors are defining the new Tom Whittaker, showing him—and anyone else who gives a damn—exactly what he can be.

Only in the outdoors could I have learned how far I'm capable of pushing myself—physically and mentally. Yesterday, with Rob in the Payette canyon, I would have gladly quit, but on a river there's a beginning and an end—with no stops in between. I had no choice but to see the thing out to the end, and in doing so I discovered something about my mental and physical fortitude. Only in the outdoors is life so filled with the possibility for transformation.

When I finally beach my boat at the North Fork, Barb and Paul are standing there, grinning. "Bloody hell, Whittaker," Barb shouts, "what in tarnation were you playing at?"

"The upside down thing?"

"I'd think so."

"Conducting a survey on fish mating habits for Idaho Fish and Game. Pays quite well, you know."

We all laugh, and as they help me throw the boat on the roof rack, Barb says, "Thank God you haven't changed."

She couldn't be more wrong, I think to myself. Part of me yearns to tell her just how mistaken she is. But unlike the old Tom Whittaker, I keep my gob shut.

CHAPTER 9
Readjustment

The day I lay eyes on my first artificial leg in late August 1980, I'm anything but impressed. It comes with a full-length metal keel and weighs in at a whopping eleven pounds. Although it's touted as a "sports" model, it feels like a sea anchor strapped to my leg. But I suppose it's an improvement over what I've been wearing lately. While I was on a whitewater trip down the Lower Main Salmon Gorge, my friend Bill Goodman, an orthopedic surgeon, found an old Prince Albert tobacco can on the riverbank, took some strips of foam rubber and my glued-together sandal, and created my first prosthesis.

The true advantage of this new artificial leg is that it allows me to attach a mountaineering or rock boot onto my stump. I decide to christen it at City of Rocks, an Idaho climbing mecca. Dave Lovejoy and I head out with Cindy Van Galder, a spirited brunette with impossibly blue eyes. With Dave, it's not clear which head is doing the thinking for him, so I'm never too sure who'll be joining us on our trips. But he has the habit of picking some wildly exciting teammates—Cindy being no exception—and I just thank God that my girlfriend, Mary, has the sense to opt out of our little excursions.

Free climbing could be difficult with an artificial foot, so I start out on aid routes and ease myself onto more difficult climbs as my muscles adjust and my rock wits return. Despite its weight, the artificial leg works well on the rock. I wedge it inside the narrow crack that extends up the granite face, and it feels as though I've regained my appendage, although I can no longer sense the texture of the rock.

Dave, Cindy, and I decide to climb a route that will allow us to install the wedges and pitons we use for protection when free climbing. Using our nylon etriers, we work our way up the rock face by skillful aid climbing. The three of us arrive on the summit just in time to watch the sun drop over the horizon.

"So now what?" Cindy asks cheerfully. Though she is only a novice climber, she has proved herself unflappable.

"Now we go down," Dave replies, aware that the onrushing darkness will make for a trickier descent.

Because of my condition, it's far easier for me to rappel down a rope than to hike back to the base. Dave heads off by foot, but Cindy decides to try her luck on a rope. As an old caver, I'm used to working in the pitch dark. The problem is, I'm not used to working in the pitch dark without a headlamp. I battle to keep our rope anchored into the rock and the two of us balanced on one tiny ledge after another. It's a precarious descent, and, though I try not to reveal how dangerous the situation is, by the time we make it down, my nerves are shot. Cindy, on the other hand, looks serene.

"For a first climbing trip," she announces, "this wasn't too shabby. Thanks for taking me."

Something about her can-do attitude nearly bowls me over. "No problem," I reply, trying to sound cool as the two of us walk back to our campsite in the darkness. "Maybe we'll do it again sometime."

"Sure," she says. "Maybe sometime."

The last time I headed up into the Grand Tetons of Wyoming, I was almost buried under two of the heartiest rockslides I've ever witnessed; thousands of tons of rock seemed to thunder out of the sky, shaking the earth like a NASA shuttle launch. So when Lovejoy and I head out in September, I'm praying we have better luck.

Dave and I start our climb at 6 A.M. from a cave near Amphitheater Lake. Because of the mixed rock and ice terrain we'll be ascending, Dave has loaded us up with all sorts of equipment—ropes, crampons, ice axes, rock gear. My pack weighs upwards of thirty pounds.

Due to the receding ice and my gammy legs, traversing onto the glacier takes far longer than we anticipated, so by the time we reach the face, a good chunk of the morning has vanished. We are, moreover, still east of our route and eight hundred feet lower than we need to be.

Climbing our way from one ledge to another, we spot a line of slings that Dave feels confident will get us back on track. After three pitches, however, we realize that the nylon webbing has been used by people getting off the mountain, not going up.

"We need to head down and get back on track," I announce.

Because the Park Service's permit and sign-out system—devised to keep tabs on who is doing what—doesn't allow for us to be overdue, Dave sees the climb slipping away from us. He convinces me that, rather than lose our hard-won altitude, we should traverse across the enormous, complex North Face. After about eight hundred feet we hit the gully, but it's now 2:30 P.M. Soon we exit the chimney onto a series of ledges and slabs leading us west, straight into a deep cleft in the granite wall. For one pitch, we are, literally, climbing inside the mountain. A millennium's worth of acrid pigeon guano coats everything in sight.

"They should call this place the outhouse!" Dave screams from above me. "It's thick up here."

Using my foot and prosthesis to bridge myself between the two walls, I work upward through what feels and smells like the slurry from a chicken coop. Despite the wretched conditions, I'm pleased with how my artificial leg is responding; I've had to slice my expensive French mountaineering boot to fit in the artificial foot, but it's been easy to wedge my boot into cracks.

When I finally reach Dave, he's looks like he is going to vomit from the stench. He desperately wants to know where we go from here, so I take the lead, taking us along a good ledge until I reach another chimney, which drops into an abyss.

"That's it for me, youth," I laugh. "Now it's your lead."

Dave peers up the steep groove, then down at the dizzying, two-thousand-foot drop that ends up on the hard white of the glacier below.

"You sure about this?" he asks.

"Perfectly. While you were frolicking in the guano, I was thumbing through our guidebook."

I place a couple of pieces of protection to anchor me to the hill and belay our rope. Dave cautiously steps out into the void. A little more than twenty-five feet later, he shouts, "Comforting to know that when I fall to my death, I'll at least be on route."

For a Marine, he can be such a drama queen. "What's it like up there?" I ask.

"A lot of ice about."

"Up or off!" I shout, hearing the words echo above me.

"I can think of something else that ends in *off*," Dave says. "And that's what you need to do."

Something about the urgency in his reply makes me check the guidebook again. Sure enough, it says, "Scramble to the extreme west end of the first ledge and make a 120-foot-high angle lead up a shallow chimney, then another up a difficult friction face to the second ledge."

Well, that's certainly reassuring, I think. *We're definitely on our way.* Then I notice a sentence I've somehow overlooked: "The large exposed, bottomless, ice-filled chimney is not recommended."

"Oops," I mumble. It seems I've been guilty of exactly what I was frustrated with Dave for. Lovejoy is one of the most gifted climbers I've partnered with, but he's also impatient. In his desire to keep moving, he sometimes doesn't think things through and makes mistakes, and we waste time backtracking or otherwise sorting through errors. It's a bit like a builder who pours the foundations of a house in the wrong place, then has to break them out and repour them. Well, in my own rush to get up, in my preoccupation with my new prosthesis, I simply assumed we were at the correct chimney and failed to double-check the guidebook.

We need to move. An icy wind whips up the wall, and overhead, the sun dips behind the jagged ramparts of the Grand Teton. What a half hour ago was trickling water has now frozen into a slick coating of verglass.

I look up at Dave and wonder why he has stalled out. Fifteen minutes goes by before I call up, "Dave what's going on up there?"

"I'm gripped," he says. "Pretty thin up here and most everything is coated in ice."

"Can you get any protection into the rock?"

"Been trying but nothing works."

"How good is the last piece you put in?"

"Bombproof," Dave replies, gazing down fifteen feet to the piece of hardware he wedged into the rock. Indecision consumes him, and I'm angry at myself for miring him in this situation. From that awful afternoon I was strung out on Slip Knot, I know how lonely and scared Dave must be.

"You've only got two options," I explain as delicately as possible. "Either you go for it or I bring you back down with a yank on this rope."

"Bastard!" he shouts. Then, after a pause, he adds, "Watch me now!"

He moves upward, locating handholds that just a moment ago didn't seem to be there. He pulls himself up over the final lip and hollers, "What was all the fuss about?"

Chilled to the bone at 13,000 feet on the North Face of the Grand Teton, I fight my way up the rock to where Dave stands. I tell myself that I should be exhilarated—with only foot I've clawed my way up to within two hours of the summit. But I'm too exhausted to care, and I'm anxious to get the hell off this face while we still can.

Under a sky full of blue-white stars, we traverse to the North Ridge, around to the West Face, then on to the Upper Saddle. The bivy hut is nearly fifteen hundred feet below. My battered legs and knees are in no shape to make the descent, and we don't even have a headlamp. Of course, the prospect of spending a night out at this altitude, at this time of year in Wyoming, is anything but pleasant. But I've run out of options.

"Gonna have to bivy here," I announce wearily. "You go on down and come wake me with a cup of hot tea and some corn flakes in the morning."

Dave just shakes his head. "You can't stay up here. It's September. You don't have any gear. You'll freeze."

"I've slept in worse places in Pocatello. Now go on. I'll lie on the ropes. Just get back up here in the morning."

"You're not going to survive the night," he snaps, before turning to make the complicated descent. Less than fifteen minutes later he's back.

"I can't do this, Whittaker," he says, sounding exhausted. "I just can't." I try to talk him out of staying with me, but he's adamant—and secretly I'm relieved. A trouble shared is a trouble halved. We coil the ropes over the rocks and crawl on top of them, pushing our feet deep into the empty backpacks. With my prosthesis as a pillow, Dave and I squirm into the spoon position, trying to prevent our body heat from leaking out into the cold night air. I can only imagine how resentful Dave must be, knowing that a warm hut awaits at the Lower Saddle. We don't speak.

As the cold works its way into my core, I drop into fitful sleep. Whenever one of our sides grow too numb, we flip ourselves over in unison. Lying here next to this big ex-Marine from Maine, I wonder who else would venture onto a face like this with a cripple on the rebound. I feel a sudden warmth within me despite the chill of the night air. If we'd been granted another two hours of daylight, we'd have summited. If this were July, I tell myself, we'd have made it to the top. After this climb, I realize, I don't have to think of myself as someone without a foot—I'm in possession of two healthy arms and an entire leg. Simply put, three out of four isn't bad. Like my kayaking debut, this hasn't been pretty, but by getting so close to the summit via the North Face in these conditions, I've made my first awkward step toward getting back in the climbing game.

By the time the morning light arrives, we're covered with frost and so stiff we can barely stand. A ranger arrives just as we crawl to our feet. "You know it's illegal to sleep up here," he says officiously, eyeing us as we pack our ropes away with numb hands.

"Don't really think sleep ever entered into what we did last night," I reply, annoyed.

After pulling out a citation booklet, the ranger asks, "Was there a medical emergency?"

"Not anymore," Dave says with a grin. "But a few months ago, he had his foot cut off."

"Oh," he says, looking horrified when he notices my prosthesis. "Do you know the way down?"

I tell him we do, but he nevertheless proceeds to give us a detailed description of the trail below. Finally, as I attach my prosthesis to my stump, he asks, "How'd you guys get up here, anyway?"

"The North Face," Dave replies.

After a long pause, the ranger chuckles and shakes his head. "So, if you can climb the North Face, I'm guessing I probably shouldn't waste too much energy worrying whether you can find your way down the trail!"

Dave and I start down the loose, rocky slope. My knees ache and pain shoots through my stump with each step. I suppose this is what I get for rushing out into the wilderness with a new prosthesis. Exhaustion comes quickly; although I've managed to rebuild 20 pounds of muscle, I'm still 20 pounds below my 185-pound target. I can sense Dave's mounting impatience as I slowly pick my way down the slope. Seven miles and 6,500 feet of descent—that would amount to two hours ordinarily, but now

God only knows how long it'll take me. I hate holding Dave back as much as I hate being held back.

"So, Tom, how you doing?" Dave asks.

"Like a centipede with a wooden leg."

"Well, I've been thinking. We need to do two things—get off this mountain and retrieve our gear from Amphitheater Lake."

"Correct."

"So I thought, if you're OK, I'll scoot across the Black Dike, grab our stuff, and meet you back at the vehicle."

Scoot across? That's certainly an understatement. Reaching Amphitheater Lake via the Black Dike is a rugged undertaking of about eleven miles; he'll have to traverse directly under the complex South Face, some 12,000 feet high, cross two ridges, and ascend another thousand feet before dropping onto Tepee Glacier. I desperately wish the circumstances were different and the two of us could make the traverse together.

"Sounds like the plan," I tell him.

He nods and says, "I was thinking, just to speed things up, that I'd drop my pack at the start of the Dike and you could pick it up on your way past."

Are you insane, Dave? I think. *Just getting to the trailhead is going to require all my strength, and now you want me to carry your pack for you?* But what do you say to someone who just dragged your scrawny arse up the North Face, slept on the rocks with you to keep you from freezing, and has now offered to "scoot across" the mountain to pick up your gear? *No, Dave, carry your own damn sack?* I don't think so.

"OK," I say. "If the rig isn't in the parking lot, it means I'm having a beer at the Mangy Moose." Dave laughs and heads off in a clatter of rattling stones.

When I reach his jettisoned pack hours later, I'm dragging my prosthesis through the dirt. I combine the two loads and shoulder the seventy-pound rucksack containing all the climbing gear we've hauled up the Grand Teton. I can't possibly do this, I tell myself. But I have no other choice.

Because I can feel nothing on the bottom of my prosthetic foot, to keep from tripping I have to focus my eyes on precisely where my next step will land. The intense concentration required for the simplest hiking drains me, and over the next few hours my eyesight blurs. Only a matter of time, I tell myself, before I'm sent tumbling down the mountain.

For hours I creep along the trail, my prosthesis rubbing holes into the tender flesh covering my stump. Sweat and tears streak my face. To keep going, I remind myself of what my father said when he damaged his back: "If I treat myself like an invalid, that's what I'll be." For years, Warren strapped himself into a steel-braced corset and soldiered on. Now it's my turn.

But the throbbing won't go away. I know that by toting this heavy load I'm damaging my already battered body. A few months ago, Dr. Bacon told me that at best my knees would be good for light duty. "You'll never run again," he told me, "but soon you'll be good enough to push a grocery cart." A specialist explained it this way: "If your knees were a radial tire with an 80,000-mile warranty, you've already put 70,000 miles on them. If you go easy, they'll last you another twenty years. If not, you'll burn them up."

Right now, I can practically smell the smoke.

When I finally hear the voice, it takes me a minute to remember where I am. It's nearly dark now—I've spent the entire day inching along this trail. "You need some help with that pack, dude?"

I stand there, teetering like a drunk, and stare at this hiker who has happened upon me.

"You OK, man?" he inquires again.

Unable to speak, I wrestle the rucksack off my back and then follow him down the trail, my eyes riveted to his tie-dyed shirt. I can't fathom distance anymore, and instead of keeping a lookout for hazards, I let my legs flop beneath me blindly.

Eventually, however, we arrive at the trailhead. When Dave sees me, tears well up in his eyes.

"Jesus," he says, lifting the load from the hiker's shoulders. "I didn't realize the load was going to be so heavy for you. I . . . I forgot about your foot."

Dave can't say anything else. But he doesn't have to. That's the best compliment I could receive.

It takes me nearly three weeks to recover from my Grand Teton expedition to the point that I can walk properly. Much of that time I spend hobbling around the confines of my squatter's lair, scribbling in my journal, and mulling over the past few months. It's been ten months since my accident, and I'm trying to come to grips with just who Tom Whittaker is, based on my handicap, my capabilities, and my dreams. Two things are certain: I seem a lot more open and less arrogant now, and being disabled has forced me to work on the edge of all my capabilities, to test my limits as I never have before.

Of course, the Grand Teton climb seems to have set me back as much as it launched me forward. I've never been one to go into the mountains because I know I can climb them; I go to see *if* I can climb them. With my North Face ascent, I've redefined what I'm capable of, but I've also learned that impatience is my worst demon, just as it is Dave's. Only by confronting my insecurities and pushing my body have I seen that my disability doesn't have to keep me from leading an active, vibrant life. At the same time, however, the condition in which the Grand Teton left me has made me see that I can push myself too far. After all my body has been through, I have to be more patient. When it's ready, I'll know.

When I am just about healed from the North Face climb, I pick up my pen and begin scribbling in my journal:

October 3, 1980: When Bruce Bistline told me that I was no longer the same person, I needed to take his comments to heart rather than deny them. If you'd shown a hundred people a picture of me in a crowd and asked them to circle the disabled person, they would all have drawn a circle around me. For me to deny I'm disabled when society sees me as disabled isn't going to get me very far. What I need to do is somehow help them to think differently when they see me. I don't want people's pity; I want their admiration. When I saw John Howie, I admired him because he could pull off maneuvers in a wheelchair that I could never hope to do or dare. Because I built the last Tom Whittaker out of the scrap heap, I can cobble together a new one out of the boneyard. But the one thing I have to realize is: what worked for the old Tom Whittaker will not work for the new one. No more "bull in the china shop"; it's time to think smart.

U.s. Immigration: those folks have been weighing heavily on my mind. I'm not about to get the boot, but I've been knocking around the States so long that I'm always worried about keeping my paperwork in order. But I've made a decision, and it's time to tell my friends.

I head across town to meet Jimmy Lane, Dave Lovejoy, and Mary over at H Hilbert's house. It's particularly important to me that I tell H and Mary, for they have become two of the most significant people in my life.

"I've decided I'm staying," I announce when we all sit down in H's kitchen.

"How's that going to sit with your folks?" H asks.

"OK, I guess," I reply. "They immigrated to Australia last month."

"So now all you need is a real job and a green card," H says.

"Right. But in the reverse order."

Mary listens with a furrowed brow. "If this thing's going where I think it is," she cuts in, "you can forget about it."

"Forget what?" H says, a slight smile spreading across his face.

"If you think that I am going to marry someone with one foot in the grave so he can live in the States, then you don't know me very well."

Although Mary and I are living together, she is adamantly against marrying me. I certainly want to stay in the States, but I don't dwell on her refusal to get married. I'm busy selling shoes, writing articles on outdoor pursuits for British and American educational journals, and traveling to conferences to present my writings to educators and professionals. I'm also enrolled in another master's degree program, this time in athletic administration. But when, after hearing of my situation, a woman in one of my classes graciously offers to tie the knot with me, I'm thrilled that my dilemma will finally be solved.

Mary, however, is less than pleased when I tell her. She threatens to kick me out.

"Look," I explain, "it's just a clerical readjustment. That's all."

Mary doesn't want to hear it. "If you're going to marry anyone, it's me."

"But," I stammer, "you said . . ." My feeble protests mean nothing, and before I know it we've filled out the necessary forms and met with the justice of the peace. After the brief ceremony, we go back to our apartment and tape a sheet of yellow legal paper onto the fridge. The sign reads: THIS IS JUST A CLERICAL READJUSTMENT. Still, we vow that if we're speaking to each other in a year, we'll get hitched in style—friends, band, open bar, church, everything.

Just as I work out my situation with U.S. Immigration, I also get the real job I've been looking for. My grand delusion of getting a half-million-dollar settlement fizzled long ago when it became apparent that the woman who hit me was barely insured. Giving me my break is Bruce Bistline, who hands me a check for $3,000 and the paperwork to the dealership he established to sell kayaks and whitewater gear out of his garage. Bruce is a struggling young lawyer, so his generosity amazes me. The business—"Rapid Transit"—takes off when Darrell Scott, owner of Scott's Ski and Sports, lets me open up a whitewater retail shop under his roof.

By the summer of 1981, sales are booming, and I'm actively rediscovering what I'm capable of on rivers and rock faces. I'm also trying to find a position in a university setting, either as an outdoor program director or an instructor for an academic outdoor adventure education curriculum. Mary has just graduated with a B.S. in nursing, and our differences have become glaring. She wants to be close to her parents in New Jersey and I yearn to be out west. But she's also a gorgeous woman who's used to having men eat out of her hand, and she finds it vexing to have to compete for my attention with the wilderness and "yard apes" (her words) like Dave and Jimmy.

One day in July I come home a day early from a river trip and find someone else's shoes under my bed. Ten days later she leaves with the car, the color TV, and the next-door neighbor. Deep down I'm not too surprised at the outcome. The marriage lasted only ten months. Despite its inauspicious beginnings, however, this was much more than a marriage of convenience, and when Mary leaves, part of me goes with her. But she has never been one to drag stuff out, and for me this is the kindest way to part.

CHAPTER 10
Outer Limits

By September of 1981 I'm ready to take care of some unfinished business: Yosemite's Outer Limits. Ever since I wrote in my journal that I would tackle this difficult climb, the idea has consumed me. I spend as much time as I can on the crags in and around Pocatello to relearn how to climb with a prosthesis and to build my strength.

I also devote myself to physical fitness and nutrition. My new maxim is: The less you've got, the better shape it has to be in. Before my injuries, I simply relied on my nonstop level of activity to keep me fit, but no longer will that sustain me. Phil Lucky's training regimen was just the start. Back then I was nothing more than a six-foot three-inch skeleton, weighing 145 pounds, but now I tip the scales at 178 pounds with 6 percent body fat. And whereas before the accident I could never do more than six pull-ups, I'm currently cranking out three sets of fifteen, three times a week.

On sunny days I head out to the basalt cliffs on the edge of town. These thirty-foot crags are plumb vertical and it's here I learn that I'm going to have to approach climbing in a new way. Because my prosthesis is fused at a right angle, it provides no push or "toe-off" to help my body transition from one move to the next, so my arms take the brunt of the burden. Yet, as all climbers know, you cannot haul your body up hundreds of feet of vertical rock by relying solely on your arms. Learning to "feel" the rock through the thin rubber soles of your boots, knowing how to use your feet precisely, is part of the climber's art. I have had to learn to trust something I can't feel—and trust is the key to climbing. If you don't trust yourself, the worst-case scenario will probably happen; if you don't trust a foothold, odds are you're going to slip. But if you trust yourself and proceed decisively and confidently, the outcome will usually be positive. To develop the necessary trust with my artificial foot, I've had to discipline myself to use small intermediate footholds.

I also learn that I can no longer simply try to solve problems on the rock, as I did when I was a biped. Painstaking planning becomes essential; I must choreograph the sequence my body has to travel well in advance of committing myself to a move. The excitement of learning how to climb all over again drives away the prima donna in me. Rather than get frustrated at not being able to knock off a route that I previously ascended with ease, I admire what I was once able to accomplish. And when I actually finish one of my old climbs in good style, it does wonders for building my self-esteem.

Having rebuilt my confidence and honed my climbing skills, I'm ready for Outer Limits. And, now that Mary has left, I want to ask Cindy Van Galder to be my traveling partner.

No matter how I've tried to deny it, I'm quite taken with Cindy. On that day we hit City of Rocks, she certainly impressed me with her spirit, her toughness, and her sense of fun. After that climb, she joined Dave Lovejoy, Jimmy Lane, and me on a number of biking, rafting, and climbing trips, and over time we have become good friends. Even after Dave went back to Maine, Cindy and I have continued to knock about together. Yet when I call her up to propose my road trip, I'm nervous because I know this would be the first time we've ventured forth as a couple, just the two of us.

As I should have anticipated, however, Cindy doesn't even flinch when I mention a road trip. Eagerly she asks, "Where you wanna go?"

On the drive south to Yosemite, I'm in great spirits: Cindy is by my side, I'm feeling strong, and my knees and stump have healed well beyond what I thought possible.

Although Cindy knows that I'm keen to climb in Yosemite, she knows nothing about my mission to tackle Outer Limits. So we spend several days climbing multi-pitch routes on the walls rising above us, including the Braille Book on Higher Cathedral Rock and the classic route on Fairview Dome.

I'm doing well up on the walls, due not only to my training regimen but also to the new prosthesis that a friend put together for me. Dennis Proksa, Pocatello's master blacksmith, grew tired of listening to me moan about my prosthesis, so he ordered a sheet of titanium from Boeing's scrap yard, got an exact plaster cast of my stump, and went to work. The fact that he knew nothing about building artificial limbs was irrelevant—as was the niggling technicality that welding titanium, hardly a straightforward endeavor, requires a special atmosphere free from nitrogen. After working closely with my prosthetist, Dale Perkins, Dennis presented me with a beautiful three-pound prosthesis with a special rubber toe and heel. The bottom portion is curved like a rocking chair to aid in walking. It feels so much better than my sea anchor I want to skip.

Cindy and I have hit it off with three twenty-something rock jocks we share a campsite with. When I first rolled into camp, to them I was just some old dude with a titanium foot and a beautiful babe, but now they realize that I've already done many of the climbs they're doing—or aspire to. The fact that I tackled these routes in the days before climbing boots had "sticky" rubber, and before the development of spring-loaded devices to jam into cracks, makes them take me a bit more seriously. They even start looking to me for advice.

By the time of my last full day in Yosemite, I've decided to slink home without attempting Outer Limits. Maybe I'll hit it some other time, but right now that route is too much for me. I try to put it out of my mind and instead enjoy our last evening under the stars. Cindy, the boys, and I have had a full day climbing on Glacier Point Apron, and we sit around the campfire, drinking beer and telling stories. But my thoughts return to Outer Limits, and before I know it I'm telling the others how my dream of doing this climb has driven me ever since I wrote it in the back of that notebook. I don't know if it's the beer or that I'm so close to the dream, but as I talk I become choked with emotion.

"But when you get right down to it," I conclude, "Outer Limits doesn't matter. It was a pretty over-the-top dream, but at least it served a useful purpose. It got me back here. Back to Yosemite."

"Hell of a story," says Matt, the leader of the young trio of climbers. "But I've got to disagree. I think Outer Limits is incredibly important and it would be a real honor to be part of this. What do you guys think?"

The other boys agree that I should go for it, and they want to help. *Damn. This is the last thing I wanted to happen.* I politely decline the offer, telling them I can't do it because of the sixteen-hour drive Cindy and I have ahead of us.

But Cindy chimes in: "Oh, that's no big deal. What's the climb going to take? A couple of hours at the most? We can pack up in the morning and be out of here by eight, then be done with the climb by eleven at the latest. That'll get us back into Pocatello by three in the morning and will give me eight hours before I have to get to work."

Gee, thanks, Cindy.

The next morning, I try again to get out of tackling Outer Limits. My heart pounds at even the mention of the climb, so I tell Matt, "Look, right now, Outer Limits is still a dream, not a reality. Nothing wrong with dreams. I can get it on my next trip out here."

Matt finishes his bowl of oatmeal, then says casually, "Well, I see what you're saying. But . . . we've decided for you: today's the day."

"The youth of today certainly are a thick-headed bunch," I mumble, realizing that protest is futile.

Forty minutes later, I'm walking to the base of the climb, remembering the first route I did here with Aussies Kim Carrigan and Greg Mortimer. Was that really only four years ago? Seems like forty.

I look up at the scimitar-like slash in the rock. To the left of the vertical crack, the face is gray, fine-grained granite with splotches of red and brown. To the right, the surface appears as if it has been blasted away by dynamite. I watch one of the boys, Ken, shoot up the pitch, only to sputter out nearly forty-five feet up; he has to be lowered down. Things don't look good: the guy is a good climber—he's solid muscle, eight years younger than me, and, most important, in possession of both his feet.

Why the hell did I let myself get pressured into this no-win situation? I wonder. I try to tie the rope into my climbing harness, but my fingers refuse to work. This whole situation is beginning to feel like my kayak trip down Staircase, only the stakes seem higher—much higher. I'm sick to my stomach and terrified. It's not so much the fear of falling, although there is a bit of that. It's more a fear of failing.

So, you've failed on plenty of climbs you've tried before. What's the big deal?

The big deal is that this is my dream. This is about how John Howie, that wheelchair hot dog I taught to kayak, felt on that day he lay crying on the shower floor. This is my one chance to climb out of the box that society has dumped me in.

"You can do this," I hear Cindy tell me as I step up to the wall. Then all sound ceases, and the only thing I see is the rock in front of me. The first part of the route leans back, just slightly off vertical. By jamming my hands into the fissure, or by using the outside edge of the crack and wedging my feet inside, I literally walk upward, by removing and replacing my hands and feet. The first fifteen feet are not difficult, but my body is tense, my movements clumsy. Then it hits me—the section of the wall that has me stressed is nearly thirty-five feet above me. If I worry about that now, I'll psyche myself out and not even get through this relatively easy section.

Focus on the now. You'll get up there soon. Then you can worry. Focus on the climb one move at a time.

After thirty-five feet the crack steepens to vertical, but by now I've found my rhythm. I use my prosthesis in the crack whenever possible and my good foot on the left wall or on the jagged outside of the flake—a thin bit of rock that overlaps the face—keeping most of my weight on my feet to save my arms for what is to come. The only danger is that I can't feel how far I'm jamming my prosthesis into the crack; I have to be careful not to apply too much force, or else it could, as it has before, become well and truly stuck. If I'm going to make it up this rock face, I can't expend precious energy trying to extricate my artificial foot from the crack.

I come to an abrupt halt when I reach the next section. Here I can no longer jam my hands and feet into the flake. Instead I have to swing out with the left side of my body against the left wall and use my feet to find whatever tiny nubbins are available. This is called lay-backing, dubbed the "technique of no technique" by well-known climber John Long. I'm like a diver in the jackknife position, with my hands grasping the flake and my feet on the wall inches away from my hands. Now I'm committed. Moving my hands up, twisting the toe of my rock boot into the crack, I stretch across the wall with my prosthesis to gain any purchase I can. The strength is draining out of my fingers. This is no place to hang about.

Move follows move until I can reach up and sink my right hand into a peapod-shaped slot in the crack. It jams like the little aluminum wedges we use and absorbs all my weight. I swing back into the crack and pause to gather myself for the next couple of moves. A generous foothold awaits. I steal a glance down at the ant-like figures of Cindy and the boys, then suck in few deep breaths and thrust my free hand back into the dark gap, working my feet higher until I can get my prosthesis on the hold.

Teatime has officially ended. I'm close to halfway there. I'm feeling good. Damn, I'm feeling good. *Not there yet, Whittaker. Don't get carried away.* But my body seems to crackle with electricity.

That I can feel the rock only with my left foot has almost ceased to matter; my prosthesis seems to know how to move, where to find purchase. I trust it in a way I never imagined possible.

Above me stretches ninety feet of the most beautiful crack climbing to be found anywhere in the world—steep and unrelenting, just a few degrees past vertical. I should feel nervous, but instead I'm exhilarated as I peel away the distance between me and the chains that mark the climb's terminus. My hands move quickly up the crack, with each handhold feeling better than the one before it. This is how the hand jive is supposed to be performed.

Before I know it, I am reaching up for the chains that are bolted into the rock at the top of the route. I pull myself onto a tiny ledge, clip my carabiner onto the anchor point, tie myself off, and lean back into my harness. Although I feel utterly spent, my spirit soars upward. *You made it, Whittaker. You bloody made it!*

In my mind I can see my blue notebook and the bold, prophetic entry I scrawled in it. I can smell the dust rising off the bleacher steps of ISU's Mini Dome. And suddenly I know without a doubt that I'll never again fall into the trap of letting other people define me or my capabilities. The only person who'll decide what Tom Whittaker is capable of is Tom Whittaker.

Tears fill my eyes as I stare off across the Merced River to Elephant Rock and up to Rickson's Pinnacle, where Smelly and I lay in the meadow together and looked up at the stars for one last night before I set off for Canada. Now I've returned, minus a foot, to exorcise my demons, with Cindy by my side.

Swallowing hard, I compose myself. "You're going to have to spot me some time up here," I shout down toward terra firma. Then I lean back against the chains, sensing the support of the folks down below and feeling the adrenaline course through my body. For the first time, I know for certain that everything is going to be just fine. As I smell the pines and damp soil, I can only grin, wondering if it's possible to get any higher than this.

When Cindy and I arrive home, I head off toward ISU's student union in search of H, a new plan bursting inside my brain.

"It came to me yesterday," I say as we grab a table in the school cafeteria. "Cindy and I were pulled over, taking a break in a park, when we saw all these people in wheelchairs."

"Yeah, and . . . ?" H asks.

"Well, these people were all parked in their chairs out on a dock, feeding scraps of bread to some ducks. And I realized, H, that it doesn't have to be like that." I then launch into my idea. The plan hinges on getting people with disabilities out into the wilderness, out into the cold, raw, uncompromising bosom of Mother Nature. No institutionally sanctioned rehabilitation program can hope to match the healing and transformative powers of the outdoors.

"The last thing we need is to be clients," I tell H. "We need to take charge of our lives, to drive our own bus. And what better motivator than living your recreational dreams in the safety of a supportive peer group?" I go on to explain how the organization I envision will be structured like a club and how the nature of our outings will be limited only by our imagination. Through cajoling, bribery, or whatever it takes, we'll tap the expertise of anyone who can assist us in our goals, whether it be dogsledding or scuba diving.

By the time I finish speaking, H is grinning. "Sounds great, Whittaker," he says. "You're going to take a group of already traumatized people and encourage them to kill themselves."

"Kill or cure," I reassure him.

Despite playing the devil's advocate, H is on board. He even hints that it might be possible to run the program through the university.

"Now you've got to come up with a name," he says. "Something catchy that summarizes the group's philosophy."

The next morning I'm back in his office. "What do you think of the 'Cooperative Wilderness Handicapped Outdoor Group,' or C.W.HOG for short?" I ask. " 'Cooperative,' because we need the cooperation of the able-bodied community. The rest of it is self-explanatory."

"Sounds catchy, all right," says H. "But do you really think anyone is going to want to be a 'Hog'?"

"They will by the time I'm through," I tell him. I also mention a motto I've come up with: "Better dead than disabled."

Soon I'm stomping around town making public service announcements for local TV and radio stations and convincing local reporters to run articles on the organization. I host a brown-bag lunch for all the disability caregivers in the region. While presenting a slideshow to demonstrate the possibilities—from horse packing to whitewater rafting—I lay my concept on them. They listen attentively, but when I ask if they'll loan me their mailing lists in order to notify their clients about the C.W.HOG program, they instead suggest that I get them some informational literature printed up on university letterhead.

"But you folks represent something like 3,500 people," I explain. "I don't think I can afford that much letterhead."

"Oh, we won't need that many," someone offers.

"So how many should I send you?"

When I take a count, I'm stunned to learn that the group will need only twenty-five copies.

"We'll hand some out to a few counselors," I'm told as my guests file out of the room. "Maybe they can get the word out for you."

As soon as they've left, I turn to H and say, "Would you want that lot in charge of your rehabilitation? They need therapy more than their clients do."

"You just fell into their 'Too Hard' basket, Whittaker," H replies. "Disabled clients are their bread and butter, and you're telling them that you're going to have the disabled drive their own bus—and that you want them to help!"

Undaunted, I plaster the town with notices for an upcoming C.W.HOG meeting, dropping off flyers at sport shops, medical clinics, hospitals, and offices for orthopedic specialists, physical therapists, and prosthetists. My first get-together, held in the cluttered confines of the ISU Outdoor Program office, is less than overwhelming. Twelve people straggle in, only half of whom are disabled. But, sitting there, surrounded by wheelchairs and crutches, I'm on top of the world. Unlike the skeptical professionals, these folks immediately get it and, more important, are eager to get involved.

When I ask what they'd like to do for our first group adventure, no one offers up any suggestions. So, to get them thinking like HOGs, I query, "What would you gladly break your leg getting good at? Because we can do anything that turns you on, just as long as it doesn't get me tossed in jail." I'm sure that no one here has ever been asked such an outrageous question. But everyone in the group grins broadly, and by meeting's end we've agreed to go inner tubing on the snow slopes of nearby Crystal Summit.

That next Saturday, our motley crew piles into several vehicles and winds its way up through the patchwork of fields and knots of silver aspens to the flanks of Scout Mountain, where some snow remains. Because the HOGs are a family affair, everyone has been invited—husbands, wives, children, even dogs. Everyone chatters and laughs as we make our way to the top of our chosen hill—the able-bodied volunteers carrying the inner tubes, the rest of us concentrating on getting ourselves up through the snow. Those who can't walk at all are carried or pulled on sleds.

Clambering onto our inner tubes, we shoot down the slope, a blur of furry-hooded parkas and wool mittens, until we crash into the muddy creek at the bottom. With each descent, any apprehension the group may have had melts away.

After one particularly exhilarating trip down the slope, I catch up with Carl Brinker, a normally wheelchair-bound father of four who now trudges up the slope on his knees, pushing an inner tube in front of him.

"Bloody good fun, eh?" I say to Carl.

He looks up at me, his eyes alight. "Haven't had such a great time since we fed little Albert to the pigs!" he shouts. That's the most deranged statement I've heard in weeks, but it makes me see that Carl is just the type of lunatic the HOGs need. I only pray he's joking.

After an hour and a half, we've scraped the hillside clear of snow, and our crew is muddied and soaked with sweat and slush. We stagger back to our vehicles and head out along the winding country roads, singing songs, telling jokes, and testing ourselves on the birds and trees we notice along the way. In the middle of nowhere we spot a clapboard building with a neon Budweiser sign glowing in the window, so we head inside to celebrate our inaugural expedition and to plot our next adventure. Marilyn Smith, whose legs were ravaged by polio, tells me she knows the coordinator of ISU's intramural sports program.

"Perfect," I blurt out. "You're in charge of organizing a swim program."

Within a week I'm upending wheelchairs into the university's swimming pool. I watch as the laughing, life jacket–clad HOGs tumble into the water and begin bobbing like corks. In the pool, they can learn what to do when they get pitched from a raft in a rapid. Of course, none of them knows yet that I have my eye set on running a seventy-five-mile stretch of the Salmon River.

Our Wednesday night meetings become more and more spirited, and much to my delight, the HOGs are running things themselves—they don't need me to come up with ideas. At each meeting we each share something good that has happened to us over the past week, then launch into whatever adventure we've been thinking of since the last gathering. As soon as one person throws out an idea, planning the expedition becomes a collective undertaking. The rapport among the HOGs delights me, as we cheerfully divide up responsibilities and costs.

Most of these folks have had the disorienting experience I first had when I was bounced from the Murtaugh River trip: as disabled people, they've had responsibility taken away from them, and since they haven't been involved in decision-making they've had their options curtailed. As a result, they had a tough time visualizing themselves playing an integral role in their own futures, and they lost their ability to dream. That is why sharing our dreams—and *acting* on them—is at the core of our mission. We continue to have a ball after our meetings let out. Often we head up to the student theater to catch foreign film night, or sometimes we just go to the bowling alley to bowl a few frames and eat some pizza.

After the cool reception I first received, I'm thrilled that the HOGs have built up so much momentum, and I do whatever I can to keep it going. When not embarking on a twenty-hour drive to our next outdoor adventure, I'm working the phones to drum up cash for the program. I call local businesses and hit up the media whenever I foresee a photo op. Meanwhile, Ron Waters, H's colleague in the Outdoor Program, spearheads an initiative to obtain government grants.

The HOG philosophy proves refreshingly simple. Our motto becomes: "Daring to be different." We treat our adventures as part of our normal lives, not as some foolish departure. So, if you need an attendant for your everyday needs, you'll need one on a HOG expedition. If you need any special medications or paraphernalia to keep healthy and functioning, you bring them along. And of course, I always know that—despite the fact that we are all members of a "common adventure" and that there are no paid guides— if something goes badly wrong I will be the one held accountable. I don't have to be in control, I just have to be in control *enough*.

Just as I did while working as a volunteer instructor for Tony Bradborne at Brathay Hall, I now get the unmistakable feeling that I've stumbled onto something worth doing. After six months, the university even sees merit in the program and begins paying

Lindisfarne days: perfecting my tough-guy look.

Every day I climbed, I felt myself exploding with life. Here I'm leading the first ascent of the Balcony route on Twin Sisters, City of Rocks, Idaho.

Charlie Rowe (left) and Greg Child on the Nose route on El Capitan, perhaps the most famous of all the multi-day climbs in Yosemite.

David Lovejoy, a tough ex-Marine I often climbed with. After my accident, Dave hitchhiked from Maine to Idaho to nurse me back to health.

December 1979, two weeks after the car accident that cost me my right foot and kneecap.

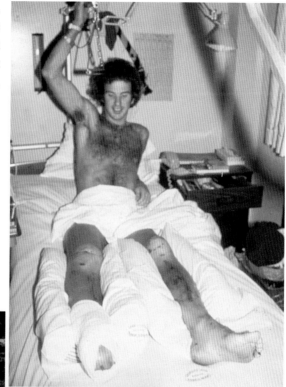

Beginning the journey back: I realized you don't need legs to go kayaking, so I stashed my crutches in the back of my boat and hit the rapids.

The accident left me penniless, so my first artificial foot was nothing more than an old tobacco can taped to my leg—great on rivers but not too hot in the hills!

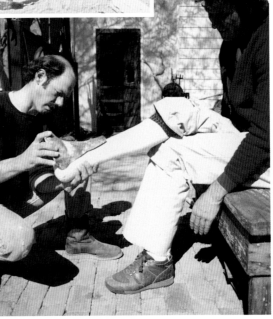

Master blacksmith Dennis Proksa fitting me for a new titanium prosthesis in Pocatello, Idaho. The new foot Dennis welded did wonders for me out on the rocks.

I refused to accept that people with disabilities have to be relegated to the sidelines, so in 1981 I started the Cooperative Wilderness Handicapped Outdoor Group ("The HOGs"). Here I'm belaying Carl Brinker as he rappels in his wheelchair.

Preparing for my first Everest expedition, 1989. I'm wearing the cutting-edge Flex-Foot prosthesis built by Dale Perkins of Rehab Systems (Twin Falls, Idaho).

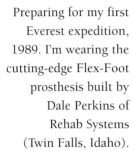

Coming through the upper section of the Khumbu Icefall. Note the spare Flex-Foot sticking out of my pack.

At 20,000 feet, negotiating the crevasses in the Western Cwm, below Everest's Southwest Face. Ski poles allow me to use my upper body and compensate for the loss of balance and power that results from my damaged legs.

After a vicious storm trapped us for five days at 21,000 feet, teammate Andy Lapkiss and I finally made it back to Base Camp.

With Greg Child in front of Everest's North Face, 1995. I had to turn back just fifteen hundred feet from the top, but Greg handed me a rock from the summit and told me, "I want you to put it back where I got it from."

British filmmaker Leo Dickinson, who documented the 1995 Everest expedition, convinced us to take the North Face route via Tibet.

HOWARD KELLEY

With my wife, Cindy, and our six-year-old daughter, Lizzie, en route to Everest, 1998. Lizzie became one of the youngest Westerners ever to travel to Everest Base Camp.

HOWARD KELLEY

Wheelchairs in the Khumbu? Led by Cindy Whittaker, five severely disabled climbers trekked over thirty-eight miles of rugged trails and glaciers to an altitude of 17,500 feet.

The All Abilities Trek to Everest Base Camp, 1998

Kyle Packer, who has cerebral palsy, often crawled on kneepads he fashioned from an old tire.

CINDY WHITTAKER

HOWARD KELLEY

Steve DeRoche, a double amputee, trekked on two Flex-Foot artificial legs.

HOWARD KELLEY

Carla Yustak, a teacher from Canada who has cerebral palsy, was an enthusiastic rock climber and backpacker before joining the All Abilities Trek.

Ike Gayfield, who in 1982 was diagnosed with a degenerative neurological disorder, ran the HOG ski program and was eager to join the All Abilities Trek.

Tom McCurdy, a paraplegic, was a hit with the Sherpa children, who had never seen a wheelchair before.

McCurdy often scooted across the splintered floorboards of the swinging bridges on his rear end.

"If we can make Base Camp, we can do anything we want!" The HOGs nearing their goal.

The entire team—HOGs, Ester-C Everest Challenge climbers, and Sherpas—together at Base Camp.

Ready to make the assault on the summit: trekking into Base Camp.

Gareth Richards, my fellow Welshman and Ester-C Everest Challenge teammate.

HOWARD KELLEY

HOWARD KELLEY

CBS cameraman Jeff Rhoads, who became the first non-Sherpa to reach Everest's summit twice in one season.

Cameraman Tommy Heinrich, who survived a fall of several hundred feet down Everest's summit pyramid.

My parents, Warren (age seventy-eight) and Bobs (seventy-five), at repose in the Himalayas.

To eke out our supplies, we dialed our oxygen cylinders to 3.5 liters per minute—only about half a lungful.

On Aconcagua, South America's tallest mountain.
I am now working to become the first amputee to climb the
Seven Summits, the highest peak on each of the world's continents.

me a salary of four hundred dollars a month, most of which I dump back into the HOGs. And yes, we still sometimes go onto the docks to feed the ducks. We just always make sure to do it en route to some rugged outdoor adventure.

CHAPTER 11
The HOGs

"**You** know, I've never been on a whitewater river before!" Warren shouts over the din of the rushing water. My father and mother have joined me on a HOG outing to Idaho's Salmon River, where I've dreamed of going ever since the group first splashed about in the ISU swimming pool. I was thrilled when the HOGs organized a trip out here.

"You'll do fine, Warren," I tell my father reassuringly. Of course, over the past few hours we've only narrowly averted disaster on several occasions, so I'm not as I confident as I try to sound. Putting a complete novice like Warren in charge of a fifteen-foot raft isn't an easy decision, but I've had to do it since most of our other volunteers are also inexperienced. And this is an unforgiving river.

I tell my father to follow Jerry Johnson, our lead boatman, who is rowing an eighteen-foot raft. "Mirror him," I advise. "If he turns, you turn. Just shadow him."

Over the next few hours, Warren gets hung up on one rock after another, forcing me to dive out of my boat and swim over to free him. Worse, when we reach Ram's Horn rapid, Jerry runs over a rock, creating a two-inch gash in the raft's floor. Water pours into the boat faster than the occupants can bail, until it levels off eight inches deep inside the raft.

Velvet Falls looms ahead. There the river drops over a riverwide shelf hole, and I have no idea how we're going to get past it in one piece. I beach my raft and clamber onto some rocks. From this vantage point it looks possible to pull hard for the big rock on the left side of the river, hit the small eddy behind it, and then catch the tongue, which should allow us to avoid the churning falls.

Once we get back on the river, however, all the gear stacked in Jerry's water-filled boat prevents him from seeing exactly where he needs to make his crucial cut into the chute. He pulls on the oars, trying to keep his sideways momentum going as the river pulls him downstream. But instead of slipping behind the rock, his raft slams into it and bounces back into the main current before dropping sideways over the falls. Miraculously, he doesn't flip, but the water that pounds the raft keeps the boat teetering at a 45-degree angle. I watch in disbelief as Jerry, who has forgotten to put on his life jacket, drops the oars and grabs two passengers just before they tumble into the ugly ledge hole, saving Sheila Brashears, an amputee, and Kyle Packer, who has cerebral palsy.

I have to get below them, so I swap with Warren, who has steered his boat over into a calm eddy. Jerry has pulled Sheila and Kyle up onto the load of gear, but I can't see Jerry's other passenger, who has multiple sclerosis and has irreverently been dubbed "India Rubber Man." Having better luck than Jerry, I hit the eddy behind the rock and pull over below him just in time to see India Rubber Man coming toward me in the current. I toss him a rope and pull him into my boat. Then Larry Zajanc and I scramble onto the bank and head upstream to the stricken craft.

Wrapping a rope around a tree trunk for leverage, Larry and I hoist Jerry's vessel free. "Jerry!" I shout. "Don't stand up in your boat!"

"Why not?" he asks. "Because from up here I can see the bottom of the river where the floor should be!"

Despite the damage to the boat, a mile and a half still separates us from Big Bend camp. We have no choice but to keep moving. Jerry takes the fifteen-foot raft while I captain the crippled eighteen-footer. At Big Bend, we drag it onto the shore and inspect the damage. Velvet Falls has turned a two-inch gash into a sixteen-foot tear in the floor.

"If this is day one," I mumble to myself, "I don't even want to imagine what the next five days are going to be like."

As we set up camp and cook dinner, black clouds roll in. Later that night, lying in my sleeping bag with Cindy by my side, I listen to the rain lashing down on the tarp that protects us. *What an idiot I am*, I think. *What kind of hare-brained scheme is it to run this river with the disabled?* The Middle Fork of the Salmon can devour river trips, and it's doing just that to us. Three HOGs got pretty shaken up today, and one of our rafts now looks to be out of commission. And—even though Sheila, Kyle, and Kristy, who had polio and is now an R.N. in training, planned this trip—it'll be my neck on the chopping block should anybody get hurt. *What the hell's wrong with just feeding ducks anyway? Why can't I be content with bowling like everyone else?*

I shut my eyes to fight back the tears. When I finally open them again, I see Cindy staring straight into my eyes. Something tells me she's been watching me this whole time, but I've been too consumed with self-pity to notice.

"This is the essence of what it's all about," she whispers, reaching up and placing her warm hand on the side of my face. "Being scared is fun—that's what you always say." Then she drops her head to my chest.

Strange, the power of another's words. Cindy may be crazy to have such faith in my ability to make things work, but she has nevertheless made the situation seem far less bleak. The doubts that have been plaguing me fade away. Soon I'm snoring so loudly that Cindy has to punch me in the ribs and tell me that I'll find my prosthesis in my mouth if I don't knock it off.

"The Cindy Van Galder School of Charm," I mumble as I roll over onto my stomach. Any doubts that this woman and I were made for each other disappear along with my other doubts.

The next morning dawns bright and sunny. Our first task is to try to repair the sixteen-foot tear in the raft—a daunting task even if we had all the appropriate tools, which we don't. But everybody wants to get down the river, and this raft is the key. We put Warren in charge of the project, and he quickly ascertains that we are long on glue but short on patching materials. Then Cindy suggests that we use our old military delousing bag, which is an excellent water-proof clothing bag made of the same material as the raft floor.

While some HOGs are cutting the bag into two-inch-wide strips, the rest of us unload the six hundred pounds of gear from the raft, remove the decking and rowing frame, and set the craft up to dry in the sun. After breakfast we deflate the raft and sand-paper the patch material and floor. Duct-taping the tear on the bottom of the raft makes it much easier to glue the patches to the reverse side, and by five that evening the raft is repaired. Everyone has pitched in, and although we've lost an entire day and the work was tedious, focusing on something else has been a welcome respite after the ordeal we experienced yesterday.

The next day the repaired raft responds perfectly, and we manage to avoid the sort of mishaps that beset us the first day—though Warren does take an unscheduled underwater photography break. The rain has returned, however, and we won't be able to make up the lost day. This puts some folks in a bind.

"Anyone who needs to bail should do it here," I tell the group as we huddle on the beach below Indian Creek guard station. "There's an airfield just above us, and there's a good chance a plane will be coming through in the next day or two."

Five of our members announce their intention to hitch a ride out of here. Strangely enough, three of the five are the ones who planned this trip in the first place. We unpack their gear from the rafts and help them up to the landing strip, pushing wheelchairs and lending shoulders to lean on. As we make our way up the bank, I grow concerned about leaving these five to find their own way back to Pocatello. We've never split up the HOGs in the middle of a trip. Then again, the HOGs have always embraced the "challenge by choice" ethic: nobody has to attempt anything he or she doesn't feel ready for.

As soon as we get to the landing strip, we see a Cessna making its descent. After landing, the pilot tells us that he has a full plane and can't take any passengers, but also that at least three more flights are scheduled to land here today. He promises to spread the word.

At this point I stop worrying. The pilot says it will be no problem to find a spot for five hitchhikers. And besides, these folks have plenty of smarts, and they've done their share of difficult whitewater rafting and camping. I started this organization to help the disabled take responsibility for themselves, and that's exactly what these people are doing. The paradox of teaching responsibility is that you first have to relinquish it. If you want people to learn to trust themselves, you have to be able to trust them, to have confidence in them. In some ways, of course, this comes down to faith in yourself: if you trust your judgment of others' capabilities, you won't second-guess yourself.

After bidding farewell to our plane-hopping HOGs, we make our way further down the river and set up camp at Sunflower Flat, where a bubbling hot spring cascades into the river. That night, as we sit in the hot pool, passing around a bottle of Yukon Jack liqueur, my mother, Bobs, leans over to me and confides, "I must say, I truly thought you were a bit daft when you first told me about your HOG organization. But I'm...I'm starting to catch on. Reminds me of the Three Musketeers. All for one and one for all."

"Pass that Yukon over to Bobs," I joke. "One more pull and I think she'll be a disciple!"

"So why do you think Kyle bailed out?" Warren asks suddenly. "I thought this trip was his idea in the first place."

"Yeah, it was," I reply. "But even though he's taking scuba diving classes and has done a bunch of whitewater rafting trips, he's scared stiff of water. I suppose he just decided he was in over his head." But I'm not worried about Kyle Packer. He's come too far.

In truth, Kyle has been a pet project of mine for a while. Not out of any "do-gooder" conviction, but because I genuinely like the guy. I first noticed him a couple of years ago in the lower level of ISU's student union. Hunched over in his fifty-four-pound chrome monstrosity of a wheelchair, with his coat collar turned up and an old knitted hat pulled down tight over his head, he resembled an angry old man, despite being a young college student. He never spoke, and he faced the wall as he pushed his wheelchair backwards with the inward-turned toes of his tattered cowboy boots.

Carl Brinker, a founding member of the HOGs, convinced Kyle to come to some meetings. Far from the sullen, aloof person he seemed in the student union hallways, he struck me as an intelligent, inquisitive sort who likes to laugh. I became frustrated, however, when I noticed that Kyle would sign up for our trips but would never actually attend.

One morning, as the HOGs loaded up the van for a trip to the South Fork of the Snake River, I decided it was time to confront Kyle's commitment problem. I drove to Kyle's house and parked with two wheels on the lawn—so the HOGs on board would have a soft landing when they piled out. "Good morning, Mrs. Packer," I said politely when his mother came to the door. "Is Kyle at home?" She looked aghast.

"Why yes," she said, "Kyle's in bed."

"That's just what I thought. Is his bedroom upstairs, Mrs. Packer?"

"Yes," she said, looking a bit hesitant, "it's upstairs."

Poking my head in through the open front door, I shouted up the stairs, "Kyle, you've got ten minutes to get dressed and get down here. If you don't, I'm coming up there to get you."

THE HOGS ▲ 159

Within eight minutes, Kyle had wheeled himself in front of our van and was ready to go.

It was on that rafting trip that I learned Kyle hated the water. Every time a wave broke over the boat his limbs would flail and he would nearly decapitate someone with his paddle. But he never complained, and when it was over and we headed to the Black Angus for some grub, I marveled at the subtle transformation in him. His normally pasty skin had some color, his hair was slicked back, and he radiated that unmistakable calm one gets after a day spent holding one's own against a river. More important, the young waitresses, who all knew Kyle, lavished him with attention when they learned that he had braved whitewater rapids.

And that was all it took. No longer a recluse, he embraced life and the HOGs. He has become a regular, and over time I've witnessed a profound change in him. By coming out from behind the wall he had built around himself, he realized that people like him and respond positively to him. In a world filled with self-absorbed people, Kyle is one of those rare souls who genuinely cares about others. What has most impressed me about him, however, is his willingness to push himself. Meeting the HOGs has impelled him to do things he never had to do before. On one of his first outings, he looked perplexed when no one moved to assist him from the van to his wheelchair.

"What are you waiting for, Kyle?" I asked. "Get in your chair."

"I can't," he replied.

"How do you know you can't?"

"I just know. I don't have the strength."

"So tell me how I can help you without actually picking you up and carrying you," I said. Kyle was clearly stumped, so after a few minutes of watching him struggle, I supported his butt while he lowered himself down. His face was lathered in sweat from this simple transfer.

"I don't have any muscle," he explained. "The doctors told me I can't do any weight lifting because it will make my spasms worse."

"How the devil do they know that?" I asked.

"Beats me."

"Kyle, less than a hundred years ago doctors used to stick leeches on people to cure them of ailments. They didn't know much then and they don't know a whole lot more now. Take what they have to offer as advice, then proceed as you think best. This is *your* life you're talking about—not theirs. Take charge. Do research. Get other opinions. But don't ever let anybody sideline you. I can't tell you what to do, but I do think that you should be able to handle transferring yourself back and forth from your chair to the van."

Clearly, no one had ever spoken to him like that before. Several days later he rolled into the HOG office to inform me that he had signed up for a weight-training class. Within a few months, muscles were visible on arms that were once as thin as pipe cleaners, and he could move himself easily from the van to his wheelchair, and back again.

The HOGs, he has told me, have been responsible for pushing him in other ways as well. Because cerebral palsy short-circuited his neural wiring, he never got the chance to test himself on a football field or a baseball diamond—never even got the chance to fail. Until he joined the HOGs, this ate at him. He felt he had been denied any opportunity to succeed, so he lived on the periphery of life, bitter, angry. Little was asked of him, and he gave little in return. By the time Brinker strong-armed him into dropping by our group's meeting, he was on the verge of flunking out of ISU. Now he's a straight-A student, and he's no longer angry about his lot in life.

"It was all just stupid vanity," he explained. "But it doesn't bother me anymore. I've run the Grand Canyon, horse-packed into the Tetons, ridden a dogsled into Yellowstone, sea-kayaked in British Columbia, and scuba dived. After I've done all that, complaining about not being able to try out for quarterback seems pretty lame."

Of one thing about Kyle I'm certain: there's no way that, even a year ago, he would have entered himself as a candidate for ISU's homecoming king. But this year he has indeed made himself a candidate. I can't say I've ever been a fan of such sophomoric popularity contests, but as a friend I feel I have a duty to be there when the winner is announced. So I cancel a kayaking trip I had planned and head over to the Mini Dome in time for the ceremony, which is being held at halftime of the homecoming football game.

From the stands I see the various contestants file out onto the football field. Kyle rolls out in his wheelchair, decked out in a tux, with a beautiful young thing in an evening gown at his side. Although it's halftime of the game, much of the crowd hangs around to check out this new action on the field. Never would I have guessed that so many folks gave a rat's ass about this contest.

From over the loudspeaker the announcer names the third runner-up—and it's not Kyle. A moment later, the name of the second runner-up reverberates across the stadium—and again, it's not Kyle. I bury my head in my hands.

Damn it, you put yourself out there, Kyle, and they didn't even have the courtesy to vote you into third place.

In the distance, a world away from my angry thoughts, a name thunders out from the loudspeaker, but I don't catch it—I don't even bother to listen, really. But as I hear people screaming and see them throwing their orange caps in the air in celebration, I look down at the field once again. Grinning broadly, Kyle is rolling himself across the AstroTurf to accept a plaque. These people, I realize, are cheering for him. Kyle has won.

To join the celebration I fling my cap skyward, never bothering to see where it lands. Tears roll down my cheeks. And it hits me: maybe it's not so bad that I lost my foot. Right now, to lose a foot but discover my purpose doesn't seem like such a lousy trade.

It's time for a HOG ski program, I've decided. But starting such a program isn't particularly simple. First, I myself have had to relearn how to ski.

On some recent road trips to Winter Park, Colorado, I hooked up with Hal O'Leary, a Canadian ski instructor who is the guru of the burgeoning adaptive ski movement. He and his staff of seasoned instructors showed me how to carve turns in a prosthesis, and, more important, they made me see that teaching skiing to the disabled is a difficult undertaking that requires patience and empathy. Hal seemed honestly impressed by my desire to take what I learned and teach it to the HOGs, and at the end of my last trip he graciously handed over a load of adaptive alpine ski equipment that, though damaged, could be easily repaired. The equipment is perfect for the HOGs, including a fiberglass sit ski that folks like Kyle can use, as well as three pairs of outrigger skis for amputees and people with lower-limb problems.

I desperately want to avoid using paid ski instructors to teach the HOGs, since I long ago convinced myself that if outdoor professionals get involved, our adventures will seem like nothing more than commercial transactions. Once again the HOGs will become clients. I want the HOGs to learn skiing from skiers. That's why I've been working to get local powder hounds on board.

When I bribe several downhill aces with pizza and beer to join me for an hour on the slopes of nearby Pebble Creek Ski Area, I can tell they consider teaching the handicapped about as challenging as skiing down the bunny slope. It's nothing they want to do soon, but I soldier on. First I pair them up and ask them to perform a stem christie—a basic turning maneuver. They each execute the move flawlessly, snickering all the while at the one-footed Welshman who's telling them what to do. "Now try it blindfolded," I say. After handing out bandannas to cover their eyes, I watch as the partners try to talk the blindfolded skiers through the seemingly simple task. As the skiers struggle and the sighted partners diligently coach them, I can tell I'm getting their attention.

"See what happens when you take away one of your senses," I laugh. "It's like that with disabled skiers, only they don't know how to ski in the first place. Each of you had the opportunity to unlock your partner's potential and help him succeed. But you couldn't do it—not because he can't do the maneuver, but because you are a piss-poor teacher. You just need to know that if people can't learn, it's not because they're stupid or don't get it or can't do it—it's because you can't teach."

When I leave an hour later, my new volunteer instructors are trying to figure out the nuances of how to distill their knowledge of the slopes into a language that the HOGs can understand. They've seen how hard it can be.

Working with Hal O'Leary and with these local hotshots has made me see that I need someone with the credentials and empathy to run the HOG ski program. I need Ike Gayfield.

Raised by his father in gang-infested projects near Oakland, Ike found a way out through athletics. In 1965 he earned a track scholarship to Idaho State, where he became an Honorable Mention All-American. After graduating with a degree in physical and special education, he remained in Pocatello and opened Mountain Folk Equipment, a shop specializing in hard-to-find climbing, rafting, and kayaking gear. He also became an accomplished downhill skier, cyclist, river rafter, and mountaineer.

The winter of my accident, Ike began falling down on the ski slopes. Something didn't feel right in his legs, as if the wires had gone down somewhere between his brain and his lower extremities, but he brushed it off. Over time, however, the tumbles grew more frequent. When he finally sought medical attention, specialists told him he was experiencing the beginning stages of multiple sclerosis. Yet when surgeons conducted exploratory surgery, they were perplexed. Nothing seemed to help him. Eventually he was diagnosed with transverse myelitis, a neurological disorder that is progressive in nature. Ike, always a perfect physical specimen, had been reduced to a broken machine. Descending into a deep depression, he lost his business and his longtime girlfriend.

In truth, Ike didn't much care for me when the two of us were able-bodied—I was too much of a showboat for his tastes, a tad too outrageous. Now that we're both gimps, he seems to tolerate me, but still, he has kept his distance from the HOGs. In fact, he has kept his distance from almost everyone since his body began betraying him.

Nevertheless, I am confident that Ike is the man I need. He certainly has the credentials—before he started avoiding the slopes and shutting himself off from others, he directed the ski school at Pebble Creek—and, just as important, he has the empathy I'm looking for. So, when Ike telephones me and asks if we can meet, I am thrilled. This is my opportunity.

A few days later, when Ike walks into the Outdoor Program office leaning on his walking stick, I notice that his clothes are wet and his hair is caked in mud. I'm immediately angry with myself. It's obvious what has happened: Ike walked all the way across town in the thawing snow. It must have taken him two hours. The highway he traveled is lined with deep, mud-splattered drifts. He clearly took a tumble or two along the way.

Damn it, Whittaker, why didn't you ask if he had a ride? I don't have the nerve to ask him about the mud, and Ike makes no mention of it. That's typical of Ike: never in my life have I known an individual with such pride, such determination.

We head up to the ISU cafeteria for a cup of coffee. Once we've sat down, Ike opens the conversation. "Whittaker," he says, "I've been denying my disability and staying away from the HOGs for as long as I could stand it. But . . . I've hit bottom. Lost nearly everything I cared about in life, everything I've worked so hard for. So I'm swallowing my pride and telling you that I'd like to help out with the HOGs."

Ike, it seems, wants to help with the swimming program. I tell him about the program, which is being run by Diane Dorman, an undergrad at ISU who is a trained lifeguard. The HOGs are involved in such activities as aerobics, lap swimming, and white-water emergency drills. I scribble Diane's number on a napkin and tell Ike that she'll be expecting his call.

Yet I can't let him escape without telling him about the ski program I'm yearning to start for the HOGs. I launch into my story about learning to ski as an amputee, about working with Hal O'Leary, and about signing up the local powder hounds to help out. Ike stares at me as I rehash my tale, raising and lowering the coffee cup to his mouth with slow, deliberate movements. Though he's a difficult man to read, I can tell my story is forcing him to contemplate things he's tried to shut out of his head.

"You'd be great for the program," I finally tell him. "Plus, I can offer you a whopping $1,000 to do the job and another $500 to cover your expenses." The HOGs are always desperate for cash, but Ike is worth the money.

Ike looks past me, places the cup gently back onto the table, and calmly considers my offer.

"OK," he says after a long pause. "I'll do it."

And with that, I have a director for the ski program. But I also sense that a real friendship is going to grow between us.

"Know what I just realized?" I say, turning to the man sitting next to me on the ski lift. "Between the two of us, you and I only have one foot . . . and it seems I've got it."

I just met Steve DeRoche a few hours ago, but I'm guessing that he's twisted enough to get my sense of humor. For a moment, however, as the lift carries us up the mountain, there's nothing but silence from this man with two artificial legs. Maybe I've goofed.

But then, finally, Steve roars with laughter. I know this man will make a good HOG.

Steve recently saw a television show about the HOGs, and he's decided to track me down. He, of course, is no stranger to disability: both his legs were amputated when he was just five years old, the result of a birth defect. Curious about our organization, he has agreed to join us on our trip to the Grand Targhee Ski Area, on the west slope of the Tetons. He remains somewhat skeptical, however, and has driven himself here rather than ride with us in the van.

Moments after my witty comment about our predicament, Steve turns to me and asks, "What the hell is it you guys actually do?"

"Anything we want," I reply. "The only stipulation is that it has to be legal and something you can share with the other HOGs." I explain that becoming a HOG is simple: all you need to do is show up. There's no membership, no fees, no officers or hierarchy. No single voice is more important than anyone else's—in fact, the weaker the voice, the more it is responded to.

We ski for the rest of the day, then stash our skis in the snow and head into the bar. The cold hasn't really affected Steve, but my stump, which goes all the way to my ski boot, has turned to ice. Eventually I pull off my prosthesis and begin rubbing it, trying to coax some warm blood down into the tissue. Suddenly a Rubenesque brunette detaches herself from a table of women and approaches.

"Are you OK?" she asks.

"Bloody thing won't warm up," I reply, still kneading the flesh.

"Where are you from?" she asks flirtatiously.

"Wales."

"I just love your accent. Here, let me help." She unzips the bib of her snowsuit, leans forward, and plunges the frigid end of my leg down into her ample cleavage. "Now that feels better," she coos. "Doesn't it?"

"You're not wrong," I say. "Just makes me wish I could wiggle my toes." The HOGs—and the rest of the bar—stare in amazement. She smiles and makes some chitchat. Then, all too soon, she lovingly removes my leg from her warm bosom and returns to her table. Nearly everyone in the bar applauds—especially me.

"Daaamn," says Steve.

"Happens all the time during HOG outings, doesn't it?" I ask the group. The HOGs nod, supporting me in my shameful lie.

"Daaamn," Steve repeats. "If I had any doubts about becoming a HOG, I don't anymore."

Sure enough, Steve becomes a die-hard HOG. His wife, Cindy— who comes with all her parts—even signs on as the organization's secretary. Somewhere along the way, Steve becomes a master oarsman. And whenever he gets a chance, he roars, "Damn, Whittaker, I can't tell you how glad I am that you lost your foot!"

CHAPTER 12
Tasmanian Devils

Up here, high above the cold blue waters of the Pacific, I'm missing home already. I'm shoehorned into this tiny airline seat on my way to Australia to lecture on the topic of opening up the outdoors to the disabled. This six-week speaking tour, arranged by the well-intentioned though poorly named Spastic Society, is a wonderful opportunity to spread the message of the HOGs, but in order to prepare for my travels I had to skip our recent rafting trip down the Green River—the first major HOG outing I've ever missed.

With hours to kill before touchdown in Melbourne, I pop into my Walkman the cassette that Kyle handed me just before I left Pocatello. After pushing the play button, I hear the sounds of a gurgling river, a crackling fire, and the relaxed murmur of exhausted, perfectly content people. Right away I know what I'm listening to: the HOGs, by the banks of the Green River.

"Tom? Hey, Tom?" chirps a voice I immediately recognize as that of Teresa Montoya, a blind woman the HOGs first met during a Winter Park ski trip. "I don't know where you are right now, Whittaker, but I just wanted to tell you that the HOGs rock." The comment prompts whistles and howls that pierce my eardrums.

"Come on, guys!" she shouts. "Shut up for a minute. This is important. I need to say this and I don't need your help."

"Give her some space," says another voice. The group quiets down and Teresa continues. "So I guess what I'm trying to say is that you guys make me feel so free. Like I can do anything— anything at all. But at the same time, I don't have to do anything. I mean, where else could a blind woman paddle a raft down a Class III rapid, yell out orders, and have everyone do just what I tell them? There I was, yelling, 'Forward all...hold right... back-paddle left,' and everybody was screaming, 'Oh, shit!' So I panicked and yelled, 'What do I do?' And Kyle shouted, 'Anything you want—you're the captain!'" She begins choking up and I hear what can only be the sound of people moving in to comfort her.

A moment later, in between gasps, she says, "You know, I feel safer and more comfortable with these lunatics than any group of people in the world. I just want you guys to know that I love you. I really do."

Teresa's words are causing my throat to swell, so I shut off the tape player. I close my eyes and try to imagine myself by the warmth of that fire I heard crackling on the tape, among the people I care about so deeply.

Hearing Teresa's message has reminded me why I've taken the path I now travel. For the past three years I've been barely subsisting. The four hundred bucks a month that ISU pays me barely covers my living expenses; if I actually had to pay rent, I'd be in dire financial straits. Yet, as Teresa has so clearly shown me, I'm not running the HOG program for the money. Funny, the things that your heart can make you do. This is something about which I'm passionate, to which I'm wholly committed. As difficult as it might be sometimes to get by on my meager wages, when I listen to such a heartfelt message of love and appreciation, I know I'm doing what I'm meant to do.

From Melbourne I set out on my whirlwind speaking tour. Wherever I go I talk about the success we've experienced with the HOGs and the benefits that outdoor adventure provides for people with disabilities. A master of logistics, Warren has volunteered to serve as my road manager and guide. Whenever my packed schedule permits, we dart off into the bush to go hiking and climbing. Over the course of my journey, numerous Australian outdoorsmen tell me of a remote, rugged river on the island of Tasmania. A solo descent of the Franklin River, I'm told, has been done only once or twice before, but never sight unseen. The more I hear about this challenging river, the more I feel as if I've been infected with a virus I can't shake.

By the time Warren and I head for the Tasmanian leg of the tour, I know that the Franklin is something I have to do. My mother, Bobs, has joined us for Tasmania, so when I set off in my rented kayak, two weeks before Christmas, she is there to bid me adieu. "If I'm not at the take-out on the 23rd of December, head back to Melbourne—I'll catch up with you when I get done," I shout to Bobs and Warren as I dip my paddle into the tea-colored water of the Collingwood River, which leads to the Franklin. Standing up there on that tiny bridge—my mother with her arms hanging down by her side, my father with one hand on his staff, the other on his hip—they both look perfectly English. But as the river takes me farther away, Bobs suddenly raises her arm and waves enthusiastically. Warren turns to look at her for a moment, then raises his hand in a salute. Something about their rapidly diminishing image makes me feel terribly alone. I wonder about the strength it must take for them to support me unconditionally, allowing me to evolve into the person I need to be rather than the one they'd like me to be.

When I'm sufficiently out of sight, I wipe my eyes on my neoprene sleeve and turn my attention to the river. My boat, weighing 110 pounds, feels sluggish from all the supplies I've stuffed inside it. One Aussie paddler advised me to bring enough food for twelve days, though he said I could expect the trip to take six. I have a hunch its only going to take four days, but to play it safe I've packed enough grub for six. After eight miles and five time- and energy-consuming portages, however, I begin to think the Aussie might have been right.

By early evening, I arrive on the Franklin. The river is hemmed in on both sides by a thick, nearly impenetrable temperate rain forest. The British used to send convicts here to chop down towering

Hunon pines, which would become sturdy masts for the British Navy's warships. The forest is so impossibly dense that guards never bothered to accompany the prisoners—there was no chance of escape. Like those convicts, I am now trapped, with my only exit being at the river's confluence, fifty-nine miles below the mouth of the Collingwood. I am committed.

According to the map, the Franklin River has three Class VI canyons around which I'll be forced to portage (Class VI in whitewater ratings denotes suicidal). There's also plenty of "serious" Class IV and "very serious" Class V whitewater. What worries me is that the map says nothing about the five portages I've already made to avoid heavy logjams—most likely because they're too inconsequential to mention. In fact, I've got miles to travel before I hit any truly challenging sections.

It is at the next logjam where I realize that I'll have to approach this river as I have no other. Quite simply, I'll need to take far more calculated risks than I ever have. At this logjam, I'm in no mood to crawl out of my boat and muscle it around the obstruction. Peering over the top of a gigantic trunk blocking the river, I decide to seal-launch myself off this natural dam and into the murky pool churning eight feet below. The risk is that there is no way to tell what lurks beneath the water's surface. If there are submerged logs, the pointed bow of my kayak could easily get jammed when I rocket into the water. Yet if I portage at every turn, it defeats the purpose of running the river, and besides, it'll eat up too much time and energy.

The river rushes over the top of the slippery trunk, and I allow the current to lift up my boat and deposit it onto the lip. No turning back now. Suddenly I'm airborne, leaning backwards, plummeting nose-first into the murk. The bow rips through the cold surface and I plunge nearly twelve feet into the brown liquid before exploding back upward, stern first. I let out a gleeful whoop. My first calculated risk was a good one.

For the next two days I move steadily, gambling when necessary. Yet I still haven't arrived at the Franklin's most difficult sections, and I have to acknowledge that the river is far more serious than I imagined.

Late in the morning of my second day, I come across a drop that requires scouting from my boat. As I ferry glide from one shore to the other, I scan the rapid and finally commit to a route. I'll drop into the heart of the falls sideways, brace hard into the violent standing wave, spin my kayak upstream, then ferry left in order to avoid slamming into a partly submerged log. Leaning downstream on a high brace, I allow the current to turn me sideways toward the standing wave, and then I steer the kayak's hull aggressively into the wave, bracing myself on its frothy crest.

Then I remember it. "My map! God, no, not the map!"

In order to orient myself, I spread my map out on the kayak's deck, but I forgot to tuck it back inside my wetsuit. With one angry, explosive paddle stroke, I pivot my kayak and frantically search the churning water. Yet the river coughs nothing up. I'm without a map on a potentially deadly river that doesn't attract solo attempts. My head spins and I hyperventilate.

No time for this, I scold myself. *Got to stay focused.*

I turn and thread my way through the rock garden below. When I at last reach calmer water, I drift into a placid eddy and consider again how I am trapped. I'm a captive on a river that's impossible to hike out of, a river that contains three potentially lethal gorges. If I miss the take-out and get swept into them, it's unlikely that I'll make it out in one piece. My survival will hinge on my ability to read each rapid and to trust my decisions unwaveringly. While images of Cindy and my parents flood my mind, I wonder if I'll live to see Christmas.

Suddenly I need out of this boat. Ripping off the spray skirt, I push myself up from the craft, then—counter to every rule of personal conduct beaten into me at boarding school—drop to the muddy ground and wail.

Never thought it would end like this, did you, Whittaker? Dying out here on a river, all alone, so far from home and friends.

Feeling helpless, and furious with myself for my carelessness, I suddenly remember something that Ike Gayfield is always saying. Ike's mantra forms on my lips: "You're in a bad place, so you best be bad." As soon as I realize there's nothing more to do but press on and face my fears, my anxiety disappears.

When I squeeze myself back into the cockpit and head back into the fast-moving current, I feel strangely alive, in sync with the world surrounding me. And when I drop through my first set of rapids without a map, it becomes clear why: all the distractions, all the wondering, all the doubt has disappeared. No more am I obsessed with the location of the next portage, or how fast I'm traveling, or where I am on the route. Losing my map, it seems, has been a gift. For once, I'm trusting solely in myself. It's just me and this wild, unforgiving river.

By mid-afternoon I've arrived at a narrow gorge, where the constriction and gradient force the river to flow faster. Eventually I come to a rapid that I remember from the map: Sidewinder. To get a better view, I beach my boat and scramble onto the rock shelf, which has been made slick by the rain that has been falling steadily since late morning. My unprotected titanium prosthesis— a tennis shoe wouldn't fit in my boat's cramped cockpit—clatters on the rock as I move about. The river, I can see, bends and creates what the map described as a "wall of death." I see why: hit it too high and I'll disappear into a strainer of rocks; hit it too low and I'll be sucked into an ugly hole.

When I turn to make my way back to the kayak, my prosthesis suddenly slips out from under me. Instinctively I thrust out my arms to break my fall, and when I slam onto the shelf I feel the unmistakable crack of bone inside my right hand. The pain is instantaneous, and I crumple into a heap. Soon, however, I pick myself up and plunge my hand into the river's cold water, hoping to keep the swelling down.

Screw it, Whittaker. No time for playing Boy Scouts. Keep moving.

Trying to grip my heavy paddle sends pain shooting up my arm. Not good. My only recourse is to begin paddling and hope that in the chaos of the rapids I will forget about the pain. Sure enough, by the time I emerge from these rapids, I've become so in tune with the river and what I need to do that the pain in my hand is reduced to a dull throb. "Today is a good day to die," I catch myself whispering. I now realize just what the Sioux braves meant by the phrase. Completely isolated, with a broken hand, and without a map on a river that is impossible to retreat from, I can't recall ever feeling more flush with life.

My third day on the river, I awaken to the dull roar of Thunder Rush. Although I intended to navigate these monster rapids, the river has risen so quickly in this rain that paddling through is no longer an option. Time to portage.

After creating a handle for my kayak by tying a line from the bow, around the cockpit, and to the stern, I start climbing up a steep bank of tree roots. I have about thirty feet of excess rope that allows me to climb ahead and pull my hundred-pound boat up after me. The higher I climb, however, the more I fear that I will drop the kayak, which is my lifeline on the river. If I lose the boat, I lose my food, my sleeping bag, my dry clothes, and my only means of escape. After pulling myself up more than a hundred feet, I take the rope, which I've been clenching in my teeth, and tie it around my waist. Now, if I lose my grip and the kayak falls, I'll go with it. End of story.

The root-covered hillside leads to a series of ladders attached to the cliff and then a narrow catwalk fashioned from twelve-inch-wide panels of aluminum. Pulling myself onto this flimsy structure, I position the kayak in front of me and slowly push the boat forward, trying to ignore the world rumbling nearly two hundred feet below. When I spot the end of the narrow walkway, I exclaim, "Piece of duff. One portage-from-hell down, two more to go."

But within a few feet I see that the walkway has not ended. In fact, the cliff face I'm traveling along takes a 90-degree left-hand turn, and this aluminum ledge follows it. "Bloody marvelous," I grunt.

Trying to push the kayak around the sharp corner proves impossible. I have no other choice but to walk myself to the front of the teetering boat. As the rain continues to pour down, I place my foot on the boat's deck and watch the opposite end rise into the air like a seesaw. My life has been reduced to three critical variables: the kayak's slippery deck, its rocking hull, and my artificial foot. Never has thirteen feet—the distance from stern and bow—felt so painfully expansive. The rock provides feeble handholds, definitely not enough of an anchor if the boat pivots too much and I lose my balance.

My movements are fluid, however, and the hull barely wiggles. Inching my way off the deck and back onto the catwalk, I collapse onto the thin aluminum flooring. Now two hours into my portage, I consider that I'd have been safer staying on the river and paddling Thunder Rush.

Being in front of the kayak allows me to pull it around the corner and move to the end of the walkway. A single stretch of red climbing rope dangles down the rock face.

"Tough bastards, these Aussies," I mutter. As I feed out the line to let the kayak dangle fifty feet below, pain shoots through my right hand once again. It's definitely broken. Threading the climbing rope between my legs and pulling it over my shoulder to create a makeshift harness and friction device, I rappel down to the kayak, which is hanging suspended in the air, and wedge the pointed bow securely into a crack in the slab. With the boat secured, I pull myself back up the rope, untie the haul line, and tie it around my waist. Painfully and slowly, I descend back down to the kayak, find something to tie the line onto, and drop the boat back to the river's edge.

Just before shoving off from the bank, I peer up at the cliffs to inspect the impossible route I just traversed high overhead.

"After that," I tell myself, "the other two portages should be a piece of cake."

Wrong.

The rest of the day feels like death by portage. This definitely ranks as the most grueling of all the days I've logged traveling through the wilderness. Just before sunset I pull my kayak ashore. I'm exhausted, and my hands barely function after being torn and rubbed raw by the polypropylene rope I've used for portaging.

Somehow, however, I've detached myself from the discomfort. My spirit is soaring, as I'm buoyed by the knowledge that no matter how grueling the situation, I possess the skills to resolve it.

After building a small fire under the lee of a huge boulder, I sit with my wet sleeping bag over my legs and watch the smoke waft up into the darkness. This, I think, is what's known as peace. Seems strange that I had to come all the way to a temperate rain forest in Tasmania to find it.

Gazing into the flames of the campfire, I catch a glimpse of Cindy. She's laughing, her blue eyes sparkling, but it takes a moment before I can place the image. Then I remember the scene: it was at the most recent HOG Pig-out, our annual fund-raising barbecue, which has become something of a Pocatello event. Cindy was there for me at the barbecue as she's there for me in everything. I can see her now, loading heavy tables, preparing food, doing whatever is necessary for this event to be a success.

And that's when I start wondering: Have I ever really been there for her? Have I ever really given her the support she needs in her life to evolve into the person she's striving to become?

The answer comes back a resounding "no."

Due to my arrogant take-it-or-leave-it attitude, our relationship has always been on my terms. I yearn for support, but I also crave being footloose. Why on earth would she put up with my nonsense?

Suddenly, panic sweeps over me. Maybe during all the time I've spent Down Under, she's decided to go off with someone else. Who could blame her? Mary took off, and I couldn't really fault her. Maybe I'm already history.

I build up the fire and crawl into my wet sleeping bag, but I can't turn my head off. So much for inner tranquility. For hours I lie there listening to the rain come down and the river rush by. Again and again my thoughts return to Cindy.

Before long, I'm drifting back to Pocatello. It's dark. I'm standing in the open back door of Cindy's house. A pair of kayaks hangs from the roof of the carport we built together. Tessa, the cat, slinks across the lawn. This, I realize, is my home now, the first real one I've lived in since I left my family's house when I was in my teens. I love this place. Dennis, who crafted my titanium foot, made the railings. Larry, with the help of a chainsaw, made the massive hole in our exterior wall for the glass-brick.

And as I lie here by the fire in Tasmania, I know exactly what I need to do. Something that should have been done a long time ago. I just pray it isn't too late. "Cindy," I whisper into the flames, "I believe in you. I love you. And if you'll have me, I want to be your husband."

The only reply I get comes from the roaring river and the spatter of rain on the protective tarp.

Stiff and cold, I limp over to the water and wait for the first light to break. When it finally arrives, I've breakfasted and packed my boat. Time to go home. Finally, after one last series of complex rapids, the seething Franklin becomes as placid as a lake. I paddle a seemingly endless stretch of flat water that eventually merges with the Gordon River.

It takes me a while before I realize that my journey is over. I've survived the Franklin River without a map, a right foot, or a functioning pair of hands.

Normally when I finish a river, I want to go right back up and run it again. But I've had my fill of this place. I won't be back. Something inside me wants to celebrate, to rejoice in conquering this river, but the elation doesn't come. All I feel is emptiness. I'm not sure what I came looking for and I'm even more unsure about what I found. There's nothing more to do but keep digging my paddle into the water.

"Thank you, Lord, for bringing this turkey back home for Christmas," I mutter.

In the distance I spot a wharf. The moment my bow makes contact with the dock, I scramble up from my cockpit.

"What the hell happened to you, mate?" inquires a grease-smeared workman who stares at my prosthesis.

"Just came down the Franklin," I reply.

He stands there looking at this Welshman with a foot missing and one swollen hand duct-taped to a paddle.

"And I'm a Tasmanian devil," he says. "So where are your mates?"

"Home for Christmas." A grin spreads across my face. "Did it by myself."

"Well I'll be buggered. You bang up your leg like that on the river?"

"No, did it in a car wreck, a few years back."

"And your mates," he asks again, still not comprehending, "where are they?"

"Couldn't find any stupid enough to come with me."

He runs his tongue across his toothless gums and grins. "Well I'll be buggered," he repeats, then ambles across the wharf and into a ramshackle shed. A moment later he's back, spinning the top off a whisky bottle.

"A mite early to be breaking into this, but I think we can make an exception here," he says, taking a swig, then handing me the bottle. Why not? I upend it and feel the liquor slide into my stomach. Something about the warmth spreading inside my belly makes me realize, at last, just how far I've traveled to arrive here.

"I'll be buggered," I say, wiping my lips with my swollen hand.

CHAPTER 13
Star and Storm

After escaping from Tasmania and returning to Pocatello, I find that everything in my life is in order. The HOGs are as eager as ever to go on new expeditions, and they're particularly enthusiastic about the ski program that Ike Gayfield has begun. These people are my adopted family, and never do I grow tired of seeing the joy that our outings can bring. Nor do I tire of witnessing the changes in attitude and behavior that occur over time. So often I've seen HOGs learn that dreams aren't just for everyone else.

Even more important, Cindy says yes—yes to that question I first posed to my campfire by the banks of the Franklin River. In 1988 we become husband and wife. The wedding and celebration is a 3 P.M. to 3 A.M. affair at a friend's ranch at the foot of Old Tom Mountain in Idaho. Ike Gayfield performs the honors at the ceremony.

I am finally home.

So, when the phone rings one afternoon in November of 1988, I have no reason to suspect that anything is missing. I am married to the woman I love, working hard at something about which I'm passionate, and active in outdoor pursuits. Yet when I hear the words come out of the phone, my head spins.

"This isn't an invitation, simply an inquiry. But I'm wondering if you'd be interested in joining an expedition I'm putting together to climb Mount Everest."

The woman on the other end of the line is Karen Fellerhoff, a Salt Lake City–based entrepreneur. She pauses to await my reply, but I am stunned.

"Hello? Tom? Hello?"

Ever since the accident, everything I've done in my life, from creating the HOGs to climbing Outer Limits, has been part of a single-minded crusade to redefine my identity and push my skills to their limits. I've also hoped, in some small way, to make people reexamine how our culture relegates the disabled to the sidelines. But hearing these two simple words—*Mount Everest*—I realize that, somewhere along the way, I buried my dream of becoming a brand-name presence in the high-stakes world of mountaineering. Despite my climbing successes, I've repeatedly told myself that a gimp has no right mucking about in the serious, high mountains like the Himalayas.

"You do realize you're talking to a guy with one foot?" I finally manage.

"Yeah, I've heard that. But I've also heard that doesn't slow you down a whole lot."

Knowing that mountaineering is as much a fiscal commitment as a physical one, I ask, "So how much money would I have to come up with?"

"Ten thousand dollars."

"That's all?" I say, feigning optimism. On my bare-bones budget, she might as well have said ten *million* dollars. Nevertheless, I tell her I'm interested. "I'm dying to do this, but I'm just not sure how appropriate it is for me," I explain, adding that I need to talk it over with some people before committing myself. "I want to earn my place on this expedition, not tag along as the token cripple. I want to be a contender for the summit."

"No problem, Tom." Just before she hangs up, Karen says, "And one more thing: we're leaving on March 25."

If I'm to climb the world's highest mountain, I've got only four months to come up with all that money. Moreover, there's that little nagging question of my prosthesis. If I'm to go, I desperately need to find one that can withstand the otherworldly temperatures and stresses of the Himalayas.

But first, of course, I need to determine whether I have any business on the mother of all mountains. I have to call my friend and mentor Bill March, who led the highly publicized 1982 Everest expedition that put the first Canadian on the summit. I've always been grateful to him for driving down from Calgary after my accident and staying by my bedside, doing his best to keep my spirits high. In addition, he has long supported the HOGs, often inviting me to Canada to give lectures about the group— and always finding a way to pay me a much-needed stipend.

Yet the main reason I want to call Bill is that he is a man of uncompromising principles; I know he will be completely—and perhaps brutally—honest with me. In 1981, when I applied for a job at the University of New Hampshire's outdoor recreation program, he refused to write a recommendation for me because he believed that my disability "might preclude me from successfully resolving an emergency situation." I desperately needed the job, so his decision was a real setback. Nevertheless, I respected his point of view and never let it stand in the way of our friendship. In fact, we often climb together, despite whatever concerns he might have expressed about my abilities. A few years ago, while we were doing the first ascent of a frozen waterfall in Canada, he grew angry with me after I soloed a particularly steep and narrow ice chimney. "What do you think you're doing, soloing that?" he demanded when he met me at the top.

"Well, you just soloed it, or we wouldn't be having this conversation," I replied casually.

"That's not the point," he blustered.

"Then perhaps you'd better explain to me exactly what the point is."

After a moment, he started shaking his head and grinning. "Damn, I've really got to stop taking responsibility for you, don't I?"

Since then, Bill hasn't uttered another word about what I can and cannot do. Still, he knows my capabilities better than anyone. That's why, when I get him on the phone, I ask directly, "Am I getting in over my head with this one?"

He doesn't say anything at first, and something tells me he's replaying images from his trip to the mountain. Although his expedition succeeded in putting the first Canadian on the summit, it also resulted in four deaths.

Finally he breaks the silence: "Whittaker, Everest is a glorious game, a wonderful thing to be a part of, but it's also a real crap shoot. You'll never know how well you're going to fare until you get up there." He grows quiet again, then adds, "Whittaker, you're always in over your head. You're in over your head with the HOGs and with Cindy. Why should Everest be any different?"

I'm relieved to hear Bill's words. Knowing that he would tell me if I weren't equipped to handle Everest, I decide I should prepare for the expedition—in case I do get formally invited. I have to locate a prosthesis that's strong enough and light enough to allow me to climb the world's highest mountain.

Over the years I've burned through seven supposedly indestructible units. Some now reside on the bottoms of rivers, others are buried in trash dumps, and still others are gathering dust in my closet. If I'm planning on climbing in the Himalayas, I'll need the best prosthesis available. Once again, I turn to Dale Perkins, who now runs his own business, Rehab Systems, in Twin Falls, Idaho. Dale recommends that I speak with another designer of prosthetics, Van Phillips, whose leg was amputated below the knee after he was hit by the prop of a speeding ski boat. Van is an avid outdoorsman who creates artificial limbs that withstand the sort of outdoor adventures he pursues. As a result, business is booming at the Orange County, California–based Flex-Foot.

Van is excited when I tell him I'm contemplating signing on with an Everest expedition. Not only will I be breaking new ground for amputees, but I'll also be pushing the limit of what's possible for a prosthesis. He's eager to design something that can withstand the subzero temperatures and extreme terrain I'll encounter. Van doesn't know a lot about the specific needs of a

Syme's amputee like me; his stump extends only a few inches beneath his knee, whereas I still have all of my leg down to my ankle. Over the next few weeks he interrogates me about what I think I'll need, trying to determine just the right combination of materials he should use. After my visit to the company, Flex-Foot's management team agrees to cover all my expedition costs and supply me with an assortment of prostheses.

Once my money troubles are solved, I have only one minor obstacle remaining: I actually have to be invited on the climb. To make my case, I mail Karen my climbing resumé and a letter outlining why I'd be a viable member of the team. In my letter, however, I lay out two stipulations: first, that my being on the team will not be published or leveraged for fund-raising, and second, that I'll be allowed to earn my summit bids like everyone else, based on my strength, my readiness, and the amount of work I've done to prepare the mountain for ascent.

A few days after I send the letter, Karen calls to tell me, "You're in." But by that point I've already started packing my duffel bags—something inside me knew I'd be going.

Over the next few months, Van works around the clock to develop a special carbon-graphite Flex-Foot, which will be light-weight and extraordinarily strong. Critical to the design is the spring, which will store energy when my foot makes contact with the ground and then release it as I remove my weight. By the time Cindy is driving me to Salt Lake City Airport for my flight to Nepal, I'm carrying three of these prostheses crafted by Dale Perkins.

Eight weeks later on the other side of the planet, I'm wedged inside a tent at 21,000 feet, listening to the thundering avalanches and the howling wind. Together with my climbing partner, Andy Lapkiss, and four Sherpas, I am perched on a moraine at the bottom of a massive glacial cirque beneath Everest's Southwest Face. Each time I hear the torrents of snow and ice, I sit bolt upright, bracing for the worst, my heart pounding. So far, however, our tents have been spared.

Andy and I force ourselves to leave the warmth of our sleeping bags and shovel out our tents to keep them from collapsing under the weight of snow that began falling here in Camp Two three days ago. The wind gusts up to sixty miles per hour and hurls flecks of shale and ice into our tent. I can't imagine how much longer the nylon will hold up in this storm, and I don't want to imagine what's going to happen when it tears apart.

We are, without a doubt, stranded on the mountain. Because of the blizzard, rescue parties won't be dispatched to find us. Besides, from what we've been able to make out, our teammates presume we are dead. The batteries in our Motorola handheld radios are so weak—we've had to warm them over the gas stove—that we've been unable to transmit for the past two days, though we can hear everything that's being said over the channel. We've heard that five climbers from a Polish expedition have perished in avalanches while attempting Everest's West Ridge, and that another, badly injured, lies marooned with his dead teammates. That brings the death toll in this pre-monsoon climbing season to seven: a Yugoslav and a Sherpa were killed earlier. Trapped up here a thousand feet higher than the summit of Mount McKinley, Andy, our four Sherpas, and I could soon be added to Everest's grizzly statistics.

Exactly how we're going to get back down through the lethal maze of snowed-over crevasses of the Khumbu Icefall to the safety of Base Camp, some four thousand feet below, remains to be seen. However, time is running out, and so are our chances for survival. We've almost burned through all our fuel melting snow for drinking water. At 21,000 feet above sea level, keeping hydrated is the key to survival because a desiccated body and brain work at only 50 percent efficiency. We pour as much water as possible into our dehydrated, oxygen-starved bodies. The only comforting thought in this seemingly hopeless situation is that, over the past month, I've performed remarkably well on the mountain. Bill March referred to Everest as a crap shoot, and I seem to have held my own against the house, thanks to my ability to perform at high altitudes. Up here, with less than half the oxygen available at sea level, everyone is disabled. As a neophyte on the mountain, I can gauge my performance only against the other mountaineers. In contrast to many of my teammates, it seems the higher I go, the stronger I become, and the less my disability becomes a factor.

Early on in our expedition, as we established our camps and acclimatized our bodies to the altitude, a lung infection caused Peter Hillary, the son of the first climber to stand on the mountain's summit, to return to Base Camp. I ended up climbing with his Australian partner, Roddy McKenzie. One afternoon I reached Camp Three, at 24,000 feet, a full fifty minutes before Roddy. When he finally stuck his bearded face into the tent, looking absolutely knackered, I prepared him some soup and helped him get situated before he fell into a deep sleep. Later, when I learned that he had made it to the summit with Adrian Burgess, it hit me: if Roddy can reach the top, so can I.

After Roddy and Adrian descended, Andy and I waited at Camp Two to provide a support role for another team heading for the summit. But when the storm began, the summit-bound climbers beat a retreat back down the mountain. Over the radio, Karen asked Andy and me and our four Sherpas to stay put at our 21,000-foot outpost to supervise the breakdown of camp and retrieve equipment and trash off the mountain. We agreed, but hardly out of altruism: Andy and I knew that if the weather broke, we would be in perfect position to make a dash for the top. These storms, though serious if you're caught high on the mountain, often blow over after a couple of days.

This storm, however, is different. When we see the dull light of day number five seep through the howling blizzard, we understand that we'd be happy just to escape with our lives. To hell with the summit.

"What do you want to tell the Sherpas?" Andy asks, now sitting up in his bag.

"We need them," I reply, "like they need us. We have to stick together if we have any hope of getting out alive."

The two of us pull our boots and windsuits on, unzip the door to our tent, and burrow our way outside.

"That," says Andy, staring dejectedly at nearly four feet of new powder, "is a heck of a lot of snow." We go to work digging our domed refuge out from beneath the accumulation. When we finish, I wade over to the Sherpas' tent and call a meeting in the two-meter North Face dome tent.

"You're free to leave when you like," I tell them as Rham, the most experienced of the lot, translates. "But I think it best that we try to stay together." The men listen to Rham, never taking their eyes off me. After some heated discussion in Sherpa, Rham says that they feel the storm has lifted enough to allow safe passage back down. Andy and I try to reason with him, telling him that the conditions are still so volatile that it's madness to proceed, but the Sherpas have made up their minds.

"We're going to wait it out," Andy announces. Although neither of us says as much, we both wonder if maybe we ought to make a run for it with them. To divide the team is madness, but to set out now is suicide.

After the Sherpas depart, Andy and I busy ourselves locating long-since-buried plastic food crates, which we cut up and tie to the bottom of our boots with parachute cord. These improvised snowshoes allow us to remain on the surface without sinking up to our thighs. We're both busy testing our creations when the Sherpas stumble back into camp.

"Could see nothing," Rham explains, looking absolutely beat. "Had to drop our loads. The going is very bad. Very bad."

That evening we listen to the radio, but the transmissions from Base Camp have ceased. After a depressing meal that all but cleans out the remainder of our porridge, Andy and I lie in our bags, saying nothing. Then, around 10 P.M., I awaken out of a troubled sleep to the sound of excited voices. I stick my head out the tent and squint in the bright moonlight that reflects off the snow.

"I think we finally got our break," I tell Andy. The Sherpas, who have made their own snowshoes, are outside surveying the terrain. Camp has already been broken down and the supplies stockpiled. All that remains are our sleeping tents and the two-meter dome. If we are on our way by 5 A.M., we should be past the worst of the avalanche danger by 9 A.M. and, God willing, off the hill by lunch.

"Wake up at 3 A.M.," I tell Rham. "Leave at 5 A.M." He smiles.

After a bowl of porridge and a cup of steaming hot milk tea, Andy and I collapse the tent and pack our gear. Everyone is keen to go by 4:30 A.M., so we strike out into the darkness, high-stepping through the deep white beneath us. Without the insulating cloud coverage, the temperature has plunged to about ten degrees below zero. Within minutes our plastic jury-rigged snowshoes that worked so well yesterday have cracked into pieces in these frigid conditions. Forced to kick them off, we have to slog through the waist-deep snow, which saps our energy. As we proceed single file, we take turns breaking trail, each of us using our body as a human snowplow to forge a deep trench through the snow. In the thin air of the Western Cwm, this is killing work. Making it even more difficult is the fact that my prosthetic foot, which is smaller than a normal boot, makes post-holes in the snow. It's like walking with one foot on the sidewalk, the other in the road. Pulling my leg out and fighting to maintain my balance is a terrible drain.

Though all of us have traveled over this stretch of the Western Cwm repeatedly, nothing looks the same after the five-day snowfall. The deeper we descend, the more it becomes apparent that we will have a difficult time locating the ladders that bridge the huge crevasses running across our path. The bamboo poles used to mark the route through the crevasses now lie buried, so we're at a loss to determine our precise location. For all we know, we're standing on unconsolidated snow blanketing a fissure that a week ago we would have crossed by ladder. As insurance against this possibility, we're all roped to one another.

As daylight trickles down, clouds swirl in and a light snow begins to fall. Nobody speaks. The only sound comes from heavy, labored breathing. Finally we arrive at our first visible crevasse—but there's no sign of a ladder. When we realize it must be somewhere beneath us, we peer down into the darkness and locate the flimsy aluminum bridge that stretches horizontally across the void. To reach it we have to burrow down through ten feet of accumulation.

After clipping into a questionable safety line and crawling out onto the ladder, I feel as though I'm walking the plank of some ghostly pirate ship. The rest of the crew stands on the end of the ladder to counterbalance my weight as I inch along. As I move, I find it impossible not to look into the belly of the chasm. Even though I have a climbing rope tied into my harness, I'm still going to take an ugly tumble if this ladder breaks or rips free.

When I finally reach the last rung, I'm nearly two feet shy of the other side of the crevasse. Glaciers are rivers of ice. This one flows at six feet a day, and in the days since it was last tended, the chasm has widened. With my ice axe clutched tightly in my mittened hand, I reach out and clear away a sentry box in the snow. Then, when I have a spot to accommodate me, I send the blade deep into the ice and pull myself across to safety. Still, I have to dig an upward-slanting trench until I am standing waist-deep in the snow once more.

At 2 P.M. we finally reach Camp One at the top of the Khumbu Icefall. It's taken us nine grueling, mind-numbing hours to travel to 19,000 feet; in normal conditions I could cover this terrain in an hour and a half. I thought that by now we'd be safe in our tents at Base Camp, sleeping off a hearty lunch. Instead we're poking into the snow at Camp One in search of our cache of food and fresh batteries. There's no sign of the tents anywhere. Somewhere below me, entombed several feet down inside one of these structures, lies one of Van's space-age feet that Dale Perkins crafted into a prosthesis. I've stashed it here as a backup for the climb and desperately want to find it. Though I've never been one to dwell on monetary figures, the artificial limb's $5,000 price tag gives me pause.

"It's gotta be down there somewhere," I mumble.

"Forget about it," says Andy. "Come on. Gotta keep moving."

In the past two hours, although the day has grown much warmer, the weather has deteriorated. The snow now falls steadily, and a mist boils up from the valley below. Nevertheless, I consider that if we spend precious time and energy digging the tents out by hand, the effort could pay off by providing us the rest, food, and rehydration we need to attempt the icefall the next day. Andy and I hash out our options.

"I know what you're thinking, Whittaker," Andy says. "But suppose we don't locate the tents and this weather turns out to be another storm in the making. Then what?"

He's right and I know it. We don't possess the resources here at Camp One or inside ourselves to repeat the ordeal of the past six days. But I don't know if I possess the reserves to make it down in the condition I'm in. For the past several hours I've been a zombie, and my body screams out for rest. Moreover, the terrain that separates us from Base Camp and safety is the most technically difficult part of Everest. The Khumbu Icefall is where the glacier in the Western Cwm topples over a two-thousand-foot cliff, then re-forms at the bottom. Since the icefall was last maintained, more than forty feet of ice have tumbled from the glacier and over the cliff. To add to the ambiguity, ten feet of snow have fallen on top of this ice. Roughly twenty of the crevasses we have to cross are spanned by ladders; some of the chasms are so wide that it takes several ladders lashed together to bridge them. To survive, we must hit each crevasse dead on, at the exact spot where a ladder is located. But even if we hit that spot, there's no guarantee we'll be able to cross.

If the Western Cwm took nine hours to traverse, we can expect the Khumbu Icefall to take twelve to fourteen hours. By pressing on now, I realize, we'll be forcing ourselves to endure more than twenty hours of continuous work. In these desperate conditions, at this altitude, and given the state I'm in, that's a number I can't even fathom. But as Andy has rightly pointed out, we have no other choice. Our forced march continues.

Fighting the deep snow is particularly difficult for me, the heaviest person in our party. The Sherpas and Andy can easily tread in each other's bootprints and never worry about sinking. But when I attempt it, I drop down into the snow, with my prosthesis awkwardly plunging even deeper. My stump has taken a pounding and a raw pain tears through my right leg, but I keep it to myself. I think back to my excruciating descent off the Grand Teton, reminding myself that I've handled it before and can handle it now. I try not to think about the unspoken law governing our every step: anyone who becomes injured or too weak to continue will be left.

For hours, Rham has led the way, divining our path through this labyrinth as if guided by a sixth sense. Whenever he appears stumped as to where to go, Andy eggs him on, knowing full well how proud the Sherpa is. "Either you find our way off this mountain or get out of my way because I'm taking the lead," he tells Rham. And each time he says this, Rham listens patiently, nods slightly, and then resumes his march down this strange moonscape.

Late in the afternoon we stumble onto a ladder so twisted that we have to cross the gaping crevasse by teetering over a single narrow edge. Rham pauses for a moment as soon as we migrate across it, but again Andy challenges him. Within ten minutes we come to another split in the icefall with no ladder bridging it. Unsure as to whether we are off route or this is a new crevasse that has appeared in the past week, we reluctantly double back to the spot where Rham believes we may have made a wrong turn.

Darkness falls, making the route even more difficult to determine. In a particularly chaotic section we're forced to jump from ice block to ice block. In my fatigue I imagine that we are in some sort of *Alice in Wonderland* fantasy and are attempting to leave a restaurant by hopping from table to table, the only catch being that the tables have thirty-foot-high legs.

I'm so fatigued that I'm not even sure who has suggested we jettison our backpacks, but we have determined that we can't keep hauling them. The situation has become desperate. With the temperature now well below freezing, stopping for the night is no longer an option. We lower our heads and trudge onward. Any delusions that we haven't crossed into do-or-die territory vanished a few crevasses back.

One by one, in the cold of the Himalayan night, the batteries in our headlamps sputter and die. We're down to just three working lamps. Vainly I search the darkness for the lights of Base Camp. After nearly fifteen hours of travel, surely our team's outpost can't be too far below. As I stare down the glacier from the top of a small rise, for a fleeting moment I see a pinpoint of light. Was this a hallucination or did I actually spot a point of light in this godforsaken nightmare of ice and snow? For several minutes I stand glued to the spot, scanning the darkness with my eyes.

Finally, knowing we have to push on, I set off again. Suddenly I hear Sonam, one of the Sherpas, call me. I turn, expecting to see him up to his armpits in a hidden crevasse, but he's standing still, staring at something below. I look down the glacier to see the flicker of incandescent light. Headlamps, four of them, moving slowly upward through the dense night. It's absolutely unmistakable, but nobody cheers, nobody even acknowledges it. Each of us knows that the others have witnessed it. We are six condemned men who have been given a reprieve.

When Wong Chu, our Base Camp cook, comes into view, I know for certain that the flickering light was no hallucination. Wong Chu grins broadly, shouts a greeting to Rham, and then yells something at the men standing behind him. Everyone breaks into joyous laughter.

It has taken them seven hours to cover terrain that would normally take them an hour, we learn. "The men wanted to turn around when the night came," Rham explains. "Wong Chu would not allow them." Along the way, they've been repairing the icefall and pulling the hand lines out from the snow.

While pouring cups of milk tea, Wong Chu, who comes from a long line of climbing Sherpas, explains in broken English that Cindy and Warren are waiting for me down in Base Camp.

"The hope had nearly gone out from everyone that you were alive," he says. "But they both refused to believe. They argued to allow us to come."

"Cinders and Warren can be stubborn pains in the arse, Wong Chu," I wheeze. "My apologies if they were in any way overbearing."

"Tom Di, we *jonny ho*," Wong Chu tells me, employing the Nepali term for "Get going."

"*Jonny ho*, Wong Chu," I reply. Traveling in front of me, he pulls up the hand lines for me to grab, then cranks back on them to provide tension as I cross crevasse after crevasse. I am grateful to these Sherpas, especially Wong Chu for refusing to allow his men to turn back; their selflessness has deeply moved me.

I concentrate on getting over this last bit of terrain to Base Camp. I never thought anything could top carrying a seventy-pound load down the Teton for eleven hours on a new stump and an even newer prosthesis. But eighteen hours plowing through deep snow at these altitudes has proved its match. When I at last reach the bottom of the icefall, I see Warren. He stands there squinting, trying to make sure that the person limping up to him is indeed his son. "Good to have you back, Tom," he says, extending his strong right hand.

"Thanks for keeping the faith, Warren," I reply. "If you hadn't sent reinforcements, coming back down would've got old!"

He smiles. "Cindy's back there," he says. "She's been pretty worried these last few days."

I trudge up the moraine and find her standing off to the side of the trail, crying silently. She throws her arms around my neck and we squeeze one another tightly, saying nothing because words have no business here. As I hold her close to me, I realize that who I am and what I achieve have a great deal to do with the confidence and faith this woman has in me. She is both my sail and my keel.

That night, as I lie in my sleeping bag with Cindy curled up next to me, I'm a contented man. Although Chomolungma took everything I had, including one of my high-tech artificial feet, I don't care. Bill March certainly hit the nail on the head. Climbing Everest is a glorious game. And even though it nearly finished me off this time, something tells me I'll play it again.

Upon returning from Everest in June 1989, I decide it's time to relinquish the directing of the HOGs to Jim Wise, my administrative assistant, who has been with the program for three years. In September I head to Colorado State University to pursue my doctorate in experiential education.

My schedule is crazed. On Friday nights, after my last class lets out at 9 P.M., I climb into my battered yellow Nissan pickup and drive the eight hours back to Pocatello to be with Cinders, who is juggling two sports retail jobs. On Tuesday mornings I turn my rig around and spend the day trying to avoid the highway patrol before staggering into class at 6 P.M. My mantra: drive fast, take chances.

I never quite grow used to this grueling schedule, but it's something I have to do. One Tuesday night, while I'm still bleary-eyed from a four-hour statistics exam, I get another of those life-altering phone calls. "Tom here," I bark into the receiver.

"It's Cindy."

"Yes, it certainly sounds like her."

"You sitting down, Tom?" she inquires, obviously not in the mood for my insipid phone humor.

"I am now."

She takes a deep breath. Something about her voice sounds peculiar. "Tom," she says, "I've got good news and bad news. What do you want first?"

"You know me, Cinders—the bad news."

"I'm pregnant."

"And the good news?"

"It's yours," she laughs.

Cinders has always had a gift for verbal delivery, but this time she's truly outdone herself. As for children, I've certainly never been opposed to them. I just never spent much time considering that I'd one day be responsible for the daily feeding and general upkeep of one.

"Cinders," I whisper solemnly.

"Yes," she replies hesitantly.

"I'm . . . I'm not sure I passed my statistics final."

She groans. "I'll see you Saturday morning," she says, then hangs up.

On the whole, I convince myself, I've reacted quite calmly to the news.

While heading back to Pocatello on Friday night, I stare out my cracked windshield at the endless expanse of snow-rimmed asphalt stretching ahead of me. Somewhere in the middle of Wyoming, I find myself pondering this next chapter of my life. With complexity, I hear myself muse, comes the potential for richness—and, of course, madness. Either way, it's time to grow up. I think about the somewhat carefree life I've led, and suddenly I realize the awesome responsibility I'm about to embrace. Yet rather than being overwhelmed, I'm elated.

Elizabeth Mary Whittaker enters the world on July 24, 1991. Twelve months later, Cinders and I take her on a six-day rafting trip down the River of No Return. Lizzie, as she is nicknamed, is voted more-fun-than-horseshoes by all the good ol' boys on the trip, proving that there is life after children.

By this point it has become apparent that I will need a more steady income to support a wife and child. I've spent so much of the past decade doing whatever I could to keep the HOGs funded, from applying for philanthropic grants to giving lectures to coming up with outrageous stunts like rappelling down the fourteen-story Cliff Hotel at Snowbird with Kyle Packer harnessed to my back. I've also taken advantage of various opportunities to put a little money in my own pocket. Right after Lizzie was born I found myself swimming down a rapid-strewn stretch of Montana's Gallatin River behind Brad Pitt. The producers of the film *A River Runs Through It* had hired me to ensure that Pitt didn't drown during a sequence in which he gets in over his head while trying to land a trout. Unbeknownst to Brad, I trailed him, half submerged, down into the heavy whitewater. The moment things looked as though they were getting out of hand, I swam up to him, grabbed him by the scruff of his neck and the seat of his pants, and literally threw him out of the water onto the steep, stone-covered shoreline. As I emerged from the river, he looked up at me and laughed, "My guardian angel."

But Hollywood isn't for me—all my scenes, I later learned, were cut from the movie—so I turn to the want ads in the *Chronicle of Higher Education*. When I stumble across a listing for professor of adventure education at Prescott College in Arizona, I know it's the perfect position for me, and I'm hired after a round of interviews. Cinders and I pack up our truck and head south to the town of Prescott, nestled a mile high in central Arizona amongst scrub oak, ponderosa pine, and an endless array of granite, basalt, and quartzite climbing rock.

From time to time I catch myself wondering about the Everest climb, about what might have happened if the storm had blown itself out after two days and Andy Lapkiss and I had been cleared for takeoff.

And sometimes Everest forces its way back into my life. The first time came in 1990, the year after my unsuccessful attempt, when my friend Pete Athans returned from summiting Everest with Peter Hillary. Athans informed me that the mountain had unearthed the detritus of my climb. The deep snowfall that had buried Camp One melted out, exposing one of our expedition tents. The tent, pushed a third of the way down the icefall, sat teetering on a towering iceberg, and when it finally broke loose, a high-altitude porter scooped up the free climbing swag—which included the $5,000 artificial leg I left behind. Athans apologized for letting the culprit slip away, but he said, "I'll be damned if I was going to wear myself out chasing after your bloody leg down the icefall."

One afternoon in November 1994 I'm walking the floor of the annual *Outdoor Retailer* trade show in Reno when I bump into Australian Greg Child, a friend from my ragtag days back in Yosemite. A wonderfully skilled climber who can tackle any sort of rock, ice, or technical problem, Greg is living the life I imagined for myself before my car accident. He has established himself as one of the world's top professional mountaineers, writing books on the sport and, as part of the prestigious North Face climbing team, getting paid to travel the globe ascending peaks. The moment I spot Greg, something comes over me—it's time to get back to Mount Everest.

"Java Man!" I shout across the hall, using the nickname Greg acquired on account of his full jaw and sloping forehead. Soon the two of us are sitting at a bar with a pitcher of beer in front of us. I lay out my scheme.

"You must think I'm bloody daft," he replies with the good-natured candor of an Aussie who has beaten the odds on many of the world's most serious mountains. "If you think I'd tie into the rope with a one-legged man on that mountain, you're crazy."

"One-footed," I correct him. Then, demonstrating my grasp of the marketing vernacular, I add with appropriate nonchalance, "Anyway, it's a sexy project."

"Sexy?!" he snorts. "It'll take a mite more than Everest for either one of us to look sexy."

"No, not *look* sexy. The project has appeal, damn it—the essence of the American dream." Greg empties the contents of his glass into his mouth. He isn't smiling. "Think about it: We both came to the United States to follow our dream of becoming brand-name mountaineers. Within months of arriving here, we ran into each other in Yosemite and eventually ended up climbing the Nose of El Capitan together. You went off to follow your star and did just that, becoming one of the world's preeminent climbers. I went reaching for my star, but before I could grab it, I got hit by an out-of-control vehicle and ended up developing a therapeutic process to help people transcend the debilitating emotional and psychological effects of disability."

"Hmm, you thought of that all by yourself?" Greg muses.

"Wait, there's more," I reply. "And now... and now our lives converge once again, only this time it's on Everest. It's a story of the heart: able-bodied friend helps his disabled mate achieve a lifelong dream to become the first disabled person to stand on the roof of the world."

Greg glances at the empty pitcher. Australians, in general, can be remarkably slow on the uptake when they believe there's another beer in it for them. From his blank expression, I can already see this will be a two-pitcher idea. After I buy another round, he plays devil's advocate, picking apart the feasibility of my grand plan.

"Look," I finally say, "I've already been to 24,000 feet on Everest on three occasions and I felt fine. And I managed to get off the mountain in a wretched storm that killed five people."

"In that case," he concedes, "this needs to be a movie."

By April 1995 we've lined up financing and a production deal with Leo Dickinson, a British filmmaker I once worked with on a documentary about extreme whitewater kayaking in Idaho. He recently completed a movie about ballooning over Everest and can't stomach the notion of facing the deadly Khumbu Icefall again, so he agrees to take on the project on the condition that we take the lesser-climbed North Face route, located on the Chinese-controlled Tibetan side of the mountain. A chance to see Lhasa and the Potala Palace? We can't say no.

After flying into Nepal, we catch another flight into the forbidden city of Lhasa. Prior to the Chinese invasion in 1950, no wheeled vehicles were allowed in this holy city, since it was thought that the depressions in the ground caused by wheels would release demons. Many who have seen Lhasa since the "liberation" trucks of the Red Guard poured in would agree that the Tibetans' fears were well founded. The uninspired communist metropolis we discover hardly resembles the medieval city described in Heinrich Harrer's classic *Seven Years in Tibet*. For centuries, monks and Buddhist deities watched over Lhasa, but for the most part they've been replaced by surveillance cameras, hidden microphones, and Chinese secret police. For two weeks we are forced to endure one frustrating bureaucratic delay after another, along with wretched food and grim accommodations.

By the time we establish Base Camp on Rongbuk Glacier at 17,000 feet, I'm awed by Everest's sheer bulk. She appears to have grown since my last expedition. The more I try to understand this mountain, the smaller and less significant I become. Staring up at the massive North Face, I understand why it took nearly a century to climb this mountain after it was discovered to be the planet's tallest. I also see why Edmund Hillary and Tenzing Norgay Sherpa chose to ascend it via the Southeast Ridge from the South Col. From this side, Everest appears to be a very different beast altogether.

When taking the South Col route in Nepal, you have to walk some thirty-eight miles to arrive at Base Camp, but here in Tibet we arrive at camp in three-ton Chinese army trucks. Instead of spending ten days tightening muscles, acclimatizing, and psychologically preparing for the next two months of mountaineering, we have a five-hour bone-crushing journey from the main East-West Highway. Of course, we then have to ferry four tons of equipment nearly fourteen miles, inching our way up four thousand vertical feet in order to establish an Advanced Base Camp at the head of the

East Rongbuk Glacier. This is the last spot on the moraine before everything turns to ice. We spend days sorting gear into seventy-pound loads and fine-tuning our equipment.

Over the past few weeks, I've become a compulsive tinkerer, constantly adjusting the fit of my chrome-moly crampons onto the bottom of my carbon-graphite Flex-Foot. Mountaineers are forever looking for ways to shave weight off their feet. I've finally found the perfect arrangement for climbing with an artificial limb. By forgoing a heavy boot and attaching a Vibram sole to the bottom of the Flex-Foot, I manage to trim two and a half pounds from the bottom of my leg. In addition, Van and Dale have refined the design, lightening the prosthesis by another two pounds. In terms of raw energy required for movement, every pound I save on my foot translates to nearly five pounds off my back. The weight I've shaved here is the equivalent of taking two oxygen bottles out of my pack.

In late April our Tibetan herders strap 150-pound loads onto the backs of three dozen grouchy yaks, and we make our way to Advanced Base Camp at 21,000 feet. Despite the constant gales ripping at its flanks, our task is to establish three camps up the northern spine of Everest: the first, situated on a flat protected shelf on the North Col at 23,000 feet; the second, located above a huge snow ramp on a crumbling talus slope at 25,000 feet; and the third, positioned at the foot of the Yellow Band, a collar of limestone that rings the mountain.

Summiting Everest involves far more than physically surmounting this pile of sedimentary rock. First, there are the logistics of getting four tons of food and equipment from Britain, Australia, Russia, Europe, and America transported across a highly sensitive international border and delivered into a communist-held country. By the time we got all our requisite permits in order, they weighed almost as much as our gear. Then there's the matter of establishing and stocking the two base camps and three high-mountain camps.

It's hardly an exaggeration to say that climbing Everest requires all the planning of a military action. Unlike lesser mountains, where attitude and fitness can often compensate for logistical snafus, in this unforgiving realm, success and failure can hinge on something as small as a fist-sized oxygen regulator not being at the right place on the mountain when it's needed.

But the physical demands of this region are even more daunting. From the moment you arrive, you're gasping for breath in the dry air that dehydrates your body, tearing up the membranes in your throat and bronchioles. A dry, hacking cough quickly descends into your lungs, and often remains for months after you return. Your skin comes under constant attack from ultraviolet radiation, and your lips, even the lining of your mouth and nostrils, fry.

Coping with the extreme altitude is most difficult. That is why acclimatization—the slow but crucial process of changing your metabolism so that it can function in the deadly upper reaches of the planet—is so crucial to Himalayan mountaineering. Above 18,000 feet, the human body loses the ability to replenish and repair itself. Even the slightest laceration or infection refuses to heal. The price for not paying your dues in this tiring process can be death. Acute Mountain Sickness (AMS) will affect the lungs and brain; if it's not remedied, you either drown as your lungs fill up with fluid or go blind and pass out as fluid gathers in your cranial cavity.

For the Himalayan mountaineer, a tricky balancing act exists between acclimatization and loss of strength. To compensate for the lack of available oxygen, your metabolism increases the amount of red corpuscles, and after roughly two weeks at high altitude the blood turns to sludge. After about three weeks it thins back down and your physiology is still robust. But after acclimatization is complete, the longer you stay above 18,000 feet, the more your strength ebbs. Every day you die a little. You travel to Everest in prime condition and return as a wasted bag of bones. Over the course of my last expedition, I melted away forty-five pounds of fat and muscle.

All of us are now engaging in this difficult acclimatization process as we try to carve camps into the mountain's flank. While we cope with the dire effects of living without oxygen, we also have to battle the elements. The eagerly awaited window of wind-free weather that enables mountaineers to make their summit bids occurs when the moisture-laden monsoons suck their way up the Brahma, Putra, and Ghanges valleys and the dense air moves the jet stream off Everest's peak. But to be prepared when this good weather comes, expeditions have to establish and stock their camps before the gales abate, and tussling with the inclement weather makes the process even more grueling.

The clock is always ticking, so we press onward. The higher we inch, the more uncertain the terrain becomes. Instead of having to contend with the snow and ice that covers much of the approach from the South Col, above 25,000 feet we move over brittle, downsloping slabs of shale. The jet stream and random gales roar along the upper part of Everest's summit pyramid, constantly threatening to rip our puny camps from the mountain.

Finally, after I've spent thirty-three consecutive days above 21,000 feet, the moment arrives. The jet stream has been pushed north over the Tibetan Plateau. Chomolungma just opened the window for us. I am sardined inside a tent along with Greg Child and Russell Brice, the wiry, rawboned, and immensely talented guide we contracted to facilitate the complicated Chinese permit process, the hiring of Sherpas, and the outfitting of the mountain. Pitched here upon a massive, gently sloping ledge at 27,000 feet, we feel the wind slam into our fragile haven and nearly tear us off the North Face. With our bulky Soviet aviator masks strapped over our faces, trickling oxygen into our lungs at the rate of one lungful every fourteen minutes, we desperately try to rest before departing for our 2 A.M. summit bid. But sleeping on oxygen is nearly impossible. Oxygen is keeping me alive, but it also exacts a high price. The oxygen canisters are heavy and cumbersome, and the mask bites into my nose and pinches my cheeks and chin. Not a moment passes when I don't wonder if I'd be better off without the gas.

I make sure my oxygen regulator, which runs from zero to nine, is set at 0.5 liters per minute so that I'm not sucking down too much of my precious gas. I shut my eyes and try to keep the twenty-below-zero night from creeping deep into my bones. Judging from the pain in my back, I'd swear we've pitched our tent atop the contents of a tool chest. The minutes crawl by, and I try desperately not to contemplate the difficulty of the task ahead.

But there's no point kidding myself. After more than a month at these altitudes, my energy is running low, dangerously low. Up here, it's not a question of whether you can move from point A to point B; it's a matter of how quickly you can make the journey. I've squandered too much time waiting for our window to open. True, I reached 27,000 feet before strapping on supplemental oxygen—something most able-bodied climbers can't do—but what does it matter now? The summit looms so far above and I'm all but spent. And of course I'm missing a foot and a kneecap, I have a quadriceps that fires at only 40 percent efficiency, and I'm always fighting to keep my balance.

Don't think about this shite, Whittaker! It's not going to get you to the top.

But I can't dismiss my doubts as readily as I would like. The mountain I'm climbing isn't just 29,028 feet high. No, because of all the extra energy that I have to expend compared to an able-bodied climber, the mountain I'm attempting to climb is the equivalent of a 40,000-foot peak. That's nearly two miles higher than any mountain on this planet.

When the time comes to move, no one has to say a word. The three of us have been watching the clock. Through our nylon wall I can see the faint glow of a light in the Sherpas' tent. It's a few minutes past 2 A.M, and since all our gear was long ago stuffed into our packs, it takes only a few minutes to prepare to climb. I pull on my boot over the thick liner I've been wearing on my left foot and adjust our flow of oxygen up to 3.5 liters a minute. Now I'm receiving a lungful of air each minute, but my lips are blue from the lack of oxygen. Whereas in my rig-diving days I got all the gas I needed, up here I have to budget the juice so it lasts the round trip.

After strapping on our crampons we are finally ready. The five of us—three westerners and two Sherpas—shoulder our packs and head out into the Himalayan night. As I step out into the frigid air, I feel the cozy sleeping bag sensation being sucked out through my thick down-filled mountaineering suit.

Working up the Yellow Band, I struggle with my prosthesis. The wind having died, the only sound comes from our labored breathing and our crampons scraping on the shale. The terrain grows steeper. In front of us, a solid mass rears up in the black night. We'll have to summit this wall to gain the crest of the East Ridge. This was the barrier that turned back many of the prewar attempts to scale the mountain.

I'm relieved to reach the fixed ropes, which will allow my powerful upper body to compensate for my seriously weakened right leg. On a steep face like this, a fixed line is something of a hedge, which as an amputee I sorely need. I'm disturbed, however, to find that the ropes are frayed and weathered. The lines have endured at least one punishing season on the mountain, and ultraviolet rays and howling winds, which continually slap the ropes against the rock, have taken their toll. Another reason the lines are in such wretched shape is that, due to the strange politics and feuding among various expeditions and guide services, none of the outfits wants to fix this part of the mountain and benefit a competitor.

"Seen washing line in better shape than this," I mumble through my mask, feeling myself out of breath before the last word tumbles from my mouth. In the darkness, Greg's eyes meet mine, and I know he feels the same way. But there's nothing to be done about it now. As I slide my ascender up the pulverized seven-millimeter line, I watch in disbelief as pitons, which have long ago worked their way loose from the rock, leap upward and dance in the air. When I catch up to Greg, he pulls off his oxygen mask and cautions, "Easy, Whittaker. Pull too hard and this breaks, all five us are going with you."

I feel a rush of anger. Fixed lines, like people, are useless if you can't count on them. I was counting on having new rope fixed on this section of the mountain, but both our speed and our physical safety are compromised because old ropes can't be trusted. The ascent is slow and difficult. By the time we're deep into a gully extending up through the Yellow Band, I feel as though I'm being strangled. My lungs bellow for more juice. Despite the fact that we've hired two Sherpas, I'm carrying two oxygen bottles plus a small load of gear. Russell's commitment to getting his climbing Sherpas to the summit seems to have taken priority over their contracted duty to serve as support. Not that I fault them for wanting to reach the top. For a Sherpa, getting to Everest's peak provides a huge career boost, allowing him to land better work and higher pay. Nevertheless, right now I desperately need someone to take one of the bottles off my back.

I stop again, trying to find some sort of balance between pulling too hard on the rotten line and grinding to a snail's pace. The moment I stop, Greg descends back to where I'm standing.

"Too heavy," I gasp, wondering if one of the Sherpas will offer to lend a hand. "My extra O_2 is killing me." Nobody bothers to move. Without speaking, Greg inches closer, unsnaps my pack, and removes the spare bottle. This puts his load up to four bottles.

What are you doing, Whittaker? You may as well just slice Greg's throat.

Both Greg and I know that the extra bottle is far too heavy a load for him to carry if he's going to reach the top, but neither of us says a word. He pivots back around and resumes his delicate ascent. Never in my life have I felt like a liability on an expedition, and I know the resentment that it breeds. Nevertheless, I feel as though I'm floating now that I have just one canister tucked inside my pack. This sensation soon disappears, however, as my fatigued body turns leaden. If only I could rely on these ruddy lines to help compensate for my missing parts.

A hundred feet later, we're moving up a steep snow ramp that leads to the ridge when my foot breaks through a thin mantle of snow. For a moment my prosthesis is dangling over a void that plummets more than two vertical miles down the North Face. A stupid misstep. I can only imagine how bad this must look to Russell.

"How you feeling, Tom?" I hear him shout from behind me, but I know what must be going through his head: *I gotta get this guy off the mountain before he kills himself and takes my guiding service with him.*

"Fine, fine," I shout as loudly as possible, but I doubt he hears me. For a brief moment, in the plastic lens of my goggles, I glimpse what appears to be Cindy's blue eyes staring back at me. When I jerk my head the image disappears, but only a moment later I see the vague form of Lizzie's face. I stop for an instant, trying to understand what they want, but I already know. A few slides of the ascender later, I halt once again. Russell and the Sherpas catch up to me almost instantly. Standing there, I try to sift through the thoughts crowding my skull.

In the three hours since leaving Camp Four, we've scraped our way up a mere five hundred vertical feet. At this pace, I don't stand a chance of reaching the top until long after our turnaround time. The only thing I've managed to do since leaving camp is slow everybody down.

"Maybe you ought to turn this thing around, Tom," I hear Russell saying behind me. "That's what I think."

Big decision, here—fork-in-the-road time. Which direction to take? Greg is now standing just above me. Does he understand what's happening? Can he? I never foresaw this ending. I always imagined it would end up like our bare-knuckle climb of El Cap on that hot afternoon two decades ago, high above the Yosemite Valley floor.

"Come on, Tom," Russell says. "It's not worth it." Greg just stands there, moving slightly to maintain his body heat in this deathly cold. It's my call. The bile rises up in my belly. It's all gone so wrong. I've become the albatross. Greg is looking strong, in striking distance of the summit, and I'm spinning my wheels. I've no other choice but to cut him loose, then watch as he chugs up the line with the two Sherpas in tow.

"You can give me the O$_2$ cylinder back now, Greg," I announce finally, incredulous that I've traveled halfway around the world only to be beaten once again by this mountain. "I'll head back."

Just Russell and me now. Without another word, we turn and start down. As the morning bleeds pink across the sky, I feebly remind myself that I've established another high-altitude record for the disabled, but the revelation does nothing to revive my crushed spirit. What took three torturous hours to ascend requires a mere forty-five minutes to descend. We heave ourselves inside the tent and crawl into our bags. Russell runs the stove and forces me to knock back hot tea before we fall off to sleep.

When we wake up, he keeps the tea coming to get fluids back into our dehydrated bodies. I can't contain my frustration and anger any longer. "I know you don't want to hear this," I gasp, "but this whole thing just went off half-cocked from the very start. I need you to hear me out."

"OK," he says, looking a little uncomfortable.

I begin my rant, focusing on the fact that, despite having two Sherpas with me, I've been forced to carry all my gear except for one bottle of oxygen. "My point is," I stammer, "what the hell are Karsang and Lobsang supposed to be doing?"

Russell frowns. Despite my pissy mood, I feel my heart go out to this stubborn, unbending man who ranks as one of the most able mountaineers I've ever been around. Amazingly, he's come within spitting distance of the summit dozens of times but never let his ambitions as a mountaineer interfere with his duties as a guide.

"They're young boys," he says, taking a sip of tea. "They've worked hard setting up and stocking camps. And they haven't been to the top. It's a real feather in their cap if they can summit. They deserve a shot."

"I don't begrudge them that opportunity. Nobody does a better job for their Sherpa staff than you. That's why those guys love you. But right now they're up there while we're sitting down here. And it just seems that the people I thought were supposed to help support my summit bid were doing nothing to assist me."

Russell is silent, and all I can hear is the hissing of the stove and the shuddering of the tent in the wind.

"Look," I continue, "I feel like a damn Judas, ranting at you, but I thought we were coming here to see if we could put the first disabled person on the summit of Everest. Instead it feels as if I'm nothing but an added frustration. It's as though if I can't climb the mountain on the same terms as you, it proves it can't be climbed."

Exhausted, feeling hopelessly angry and frustrated, I start to weep. Russell still says nothing, but I can see that he is carefully considering everything I've said. After spending the past month with me, he must have seen my outburst coming. To his credit, he hasn't countered with verbal backpedaling.

I wrap my hands around my cup of tea and feel the warmth seep into my hands. "How about this for a Plan B?" I stammer. "We got a false start this morning, but we weren't going so long that I burned myself out. If we hang here for thirty-six hours, I can rest on low flows of O_2, rehydrate, and recuperate. This will give you time to move a couple of new boys into place, and, weather permitting, you and I can give it another shot."

Russell shakes his head slightly. It's clear he believes we just shot our bolt and now need to descend. When Russell makes up his mind about something, he's a fairly rigid sort. Up here, this inflexibility is key to survival. To vacillate and second-guess yourself is suicidal.

Surprisingly, however, he retrieves his radio and spends the next thirty minutes dredging up the requisite supplies and manpower to make my Plan B work. When he finally clicks the radio off, he says, "Right, Whittaker. Everything is on standby for tomorrow night. But there's one thing you have to agree on: If Greg thinks the terrain is too challenging for you, you go back down. No ifs or buts. Agreed?"

"Agreed," I reply, wanting to reach out and hug this smelly New Zealander, but realizing it probably wouldn't be appreciated. The mood in the tent has shifted from tense to convivial.

At 3 P.M. Greg sticks his head through the door of the tent.

"Bloody hell," he grunts, looking absolutely wiped out. "This mountain's harder than K2."

The news hits me like a cricket bat between the eyes. K2 is known as *the* tough mountain, and Greg isn't the type to mince words. To hear such a blunt assessment from an accomplished mountaineer like Greg can mean only one thing.

It's over.

Back down at Base Camp, I put on a brave show, but the disappointment of choking just fifteen hundred feet from the summit consumes me. As I think it over, however, I decide that I won't be returning to Everest. This, I tell myself, was my swan song. I've left my mark, and there's no need to keep trying to better it.

As I lie back in my tent, I listen to the soft gong of the bells tied around the necks of our yaks. I hear boots approaching and without even having to open my eyes I can tell they belong to Greg. The two of us haven't said much since the upper camps. Nothing to say, really.

"Greg, my little basket of strawberries," I say as he pops his head inside, "what brings you to this side of town?"

Sitting down in the vestibule, he just smiles. "I've brought you something."

Anticipating a tattered envelope from Cindy or Lizzie, I feel my depressed heart start to pound. "Thanks," I reply, sitting up and reaching out my hand. He presses a thumb-sized shard of dark gray shale into the center of my palm and stares deep into my eyes.

"Whittaker, I picked this up on the summit," he says. "I want you to put it back where I got it from."

"You're kidding me, right?"

"No. I'm deadly serious."

Greg scratches his whiskered jaw and glances over his shoulder at the vast bulk of Everest, which looms behind him in the darkening sky.

"Don't you see? We were on the wrong side of the mountain. When we were moving on snow and ice, you were strong. But as soon as we got into the shale, your foot was working against you. If we'd been on the South Col, climbing on snow and ice, you'd have it in the bag by now."

He pauses to eye the rock still resting in my open palm. "Too bad we had to get to 27,000 feet to find out we were on the wrong side of the mountain," he adds with a grin. "Besides, I've had to go back to some mountains three times to get the job done. What makes you think you're so different?"

Without another word, he stands up and leaves.

Finally I allow myself to squeeze the rock in my hand. Just as I shut my eyes I hear Greg call, "If you want it bad enough, Whittaker, you'll find a way to do it."

I notice the yaks have grown quiet now. Night will soon be on us, the time when they stand as still as statues to conserve heat. The next twelve hours will be cold, no doubt. Still exhausted from my ascent, I strap on my foot and head over to the dining tent, Greg's rock clutched tightly in my palm. I know I should fling it as far as I can out onto the glacier, but something makes me hang onto it for dear life.

CHAPTER 15
The All Abilities Trek

One foggy morning in December 1996, I steer my van into Steve DeRoche's driveway and kill the engine. Cindy and Lizzie are still asleep in the back as I stare out at Steve's ranch-style home here in the suburbs of Pocatello, where he lives with his wife and three kids. No one's home, so I sit back and rest my eyes after the twelve-hour drive we've just made from Prescott.

Ten minutes later, Steve roars into the driveway after dropping off his wife, "Little" Cindy, at the HOG office, where she works as secretary. She's earned this nickname to distinguish her from my Cindy ("Cinders"), who towers over her by a full five inches.

I haven't seen Steve since I left for Everest with Greg Child, more than a year and a half ago. He looks surprised to see me.

"Whittaker," he says, climbing out of his car, "I had a dream about you last night. The two of us were sitting around the kitchen table, drinking tea, talking about your climb."

"Amazing, DeRoche," I reply. "In the year and a half since I last laid eyes on you, you've gone from psycho to bloody psychic."

Steve, whose deformed lower legs were amputated at the age of five, now bounds around on a pair of Flex-Feet. He races up the steps and into the kitchen.

"Come on in," he hollers. "I'll put the kettle on. Where are Cinders and Lizzie?"

"Sleeping in the van," I say. Soon the two of us are sitting at his oak kitchen table, getting caught up, while the kettle boils. Before long, the talk comes around to Everest and my climb with Greg.

"Steve, something happened to me up there," I say. "Greg made it and I didn't, but he ended up giving me something way more important."

"What?"

"A rock—a piece of Everest, from the summit. He told me to put it back where he got it from!"

"You gonna do it?" he asks as he gets up to fetch the kettle.

"I'd like to try."

He laughs as he pours the hot water into my cup. "We're a lot alike, Whittaker," he says. "Tell us to do something and we just might; tell us we can't and—look out!"

I tell him about when I knew, when it came to me that I had to return. The day after Greg dropped that damn stone into my hand, I hiked up on the ridge overlooking the glacier near Base Camp and felt the excitement start to boil up inside me. I realized that I had wanted to stand on top of the world so badly that I had compromised why I go into the mountains in the first place. I had assumed the role of a client and allowed other people to make decisions for me, letting their expectations of my capabilities define me. After climbing Outer Limits I had sworn that I wouldn't let this happen to me ever again. But it had. I gave up the decision-making and the logistical planning to someone else, and all I had to do was get to the top. Even if I had reached the summit, it would have felt like cheating to pass an exam. Turning back from the summit was, in fact, a blessing in disguise.

When I met Cinders in Kathmandu a week later, I delicately broached the subject with her. As usual, she made it easy for me, telling me that I should go back, but only with people who knew my capabilities and wanted to be part of a dream bigger than any of us. She was right. If I go back to Everest, it must be first and foremost as a mountaineer who wants to see if he possesses the physical, mental, and emotional toughness to summit. But it must also be as a HOG—to prove that most of our limitations are in our heads and in the eyes of others. Mountaineering should never be a publicity stunt, but if it is done right it can have a higher purpose than just bagging a peak.

"Going back and doing this thing right," I tell Steve, "is more important than merely doing it."

Steve nods and takes a long sip from his mug. "Well," he says carefully, "maybe we should do a HOG trip to Base Camp, to see you off before you head up the mountain."

I try not to smile, as I think to myself that maybe Steve has turned psychic after all. This is just what I've been thinking for the past year and a half, ever since Cinders suggested it in Kathmandu.

Steve just sits there, trying to gauge my reaction. "A HOG trek to Base Camp?" I finally say. "You really think we could pull it off?"

"Listen, if you haven't managed to kill us off by now, Whittaker, then we're pretty much unstoppable."

He's got a point there. "Well, if this one doesn't finish you off, I'm gonna stop wasting my time trying."

In June 1997, after finally getting Little Cindy to sign off on the idea, Steve telephones Kyle Packer, who now lives in Illinois with his wife, Cheryl, and their two boys. Kyle is intrigued, but the financial cost of the trek worries him.

"Five thousand dollars?" Kyle says. "That's a lot of money."

"How often do two fellows like us get a chance to hike to Everest Base Camp?" Steve asks. "I wouldn't miss this for the world. Besides, Tom and Cinders need us. I'll borrow the money if I have to."

Kyle agrees to sign on. Cinders then goes to work recruiting HOGs, and she eventually signs up Tom McCurdy, a wheelchair marathon racer; Ike Gayfield, who suffers from a neuromuscular disease; Carla Yustak, a teacher from Canada with cerebral palsy; and Sheila Brashears, who lost a leg to cancer. Between the six of them, they're missing three legs and will be traveling with three wheelchairs and four pairs of crutches.

Also joining the group will be two Prescott College students, Alison Orton and Nathan Barsetti, who will use the trek for a senior studies project; Jeff Brandt, the HOG director; and Bob

Meyer, an able-bodied HOG volunteer. Cinders will serve as trek coordinator, and at the ripe old age of six, Lizzie will become one of the youngest Westerners to travel to Base Camp.

Even for a group as nimble on their artificial feet as the HOGs, this latest adventure has all the trappings of a mission to Mars. Climbing to an altitude of 17,500 feet—in a Third World country where medical help can be days away—is an extraordinarily difficult task, even for someone possessing all of his body parts. In fact, nearly 50 percent of the people who start out for Base Camp are forced to turn back. If the rugged terrain or intestinal disorders don't stop you, chances are the debilitating effects of the altitude will. But the HOGs are a team, and they all know that they'll have to do their utmost if the "All Abilities Trek" is going to succeed.

The first obstacle, of course, is for each member of the team to raise the necessary $5,000, which is a hardship for all the HOGs. To keep costs down, some HOGs hit the *Outdoor Retailer* trade show in Salt Lake City to sweet-talk gear out of various manufacturers. Late one afternoon, Steve stops at a manufacturer's booth to ask about a possible sponsorship.

"You want to do what?" the woman asks.

"Six disabled people," Steve says patiently, "with disabilities ranging from cerebral palsy to double-leg amputations, are going to hike to Everest Base Camp."

"To Everest Base Camp?" she stammers. "Why the death wish?"

Steve has spent a lot of time pondering that one. Why is it, after all, that he and the others are willing to lay everything on the line to travel to the other side of the planet and hike up into the ice and clouds? It's not as though people like Carla, Kyle, and Sheila are starved for adventures. Their daily lives are packed with more challenges than some people encounter in a year.

"If it makes a difference to just one person," he says, "then it'll be worth it."

The sales rep waves her hand in the air and says, "Listen, I did that trek two years ago, and of the eleven people who started out, five didn't make it—five *healthy* people." There are the statistics again. The HOGs have heard such depressing figures countless times since they decided on their mission, and even someone as stubbornly optimistic as Steve finds it hard to argue with them.

"Tell your friends that what they're attempting to do is noble, really noble," the woman continues. "But they're getting in way over their heads."

Steve nods thoughtfully, then brushes the comment off with a chuckle and resumes pressing the sales rep for sponsorship.

"Let's pretend we're being open-minded about this," Steve says with a grin. "Think of the publicity you'd get. We have the BBC on board for a two-hour documentary, we'd post your name on a Website accessed by thousands of schoolkids every day as they follow our progress, and we'll take your brand logo to Base Camp as well as do promo shots. Or you can just donate some gear and use it for a tax write-off. How about that?"

The sales rep just laughs, shakes her head, and walks away.

The reaction is hardly unique. Few manufacturers want to align their products with disability. Most people, I've noticed over the years, think in terms of winners and losers—and you know which category they put the HOGs in. Companies are particularly resistant in the wake of the May 1996 storm on Mount Everest that left nine climbers dead; since then, businesses have shied away from the mountain, treating it as a potential public relations liability. Thus, despite logging thousands of hours writing sponsorship proposals and making phone calls, Jeff Brandt, Little Cindy, Steve, and Cinders have had little success drumming up support.

Eventually, however, Steve and the others manage to get promises of gear from several manufacturers who seem to understand what they're attempting to do. Among those contributing are

Cascade Designs, Eureka, Life-Link, Adidas, SmartWool, Swiss Army, Coyote Wear, and Croakies.

The All Abilities Trek is off the ground. Members have taken out loans and struggled in the gym and on hills near their homes, all the while raising families and working extra hours. They have the cash in hand and are fit and ready.

Everest Challenge '98 also manages to land a few sponsors, including Prescott College; Pride Industries, a nonprofit organization whose mission is to train and employ people with disabilities and that also owns Yuba, the snowshoe manufacturer; and the travel store Changes in Latitude.

Then, in February 1998, six weeks before the expedition is due to leave for Nepal, the BBC is hit with a restructuring crisis. Because our contract is not yet signed, we get axed. My business friends tell me there's no way I can pull this off now, with so little time to go until the climb. They suggest I return the funds to our sponsors. But, as Steve DeRoche pointed out when we first talked about this expedition, telling me I can't do something is the least effective way to stop me.

Neal Mangham, the president of Prescott College, agrees to run Everest Challenge '98 through the college's books so that we can offer the expedition's supporters a tax write-off. Eric Howard, an experienced fund-raiser and marketer who was working for the Grand Canyon Trust, signs on to manage the expedition accounts and spearhead our fund-raising and publicity efforts. After a hasty council of war with Eric, we use his frequent flyer miles to head to New York to talk face-to-face with my contacts. Sleeping on floors, hopping subways from one meeting to the next, we ink deals with the New York Times, CBS's Public Eye with Bryant Gumbel, and Merrill Lynch. By the time we catch the red-eye back to Phoenix, our whirlwind trip has reeled in $63,000. That's still not nearly enough to fund the entire trip—we have only half of the $300,000 we'll need—but we definitely have hope now.

Just three weeks before we're due to leave, the Prescott-based Inter-Cal Corporation, which manufactures a vitamin C product known as Ester-C, agrees to take the title sponsorship role, and the expedition officially becomes the "Ester-C Everest Challenge." Even with Inter-Cal's support, it's clear this will be a bare-bones adventure. A typical HOG undertaking.

The Ester-C Everest Challenge is a mission of two parts. First, while I acclimatize on the mountain, the HOGs will make the long trek to Base Camp, to arrive in time to see me off for my summit bid. I consider getting the HOGs to Base Camp, at 17,500 feet, just as important as my own climb to the peak.

So, after I head to Everest to begin the acclimatization process, the HOGs fly into Kathmandu to begin their own trek. Two days after they arrive, however, fifty-year-old Sheila Brashears stuns Cinders by confessing that she is dropping out and catching the next jet back to her home in Kansas City. Sheila epitomizes everything I dreamed the organization might come to stand for. Over the years she's initiated and managed some of our most hair-raising odysseys, and despite her amputated leg, she moves deftly on her crutches. Cinders is unable to convince her to reconsider, and Sheila's departure sends the group into a funk.

After learning of Sheila's decision, Ike Gayfield sits alone in the hotel lobby, now dwelling on his own choice to come to the Himalayas. From across the room he hears a European trekker inquiring about all the wheelchairs and crutches he's spotted around the lobby.

"That's absolutely ludicrous," the gentleman stammers after the hotel manager informs him of the HOGs' intentions. "They will never make it. Never." Hearing this discourse, Ike feels the doubt well up inside him.

The next day, by the time the HOGs' twin-engine plane slams down on the tiny airstrip in Lukla, the main jumping-off point for trekkers and mountaineers going into the Khumbu region of the Himalayas, Ike is wondering whether the HOGs have made a major mistake in coming here. The grim, crumpled reminders of flights that didn't make the landing have been pushed to the sides of this remote airfield, where Sir Edmund Hillary lost his wife in a tragic accident.

Word travels fast in these hills. Nearly everyone in this mountain village has turned out to see the disabled foreigners who are attempting to climb to Everest's Base Camp. Wheelchairs in the Khumbu? The trails, set into the hillsides centuries ago, are steep and feature many stone steps. Humans, horses, and yaks all travel by foot, and the HOGs are pretty short on feet.

After piling his duffel bag onto his wheelchair, Tom McCurdy muscles his way toward a group of gray stone houses. But within seconds, the bag is lifted from him and deposited at the teahouse. The Buddhist villagers firmly believe that the more altruistically you behave in this life, the more pleasant your next incarnation will be. Needless to say, they're happy to be of service.

"The circus is in town," laughs Steve as he hikes up his pants to reveal his artificial legs.

The group makes its way to the teahouse to meet Tindi from Asian Trekking, the *sirdar*, or head Sherpa. A short, slight man who understands more English than he speaks, Tindi is kind and thoughtful. Sitting on the steps, two Sherpa women, known as Sherpani, groom a little girl's dark, snarled hair. The HOGs smile at them as the group files inside to a lunch of noodle soup and chapati (an unleavened bread) with honey.

Kyle eats outside, but when he finishes he gets out of his chair and begins climbing the stone stairs of the teahouse. His legs are covered in thick kneepads he's fashioned from an old tire. When they see him, the women and the little girl jump up and run giggling down the street. After two steps, Kyle tumbles back down and slams into the dirt. Tindi runs outside to help him, along with Bob Meyer and Cinders.

"First blood," Kyle winces, proudly holding up his scraped wrist.

"Way to go, Kyle," Tom McCurdy cheers. Kyle chuckles, as only Kyle can, and he's helped to a bench under the window. After he puts antibiotic cream on his scrape, the HOGs set off for the village center.

The group has leased three Tibetan ponies, all stallions, which McCurdy, Kyle, and Ike will ride. Each animal is fitted with color-fully woven wool blankets, wooden saddles, and hemp bridles. Although none of the ponies has a bit in its mouth, each has a sixteen-year-old boy leading it on the trail.

Kyle's horse sidesteps as he tries to mount, sending him sprawling. But his foot is still in the stirrup, so Babu, the Sherpa who will travel with him, grabs Kyle and pushes him up into the saddle so forcefully that he nearly goes over the other side.

When McCurdy is helped to his mount, he has to fight to balance himself in the saddle, since he has no muscle control below his powerful chest.

Once Ike is on his pony, the HOGs head out of town, moving under a string of prayer flags and past the stupa, a Buddhist monument containing holy relics. The same mist that has been falling ever since they landed swirls around them. The trail they're following runs downhill to the Dudh Kosi, Nepali for "Milk River," whose freezing water, the runoff from glaciers, tumbles savagely over truck-sized boulders and cascades down steep ravines.

When the group reaches the outskirts of Lukla, Ike and Kyle's ponies begin bickering, trying to slash one another with their sharp hooves. Both men are thrown off their mounts, but fortunately it is to the side of the trail forested with rhododendron trees—on the other side, the rocky trail drops several hundred feet to the river. The Sherpas rush to their aid, relieved to find that they haven't been injured. After Ike gets to his feet gingerly, he stares down his pony and says menacingly, "That's it, sucker. Do it again and you're fired!" With a foot-up from his Sherpa, he slings himself over his saddle and continues down the trail toward Phakding, mumbling, "I best be bad." Against his better judgment, Kyle lets the HOGs bully him back onto his charge.

McCurdy makes it to camp ahead of the others, but the downhill, side-to-side lurching has wreaked havoc on his forearms, which he has used to stay in the saddle. As he enters the yard of the Guest House, Kyle is almost catapulted once again when the pony begins jumping and pawing at the ground after spotting Ike's mount. Kyle scrambles off and to his wheelchair.

"I can't do it," he announces, after brooding for several minutes. "I'm not getting back on that pony." After a short discussion, Tindi and Cinders decide to get rid of the high-strung animal, which seems to be making the others nervous.

Nobody blames Kyle, but it's clear that without a horse he's not going anywhere. At dinner that night, he looks dejected and beaten. When he rolls off to his bed, he seems resigned to returning to Kathmandu alone.

Over the course of the night, McCurdy's intestines go haywire, causing him to foul the inside of his sleeping bag. Jeff Brandt helps get him cleaned up, but both men grow skeptical about the trek ahead. It's only the first day on the trail, and the HOGs have lost one teammate, at least. If McCurdy's condition is serious, he's out as well.

The next morning, the group is glum. By 7 A.M., most of the HOGs have been awake for an hour or more, but Kyle has yet to show his face in the dining room. Finally Babu wakes him with milk tea and a bowl of warm water to wash with. Once Kyle is up and about, several of the other Sherpas approach; they're carrying a huge woven basket, which they've cut a rectangle out of and padded.

"You ride in this," Babu says, grinning.

As Kyle looks over the contraption, a smile spreads across his face. While he was sleeping, stewing in his juices, these men he didn't even know took it upon themselves to ensure that he can keep going, that his dream doesn't slip away because of a spooked pony. Fighting back tears, he agrees to give it a go.

After Kyle climbs into the basket, Babu hoists it on his back, secures it with a padded tumpline, or strap, across his forehead, and stands upright. Balanced squarely upon the porter's head and back hangs Kyle's 140-pound frame. The Sherpas laugh proudly, and all the HOGs smile as well. Kyle is back.

As Kyle is carried up the rocky trail, however, this basket becomes something of a prison. He knows his success depends on it, but the helplessness that comes with being strapped on a stranger's back scares him horribly. Particularly disturbing is the deep chasm that is just beside the trail. If this dedicated Sherpa stumbles even a little on the stony terrain, Kyle could go plummeting down into the river hundreds of feet below. On two occasions he grows so scared that his shaking throws the porter off balance. Prescott College senior Ali Orton begins walking beside Kyle, telling him when he's approaching any changes in the topography and peppering him with questions about his life and family, anything to take his mind off the exposed trail. Just knowing what lurks ahead seems to give him a sense of control.

The trail through the Khumbu, winding thirty-eight miles up to Everest Base Camp, crosses a handful of deep valleys cut into the earth by the rushing Himalayan rivers. The suspension bridges that span these valleys are in various stages of repair (or disrepair), but even those that are in good condition are unsettling to Westerners unaccustomed to venturing out on such swaying structures. On some of the bridges, pieces of the wood planking have dropped into the gorge and been swept away by the river. If

the holes haven't been covered with strategically placed flat granite rocks, the HOGs must step over gaps in the planks, doing their
best not to look down through the holes at the long drop below.

The villagers have strung colorful Buddhist prayer flags that
flap in the wind, sending blessings up into the heavens. Although
the HOGs aren't followers of Buddha's teachings, they'll take
whatever spiritual and karmic power they can get.

The group develops a ritual for bridges. The Sherpas chant the
widely used Buddhist mantra *Om Mani Padme Hum* and the HOGs
say the group's battle cry, "Better dead than disabled!" Each person
then heads out on his or her own, however he or she sees fit.

Kyle generally travels in his basket, but the crossings are particularly nerve-wracking for him. The more nervous he becomes, the
more likely he is to twitch violently. The twitching is likely to throw
his porter off balance on the swaying bridge, but knowing this only
makes Kyle more nervous.

Ike prefers to use his crutches. On one unusually long bridge,
two porters rush to his aid, but when they grab him they cause the
bridge to sway, nearly sending all three of them plunging hundreds
of feet into the river. Ike sends them back and gingerly makes his
way through the heaving obstacle course, praying his wobbly legs
stay balanced and his crutches don't disappear into the holes.

Sometimes Tom McCurdy maneuvers himself across in his
wheelchair, a feat that puts everyone on edge. One slip of his wheel
and he'll be pitched over the low rail and into the river. Other times
he scoots himself across the splintered floorboards on his butt.

Carla just cruises across in the same way she travels everywhere: fearlessly. Her gait is a little lacking in control and she
sometimes seems to be on the verge of falling off, but she always
recovers without missing a step.

Steve is so sure-footed, despite walking on two artificial legs, that
he doesn't even look at his feet as he crosses. Using his adjustable
ski poles, he blows by his wife and waits for her on the other side.

As the days go by, the HOGs realize that there's a real technique to bridge crossing and that if they travel one at a time, they can pick up the rhythm and move with the sway. Every time they arrive safely on the other side, they remind themselves that they have one less bridge to cross—until they come back down.

Everyone waits and watches until the last person makes it across the bridge. Then heads are lowered, lungs are filled with the thin, clean Himalayan air, and the slow uphill grind continues. The HOGs proceed at their own pace, and the group is soon scattered along the trail.

Word of the HOGs' quest spreads, and villagers, and even other trekkers, often gather to watch the group's slow procession. Steve never tires of yanking up his trousers and showing off his lack of legs to get a rise out of the crowd. Sometimes children run out to touch the spokes in the wheelchairs. "No one ever told these kids they're supposed to be afraid of us," Kyle shouts to Babu. When Kyle was a child, parents often wouldn't allow their children to play with him out of the misguided fear that cerebral palsy might be contagious.

The closer the HOGs get to Namche Bazaar, a maze of houses, hotels, and shops that serves as the local trading center, the more crowded the trail becomes. One by one, tall, nomadic Tibetan traders, many of whom wear their long black hair in unkempt ponytails tied back with silver and turquoise clasps, push past the group as they make their way up the hill. The HOGs quickly learn to move to the inside of the narrow trail to ensure that, after the merrily decorated mule trains and goods-laden goats have passed, they'll still be on it.

Because of its steep, two-thousand-foot vertical grind out of the Dudh Kosi valley, the Namche hill is the first of the major challenges en route to Base Camp. The hill represents a doorway from the relatively lush lowlands to the stark, alpine highlands. From this point on, the blinding white Himalayan peaks slice the heavens.

After six hours of toiling uphill, staring back at where he's been, Kyle can't take the basket anymore. He's exhausted from his frequent muscle spasms. Nearly three-quarters of the way up the hill, his porter squats down to rest, setting the contraption onto the dirt. Kyle unties the strap around his waist and hops out of the basket.

"Knock it off," Steve tells him. "Get back in your basket."

Kyle looks up at him with a grin. "I'm not riding in this basket anymore today. I'm walking!"

And before anyone knows what's happening, Kyle—his hands protected with bicycling gloves, his knees and legs covered in his makeshift Michelin pads—strikes off up the trail. He's hardly graceful—in fact, it's looks as if he's been rehydrating on copious amounts of Chang, the local rice beer—but at moments like this, only a fool would concern himself with appearances. Some folks cry as they witness another display of Kyle's indomitable spirit.

He moves slowly, contorting his body in ways that make sense only to him. From a switchback high above, Little Cindy looks down at the cloud of dust trailing behind him. The two of them have formed a close bond on this trek, and he has opened up to her in ways he hasn't to anyone else. But as much as she wants to run down the trail and help him, she realizes that this uphill slog is something Kyle must do for himself.

Kyle continues lurching upward, dust flying everywhere. An hour after he starts, amidst cheering and clapping from the other HOGs, he reaches the top of the hill and arrives at the ancient arch that leads to the Solo Khumbu, which protects Namche Bazaar from evil spirits in the valley below. He is covered in mud and drenched in sweat. Sitting back on his heels he gratefully accepts a proffered water bottle, trapping it between his fist and forearm, and gulps the cool, fresh water.

"One hill down," he grunts to his fellow HOGs, "only another 237 to go."

Not long after the HOGs leave Namche Bazaar, a trekker and his wife wander into a teahouse where the group is devouring lunch. They stare disgustedly at the crutches and wheelchairs scattered around the property, and, after clumsily tripping over Ike's crutches, the husband shouts, "What the hell is all this junk lying around here for? I feel like I'm in a damned hospital ward. Who's in charge here?"

The porters point at Jeff Brandt, who sits at a nearby table with Kyle, McCurdy, Ike, and Carla. The trekker storms over and confronts him.

"You people have no business being here," he yells.

"That's funny," replies Jeff, staring directly at the blowhard. "That's the very reason we came."

The man looks at his wife as if he can't believe what he just heard, then shouts, "None of you belong here! Pick up your toys and go home before you get hurt."

"Back off, little man," Steve says quietly. Standing up, he towers over the opinionated trekker; Steve outweighs him by more than fifty pounds. The HOGs brace for a confrontation, but the man turns on his heel and storms out.

Nights are also fraught with activity. One evening, a snow leopard creeps into camp in search of a meal and spooks the animals. During the ensuing mayhem, one of the ponies gets gored in the flank by a yak horn. Later, after hearing accounts of a seven-foot-tall Yeti attacking a female hiker further up the trail, the Sherpas sit up all night guarding the tents with machete-sized meat cleavers and large stones.

Because it's springtime, the forests are filled with amorous wild fillies searching for a good-looking stallion. Once, just before dark, a female emerges from the trees and stands in the middle of the encampment, neighing excitedly at the group's ponies. The horses break loose and chase the lusty female back into the dense rhododendron trees. These animals have disappeared entirely, and without them, the trek is over. But just as quickly as they disappear, they reemerge from the forest—only they're being chased by an enraged, wild black stallion. Fortunately for the HOGs, this other horse wins the fight; he gets the girl and the Sherpas get their ponies back.

The higher they move, the colder it gets during the night. Usually they wake up to find the remnants in their bedpans frozen solid. Every morning McCurdy has to scrape the ice off his wheelchair, and Steve must slide his stumps into his bitterly cold prostheses, which he normally stands outside his tent during the night.

Before the HOGS reach 15,000 feet, the Sherpas inform them that their ponies' lungs will explode above that altitude, so the animals are swapped for yaks, affectionately known as Himalayan Harleys. Neither McCurdy nor Ike is especially eager to hop on the back of one of these longhaired, crotchety beasts. On the morning of the switch, the two of them try to convince the other to be the guinea pig.

"You go first, Ike," McCurdy says.

"The last time I sat on a cow it ran off and left me in the dirt."

"That's no cow, Ike."

"You're telling me. Look at those horns—they're sharp and pointed straight at me."

Neither budges from his wheelchair until Lizzie skips onto the scene and stares at the two men. Quickly sizing up the situation, she puts her tiny foot in the stirrup and pulls herself up onto the yak.

"They're OK, you guys," she giggles as she rides. "Tom, Ike, they're OK."

Both men look at each other and shrug. Looks like they'll be riding yaks after all.

"A chip off the old annoying block," McCurdy says, laughing.

The Sherpas cover the wooden saddles with inflatable camping pads and sheepskins. Being a paraplegic, McCurdy could develop debilitating sores on his lower body long before he ever was aware of the problem, and at this altitude, wounds fester quickly and seldom heal. One sore could be enough to send him back down the mountain.

No one stops to think about the fact that Lizzie weighs less than forty pounds; chances are, the yak never even noticed she was on its back. No sooner does Ike reluctantly climb onto his yak than the animal begins violently shaking its head from side to side. The tip of the beast's curled horn gouges his leg. Ike stares down at the blood, then slides off the animal's massive back and waits for it to mellow. The moment he crawls back up, the yak bolts down the trail as Ike shouts, "Whoa! Whoa!"

By the time McCurdy catches up with him, Ike is seated on a rock, rubbing his leg. He's smiling, looking strangely tranquil.

"I got me a yak with attitude."

As the journey continues, the HOGs learn how serious it is to venture into the hallowed, upper reaches of the Khumbu. Several of the Sherpas, the group discovers, have traveled to Base Camp once before, but because they weren't part of a climbing expedition they were permitted to remain only long enough to deposit their loads. One of the porters, who has previously made the trip, recently spoke with a lama (an elder of the Buddhist church) about his desire to become a climbing Sherpa. The lama assured him that he had nothing to fear from the mountain because he was one of the chosen ones who would be accepted by *Sagarmatha* (the Nepali name for Everest, meaning "goddess of the sky"). The message to the HOGs is clear: if the mountain gods don't think you belong, they pull your ticket.

When the HOGs find themselves standing before this same lama in a dark temple, he showers them with sacred rice, blesses Steve's ski poles, and hands each member of the group a yellow string that he has prayed over and blown across. Afterwards he motions to them with his hand, showing them how the prayer now travels up into the heavens. Any apprehension that the gods aren't happy with the HOGs' mission is finally put to rest. Their quest, he assures them through an interpreter, is a pilgrimage of the spirit. The HOGs knot the yellow cords around their necks and file out of the dark room, which is lined with figurines depicting all the previous lamas who have served there over the centuries.

The days grind on, and they fight their way up through the cold, thin air, up toward one of the planet's most desolate spots. This trail has come to stand for the uphill battle all of them have been waging for much if not all of their lives. Leave it to me to drag them halfway around the world just to remind them of this.

The HOGs have been on the trail for three weeks. On this day, snow falls from the sky and an approaching storm roars in the distance. A layer of white coats Kyle in his basket, and he looks unbelievably haggard.

"You feeling all right?" Steve asks. Kyle glances at him, then looks away.

"No," he mumbles, diverting his eyes from the steep drop beside the trail.

As Kyle disappears up the trail on the Sherpa's back, Steve looks down at the path they are traveling. To the left, the drop is lethal; to the right, crippling. In the past three weeks the Sherpas haven't made a single misstep, but in a journey of thirty-eight miles, even the surest foot has to stumble occasionally. The laws of probability demand it. Only this can explain the pained grimace on Kyle's face.

Walking beside Kyle is the willowy, blue-eyed Ali. She speaks to him reassuringly, trying to talk the fear away, explaining every aspect of the terrain coming up so that when he sees it, he won't be afraid. But when the porter puts down the basket to rest, Steve, knowing only too well that the only person who can exorcise Kyle's fear is Kyle, reaches in and grabs Kyle by the jacket.

"We're right here, Kyle," he shouts. "*This* is where we are right now. Right here! You gotta look at this stuff. Open your eyes and breathe. You've earned the right to see it, now take it in."

Nearly three hundred feet below them on the glacier lies a pool filled with cobalt blue liquid. Steve tugs on Kyle until his head pivots around, then thrusts his hand down in the direction of the glacial pond.

"We're never going to see that again as long as we live," Steve says, his face just inches from Kyle's. "Can you see it? Can you?!"

Finally Kyle screams, "Yeah, I can see it! I can see it."

When the Sherpa stands back up and resumes walking, Ali continues her monologue. Steve marches back over and shouts at her, "Kyle can handle this! Stop coddling him. Start treating him like a man."

Ali is stunned momentarily, but then she bursts into tears and rushes up the trail as quickly as her oxygen-hungry lungs will allow her.

"Shit," mutters Steve. "That's the last thing I wanted to happen."

Kyle and Steve say nothing as they continue up the trail. In the last hours before they reach Base Camp, the full fury of the storm hits them, blowing snow from every direction. The Sherpas seem to feel their way forward, since the snow has almost completely obscured the trail. They can't rely on past experience either, since the trail into Base Camp changes from year to year. Until the tents come into view, all the HOGs can do is stick with the leader over the winding route and fight through the blizzard.

After hours of plodding through the snow, the Sherpas suddenly stop, step carefully onto a boulder, and point off into the blurred distance. Through the snow can be seen the fuzzy outline of several tents.

"We're going to make it!" Kyle yells.

"Damn right, we're going to make it," shouts Steve, wedging himself against a massive obelisk of granite to hide from the wind and snow. "Thank you, Cinders," he yells to my wife through the blizzard. "Thank you for this."

Eyes narrowed, I peer into a Himalayan gale. Somewhere out there in the maze of ice pinnacles and moraine debris is a small band of intrepid adventurers who are very close to my heart. I know the HOGs are due to arrive soon.

As I stand sentinel in the thin air of Base Camp, I shudder in the frigid storm winds. The pragmatist in me knows that it's time to seek the shelter of my tent, especially because I've been battling a virus known as the "Khumbu Crud," which feels like someone has poured pancake batter into my lungs. But my longing to see my wife and daughter and the other HOG trekkers makes me stay just a few minutes longer.

Finally, after the feeling has drained from my extremities, I reluctantly turn to go. Casting one last look backward, I stop dead in my tracks. Through the storm I can see two massive beasts coming up the trail, their long, shaggy coats covered in snow. These yaks are loaded with food and equipment, and I know that they must be the advance party for the HOGs. Looking closer, I notice a small figure urging the Himalayan oxen forward.

"Lizzie?" I call out uncertainly.

"Daddy!" the little snow-covered figure says joyously. Rushing ahead of the yaks, my daughter runs up the rock pile I'm standing on and flings herself into my arms. This six-year-old girl from Arizona has not only made it to Everest Base Camp, but she's made it well ahead of the rest of her group.

Together we head to the mess tent and wait for the HOGs to come into camp. Watching Tom McCurdy move over the rocks on his butt pad, and Ike walking on his crutches, reminds me what brave souls these folks are. When Steve and his wife arrive with Bob Meyer right behind them, my heart swells even more. I look at Steve and ask, "What took you so long?" He gives me a bear hug in reply.

By now all members of the climbing team have turned out to the tent to see these heroes reach their goal. Everyone whistles and cheers when Carla pokes her head through the door of the tent, with my wife right behind her. Cinders gives me a hug so tight that I practically burst. No need to ask how she feels. I can see it in her eyes.

When Kyle Packer arrives, he is secured to a Sherpa's back in his padded basket, but twenty yards out from camp he insists on being put down. This is a point of pride for Kyle. With awkward, jerky movements, he wills his body over the rock and ice toward the tent. By the time he arrives, his beard is full of icicles and he is covered in snow. Still on his knees, he moves into the tent and is greeted by applause and whoops of joy. "You're amazing, Kyle!" one team member says. Kyle looks up at the assembled mountaineers and announces, his voice choked with emotion, "Like Whittaker says, if we can make Base Camp, we can do anything we want!"

The HOGs have pulled it off. The five of them have come into the heart of the Himalayas from Illinois and Canada, from Boise and Pocatello, and all five have made it over thirty-eight miles of trail to an altitude of 17,500 feet. It's a feat I wouldn't have even dared dream about that night so long ago that, while driving back from Yosemite with Cinders, I first sketched out my idea for bringing the handicapped to the great outdoors. The essence of the HOGs has always been building self-esteem while challenging the concept that disability is something to be ashamed of. I never realized just how far they'd take it.

That night, as I lie in my tent with my wife and daughter snuggled up to me, I listen to the storm howl over the peak that I must soon climb. Summiting Everest has been a dream of mine for so long, and I've been thwarted twice, but despite the challenge I face, I am calm. Watching my wife, my yak-herding daughter, and my close friends on the All Abilities Trek has given me the courage and resolve to climb this mountain. Despite all the skepticism they encountered along the way, the HOGs have reached Everest Base Camp, and by doing so they have passed the baton on to me. Seeing them live their dream has empowered me to live mine.

Years ago I set out to somehow repay the community of Pocatello, Idaho, for helping me in my darkest hour, and the HOG program became my small contribution. Reflecting on Kyle's triumphant entrance this afternoon, on all of the HOGs' heroism and determination, I recognize for the first time the meaning behind the words "Your gift to the world will be the world's gift to you."

CHAPTER 16
The Three Pouches

Gasping to catch my breath, I jerk myself upright inside the tent, trying to remember where I am. Desperate to drag precious oxygen into my soggy lungs, I fumble for my mask. In the few seconds it takes me to pull the oxygen mask over my nose and mouth, reality comes crashing back.

After the HOGs left Base Camp, the virus that I had been battling became worse, and in order to recover I descended to the village of Pheriche, at an altitude of 13,800 feet. Once I felt better, I climbed more than thirteen thousand feet up the mountain in order to beat a storm predicted to dump thirty feet of snow on the upper reaches of Everest. But three hours ago, just before dawn, I lost it. My quest to be the first disabled man to stand atop the world's highest peak has been dashed for the third time. And once again, I didn't even reach a named spot on the mountain before turning back. Worse, it now seems as though the documentary film I promised my sponsors isn't going to get made. Nearly two years of work and $30,000 of my hard-earned cash have just been flushed down the toilet. Even more disturbing, my longtime friend Jeff Rhoads and Tashi Tsering, one of our Sherpas, are still up on the mountain, inching their way toward the summit. Helpless to do anything to assist them, I can only pray that they get down before they're buried in the storm.

I spot Tommy Heinrich pointing his video camera at me through the open tent door, but before I can utter a word, my chest erupts into a paroxysm of coughing. I have to pull off the oxygen mask and retch up a mouthful of stringy mucus. Feeling as though I'm suffocating, I lean over and spit it outside the tent.

"Jesus, my lungs are filling up," I whisper, my voice ruined by laryngitis. I inspect the liquid that I just spit outside for the tell-tale sign of pulmonary edema—a pink, bubbly froth. Since pulmonary edema is often a death sentence in this remote section of the mountain, I'm relieved to see that the warning signs are absent from my mucus. But a look of concern spreads across Tommy's face, which is still swollen and bloody from the three-hundred-foot tumble he took yesterday when he was retrieving the wedding ring and a bracelet from the frozen body of Scott Fischer.

"It's pulmonary edema," he says while searching frantically for the radio. "You've got pulmonary edema."

"Now wait a minute, Tommy," I whisper. "I've definitely got fluid in my lungs, but it's not pink or frothy. I need to talk to our doctor down in Base Camp, and then I need to get down."

Tommy doesn't appear concerned with such technicalities. He locates the radio and starts chattering to Doug White, our expedition doctor.

"Yeah, it's pulmonary edema, all right," he tells the doctor. "He looks horrible."

An enthusiastic mountaineer with an encyclopedic knowledge of this part of the Himalayas, Tommy was added to the trip at the last moment to work as a cameraman for our title sponsor, Inter-Cal. As I listen to him jump to conclusions over the radio, another spasm of coughing grips my chest. Turning my oxygen up to three liters a minute, I pull the mask back onto my face as Tommy reaches into his down suit and retrieves a tiny zip-lock bag that we all carry for such emergencies. He pulls a tablet from the bag and shoves it into my hand.

"Take this," he insists. "This is the pill the doctor says you need. You've got to take it now."

I stare at the pill, which is actually just one of two tablet-form medications in the plastic bag Tommy carries. The pills are meant to stave off the effects of the two types of edema that can hit climbers at high altitude. One pill is meant for cerebral edema, when the brain literally swells, which can lead to blindness and eventually death. Tommy wants me to take this pill to treat pulmonary edema, which occurs when the lungs don't function properly due to the lack of atmospheric pressure and are transformed into a fluid-choked mess. If the condition goes untreated, a person can drown in his own lungs—altitude-induced pneumonia, if you will.

For all his good intentions, the last thing I plan to do is trust Tommy's judgment. To begin with, I'm unconvinced that I'm suffering from full-blown pulmonary edema. Some fluid has definitely collected in my lungs, but I feel certain that if I can just stand up and move around, my condition will sort itself out. I also know that dropping to a lower altitude and breathing bottled oxygen will take the strain off my stressed lungs.

The other issue is that, if I swallow the wrong tablet, I won't be in any shape to get off this mountain before we're all buried by the approaching storm.

"You sure this is the right one?" I ask, staring at the small, fuzzy white tablet in my hand.

"Yeah, yeah, that's it," he says. "Go ahead, take it."

Without my reading glasses I can't read the writing on the tiny zip-lock bag the tablet came out of. I can't take the risk that it's the wrong pill. I need a second opinion. "No, Tommy, I'm not going to take it until I talk to the doctor."

Tommy nods, then begins jabbering into the radio, "Whittaker's not taking his meds. He's refusing to take the tablet."

"Give me that," I wheeze, snatching the radio out of his hands.

"Doug, are you there?" I rasp into the unit.

"I'm here, Tom," he says. "Why are you refusing to take the Nyphedapene?"

"Look, I'm not refusing to take anything. I just want to make sure I'm taking the right tablet. What does it look like?"

"It's the brown, hexagonal tablet."

"Not the white tablet?" I inquire, looking pointedly at Tommy.

"*No!*" Doug says emphatically. "Not the white tablet. Make sure you take the brown, hexagonal tablet. On no account are you to take the white tablet. Do you understand?"

"Perfectly," I reply. "Whittaker out." I throw the now silent radio back to Tommy and say, "Now give me the other tablet."

The radio crackles to life again. "I'd leave in the next ten minutes, if possible. Seriously. Ten minutes."

After swallowing the tablet, I stagger out into the five-below-zero sunshine, balancing on one leg, clad only in my three pairs of long johns. Within seconds I feel the frigid air snapping me out of my fog. I crawl back into my nylon dome to pull on my windsuit and wedge my cold prosthesis back over my wool- and neoprene-covered stump. With the storm coming, I ask the Sherpas—Dawa, Norbu, and Pema Temba—to break down one of the tents and leave the other for Jeff and Tashi. Tommy and I start down toward the fixed lines of the Lhotse Face. As we traverse the Geneva Spur on a faint trail worn into the black shale, I scan the horizon to the south and west for any signs that the tranquil weather is ending, knowing that the storm will move up the mountain from the lower elevations.

The hand that has been squeezing my lungs all morning seems to be loosening its grip. Still, I have to focus all my attention on my movements when we reach the edge of the Geneva Spur, an exposed shale outcrop where we lower ourselves down onto the Lhotse Face. If I take a tumble here, the next stop is the Western Cwm, five thousand feet below. Once at the bottom of the drop, I clip my leash into a fixed line and begin a long, downsloping traverse across this massive face of ice and snow.

After an hour, I sit down and wriggle out from my Gore-Tex windsuit. Not a breath of wind here. Looking back across the Lhotse Face, I can make out the dark shape of Tommy, who creeps toward me. As I suck down some water and a Sherpa

Shake, a nutrient-rich drink that Inter-Cal nutritionist Jack Hegenauer created for the expedition, I wonder if Tommy's fall rattled him more than he's admitting. Given that he is twenty years my junior and has all his various parts, he should be ahead of me. I decide to wait and check him out.

"You OK, Tommy?" I ask when he finally catches up.

"Yeah, fine. Just a little stiff and sore."

"Well, let's pick it up a bit. We still have most of the mountain ahead of us, and the storm's going to be closing in."

Two hours later, we stagger into Camp Three with the Sherpas struggling under huge loads. Here at 24,000 feet, while I brew some miso soup and mix another shake, I try to psyche myself up for the ten hours I expect it will take me to get to Base Camp. All too soon we're back at it, moving down an undulating ice face. In some places the pitch is vertical, and I'm often forced to swing around and descend backwards on fixed lines. My progress is awkward and slow because my prosthesis is locked at a right angle. Thanks to my overloaded nervous system, I feel a stabbing pain in the big toe of my right foot, or what used to be my right foot. Phantom pains. But knowing that my big toe hasn't existed for nearly two decades does nothing to alleviate the excruciating pain. I have to stop and wait a couple of minutes before it subsides.

An hour and a half later, I disconnect from the last of the fixed lines and run into Ang Temba, the leader of our Sherpa team, who has trudged two hours up from Camp Two to assist me in my descent. He hands me a thermos of hot lemonade and watches me carefully as the liquid soaks into my cracked lips.

"Up there, what happened?" he asks, while transferring my gear into his pack, leaving me to carry just my oxygen bottle. "Why turn around?"

I tell him about my crampon, the fallen climber, the rescue, my loss of resolve and confidence, the deadening cold in my stump. As the two of us navigate the terrain below, I'm struck by how this is the second time a Sherpa has ventured up this mountain for the sole purpose of helping me down. I wonder if I could ever possess such a selfless sense of duty.

When I plod into Camp Two at 21,000 feet, I'm shocked by the number of tents still standing. With the cyclone only hours away, it seems odd that the place hasn't been cleared out. Walking toward me from the mess tent is my old friend Rham, a huge grin spreading across the Sherpa's round face. My two teammates stand behind him—Angela Hawse, her skin burnt dark by the sun, and the always immaculate Gareth Richards.

"What are you guys still doing here?" I ask. "I thought you and most of Camp Two would be long gone by now."

"You didn't know?" Angela asks. "A ridge of high pressure has diverted the storm. We've got good weather for the next week."

Hardly able to contain his excitement, Gareth grins and says, "We want to go for it. You with us?"

"Gareth," I croak, "I need to sit down for at least two minutes before I answer that." My head spins from the ride of the past three days. Thinking that the mother of all storms was about to hit, I pushed myself to the absolute limit to try to summit in two days; out of the past fifty-eight hours, I've been on the move for thirty-seven. Then, told I have pulmonary edema, I dragged myself down the mountain, only to be asked if I want to head back up for another crack at the summit.

A moment later I'm sitting in the mess tent with Sandeep, a young, U.K.-raised, Special Forces–trained physician whose parents are Indian by birth. After listening to my chest with a stethoscope and inspecting the crud I cough up, he says that there's no sign of pulmonary edema. My lungs are clear; it's just a bad case of dehydration, exhaustion, and laryngitis. Sandeep says he'll monitor my progress until he heads up the hill, but in his opinion, if I rest for three days on low flows of oxygen, I should be in good enough shape to head back up the mountain. Jim Williams, a seasoned guide with years of experience in high-altitude sickness, agrees with Sandeep's assessment. But right now I'm too exhausted to contemplate another summit bid.

Before I crawl off to sleep, Jeff Rhoads appears in camp and recounts fantastic tales from his journey to the peak. At one point, he took a tumble off the summit ridge. All that prevented him from shooting thousands of feet down the Southwest Face was a single fixed line. He hung upside down with his pack around his ears as he struggled to get back up. Then there was the mysterious woman he spotted. She was traveling so slowly that he asked if she'd let him pass. Instead, she sprinted up the mountain ahead of him. When he reached the summit, however, it was deserted.

"It's amazing up there," Jeff tells me, looking wasted and spent, but elated. This is his fourth expedition, and he has finally reached his goal.

When morning comes, I wake up feeling remarkably fresh. Whatever creature resided inside my lungs yesterday seems to have crawled off. Poking my head out through the door, I spot Ang Temba preparing to descend to Base Camp with the Sherpas who supported our two summit bids. I head outside to wish them well.

"We will go down to rest," he tells me as we shake hands. "I will call you on the radio."

Meanwhile, Sandeep stands on the outskirts of camp, locked in a conversation over the radio. I can only assume he's speaking with Doug, our camp doctor. After nearly twenty minutes he walks over and hands the radio to me.

"They wish to speak with you," he says with a frown.

The next thing I know, I'm speaking with Dr. Kenneth Kamler, the renowned physician who treated Beck Weathers, the climber who had been left for dead in the famous storm of May 1996 and eventually lost all of one hand and most of the other to frostbite.

Now back on the mountain as part of an MIT expedition, Kamler doesn't mince words.

"You need to come down, Tom," he says. "You've got to really rest up and be sure you're OK." All at once it hits me. Faced with mounting pressure from below, Sandeep has recanted his diagnosis and prescribed treatment. People who sit down in Base Camp—who haven't examined me or even interviewed me about what I've endured and what my symptoms might be—are now diagnosing me as suffering from pulmonary edema. To make matters worse, everyone in Base Camp now believes I'm gripped with a case of summit fever, that potentially suicidal disorder that strikes climbers who decide to bag a peak no matter what the cost. Lord knows I've got plenty of shortcomings, but such lethal madness has never been an issue for me. I have a life wish, not a death wish. All the time and money that I and others have invested in this expedition are just that—time and money. Neither is worth dying for. I've always climbed mountains just to see if I can climb them—simple as that. But if my abilities are no match for the mountain or the conditions are too wretched, then I back off. As the saying goes, "There are old mountaineers and there are bold mountaineers, but there are very few old, bold mountaineers."

"I will take your advice," I tell Kamler, "but I will take it as that—advice. I truly believe that if I rest up here for a few days on low oxygen flows, I'll get my strength back."

"No," he replies, "you've got to come down."

Our conversation volleys back and forth like that for a while, growing more heated with each exchange. The last thing we want to do is burn up two days of good weather and what's left of our energy by returning to Base Camp only to have to come back up once they see I'm fit, so I dig in. I'm bolstered by the fact that neither Gareth, who trains mountain guides, nor Angela, who is paid to lead climbing expeditions, has any qualms about heading on another summit bid with me. In fact, it was their suggestion.

"Listen, Tom," says Kamler, "I see I can't talk you out of it. I admire your determination. Just be careful, and Godspeed."

Angela and Gareth have been listening to the conversation, and they smile cheerily. "That's great," Angela says. "You didn't cave in."

I shake my head gloomily. "No, it's not great. This isn't a victory, only a brief respite. What they're going to do is poison the well. They'll go to our Sherpas and tell them that if they support our summit bid, they're going to be dealing with a body."

My two teammates shake their heads in disbelief. "That's not going to happen," Gareth insists. "You're being paranoid."

I stare at Everest's brooding mass jutting above us into the blue sky. For Gareth, Angela, and me to head up there with three Sherpas would be the perfect scenario. It is what the three of us dreamed about when we planned this trip.

Four hours later, just after 2 P.M., the call comes through on the radio. Ang Temba, who has been in Base Camp for a couple of hours, delivers the blow I felt sure was coming.

"Tom," he says sternly, "my Sherpa, we are not going to summit with you." Who can blame him? Knowingly helping a climber commit suicide is not only bad for his—and his men's—professional reputation, it also carries some fairly heavy karmic implications. There's no use trying to talk my way out of this corner, not now.

"Well, in that case, Ang Temba," I reply, "will you tell Ming-Ma to put the kettle on? I know some people who will be ready for milk tea around five this afternoon."

With nothing left to do, we pack up our gear and head down through the Western Cwm. Not long into our descent, I can hear an angry, choked-up Angela speaking to Jeff Rhoads's camera: "Now I know what it's like to be disabled—having other people make decisions for you. It's wrong."

Once again, I push the anger and self-pity out of my head and focus on the task at hand, trying to keep my boot out of the icy runoff cascading down the glacier. We walk together in sad, strained silence, until my two teammates and I huddle under the polished ice and granite walls of Nuptse. I hug Angela and Gareth. If we stand a chance of getting another stab at this mountain, I explain, we've got to put on a brave face when we arrive in camp. Let's focus on the good things. We have a great deal to celebrate: Jeff and Tashi have summited, and Angela, Gareth, and Tommy have all reached the South Summit.

"Today we celebrate," I whisper. "Tomorrow we try to salvage the expedition. Right now, we've got to put our dreams aside. Tomorrow we'll regroup with Ang Temba and talk about this in a calm way. But right now, it's over as far as I'm concerned, and we should celebrate our successes."

With tears streaming down our cheeks, we hold each other tightly, trying to collect ourselves before proceeding. We continue down through the icefall, and when we hit the bottom of the fixed lines we find that everybody involved with our expedition has gathered to cheer our arrival. Back at Base Camp, our cook, Ming-Ma, not only has prepared milk tea, but he's even baked a chocolate cake. By looking at the smiles on our faces, you'd never know that Angela, Gareth, and I want to cry.

After dinner I walk to my tent and peel off the clothes I've been living in for the past four days. I crawl into my sleeping bag and stare blankly into the blackness of my tent. Right now, I want no more of this mountain. To head back up would be to tempt fate once too often; I want nothing more than to run away. Never mind the documentary film, the Webcast, the environmental cleanup, the expectations of my teammates—I just want to find my wife and little girl and forget about this place once and for all.

Morning drifts into camp slowly, but by 8:30, the sun has transformed my tent into a sauna. Wandering out to get some breakfast, I look up at Everest's massive peak and realize that I cannot turn my back on this mountain as easily as I would have liked last night. It's time to talk to Ang Temba.

When he's finished eating, I invite him to meet with my teammates and me about the possibility of another summit bid. At 10 A.M., Angela, Gareth, Jeff Rhoads, Ang Temba, and I circle up in the mess tent. I remind Ang Temba that the only thing I asked of him during this whole expedition was to have the mountain fully stocked to the South Col by May 1, so that if we got an early window, we would be ready to go. Other than that, I allowed him to call all the shots regarding the Sherpas' work schedules, rest days, and load allocations.

"Now, I'm asking one favor of you," I say calmly. "Support one more summit bid." We all know that we have less than a day in which to act if we are to go back to the summit. Because the climbing season is drawing to an end, we can leave for the top no later than tomorrow morning.

Ang Temba studies me for a long time. Although I'm still hoarse, he can tell that I'm certainly not in as horrible shape as the doctor claimed.

"My men, I cannot tell them to do something," he says. "You should propose something to them."

"What proposal would you be prepared to support, Ang Temba?"

Again he pauses before replying, "You and four Sherpa to make the summit bid."

This is hardly what I hoped to hear. The plan from the outset was for Angela, Gareth, and me to climb this mountain together.

"We need to film this attempt," Jeff announces. "How about I go to Camp Three, then hand the camera off to one of the Sherpas?"

Ang Temba nods in agreement, then heads off to gather the Sherpas for a meeting. Jeff wanders out to locate the redheaded CBS producer, Liza Finley, who has become a valued friend, to tell her what has transpired. At last, Angela, Gareth, and I are alone and I ask the question that has been weighing on my heart.

"So what do you guys think?" I inquire of these two individuals who now feel as close as family.

"Actually, I'm OK with it," replies Gareth. "When we were up at Camp Two, we were in perfect position. But now, from down here, it hardly seems worth it for another 250 feet."

Angela nods her head in agreement. "For the first time on the mountain, the South Summit feels pretty darn good. Another round trip through that icefall? No thanks!"

I study their faces for a few moments, not sure what to say. Over the past few months, the three of us have been through a lifetime's worth of headaches and joys. Gareth and I have often spoken about how great it would be for two Welshmen to stand together on Everest's peak. "Without your blessings, going back up just wouldn't feel right," I say. "It means a lot to me, and I thank you."

As the three of us walk out into the sunshine, I reflect on how much their support and their personal sacrifice mean to me. But their words have made me recognize something else, as well: if I had made it to the South Summit, as Angela and Gareth have, I too would probably not be so intent on taking another crack at the peak. My sense of failure up in the Death Zone had much to do with my inability to reach a recognizable point on the mountain. Suddenly I recall Greg Child's words to me: "If you want it bad enough, Whittaker, you'll find a way to do it." Maybe what at one time seemed like bad luck has just given me the determination to succeed, has made me want it bad enough.

I head to our communications tent, where Base Camp manager Eric Howard looks grim. His father's cancer, he tells me, is progressing more rapidly than first expected. I support his decision to return home.

After checking on the latest weather reports and reading a few e-mails, I wander back outside to find Tommy Heinrich and do what needs to be done. Our Sherpas believe that removing items from a dead body on a mountain is sacrilegious and that the protective spirits surrounding Scott Fischer's body were responsible for pushing Tommy off the mountain. His life was spared because his intent wasn't malicious. But the Sherpas will not climb with him until he has been cleansed by the monks at Pangboche monastery.

The bigger problem, however, is Tommy's maverick behavior. Although the decision has been made that only Jeff, four Sherpas, and I will venture back up the mountain, I suspect Tommy intends to go anyway.

"Look, Tommy," I explain, when I finally spot him sitting on a rock not far from the communications tent. "I can't afford to expend any more energy worrying about what you're going to do next. The only way I can ensure that you don't further compromise your life and the safety of my team is to officially remove your name from the expedition permit. You're welcome to use our supplies and hang around Base Camp, but you're not to use any of our camps, equipment, or supplies above Base Camp."

Tommy grows quiet and stares down at the slush and gravel around his boots. Like it or not, he knows I hold the trump card. If he goes back onto the mountain after he's removed from the permit, the Nepali government can ban him from climbing for three years and fine him. That's the last thing Tommy wants.

After I have completed that unsavory task, I locate Ang Temba, who informs me that his men are ready to listen to my proposal. We wander over to the cook tent, where our seven climbing Sherpas sit on carpeted benches built into the stone wall of their dining area. Many of these men are second- and third-generation climbing Sherpas. Their grandfathers supported the early attempts by the British to reach the top by taking the North Ridge. They're intensely proud men who enjoy considerable wealth and status in their communities. With bonus and pay, our top performers will each take home what a Nepali schoolteacher earns in three years.

Ang Temba nods at me, ready to translate. I take a deep breath. Everything rides on these next few minutes. "Because of sickness and the expected storm I was forced to try to summit and come back down in three days," I say, pausing as Ang Temba translates. "For top Sherpas, maybe this is OK. But it's too much for a fifty-year-old with one foot. After the rescue, I was too cold, too tired. I lost my drive. I became like a *jinjaput*. I was a danger to myself, to Norbu, Tashi, and Pema Temba. So I turned around.

"I came to this mountain, to Sagarmatha, with a dream: to show that handicaps are as much in people's hearts as they are in their bodies. I have not had a real chance to summit. Without your help, to make this climb is impossible. So I come to you for one last chance. I know you have children and crops that wait for you. I too have a home, but this dream is bigger than me. It is bigger than Sagarmatha. Together we can show that handicapped people want to be part of the world, to work hard, to do our best. Because of this, I ask for one more chance. Maybe I won't get anywhere this time, but all I ask is one last try. You will be in charge. If the conditions are unsafe or I'm climbing like a *jinjaput*, you can finish the climb and we'll go down. No argument. This is all I have to say. I leave the decision in your hands."

When Ang Temba finishes translating my words, I wish the men "*Namaste*" ("I honor the sanctity within you") as I press my palms together in front of my heart and bow my head. I turn and leave. I have no idea how my words have been received. The Sherpas are like seasoned poker players: you never know what they're thinking until they're ready to reveal it.

Back in the main mess tent, sipping a cup of milk tea, I suddenly feel queasy. My fate is again being determined by others. I can't decide whether I'll be more relieved or disappointed if the Sherpas say no. If they do reject my proposal, I'll be able to join Cinders and Lizzie in Kathmandu, and I'll have a clear conscience, knowing that I've done my best to climb the mountain and that circumstances beyond my control have conspired against me. Ang Temba finally enters the tent and sits beside me. I suck in a lungful of air and hold it.

"Norbu, Tashi, Dawa, and Lhakpa—they have agreed to climb the mountain with you," he says matter-of-factly. "They will leave the day after you and Jeff." His face softens into a broad smile and he stretches out his hand to grasp mine.

"How did you do it, Ang Temba?" I ask. "Was it difficult to get them to volunteer?"

"No," he replies. "All seven want to climb the mountain with you. I chose my strongest men."

"All of them? What do you make of that?"

For a moment, Ang Temba doesn't utter a word, doesn't even blink. When he finally finds a way to put his words into English, he says quietly, "Tom Di, because you did not offer them more money. If you had done that, none would have gone with you. You gave them a better reason. You reminded them who they are: they are climbing Sherpa."

Over the next few hours, Angela tackles the complex task of ensuring that we have enough infrastructure in place at 26,000 feet on the South Col. Tents and oxygen bottles can get quite expensive when another expedition knows you're in the market, which is where Angela's negotiating skills come in handy.

That evening I obsess over each component of my gear. Any seasoned Himalayan mountaineer will tell you that when a summit bid fails, it's usually not because of a single dramatic event but rather it's due to a number of small, seemingly inconsequential factors that conspire together. In particular I'm focusing on the interface between my crampon and prosthesis. In an effort to save weight, I've glued a boot sole to the bottom of my laminated carbon-graphite Flex-Foot. Earlier in the expedition, however, the rugged mountain terrain ate through the rubber soling and destroyed my laminated foot. The lack of atmospheric pressure caused the closed-cell foam liner of my spare leg to swell, so I couldn't wedge my stump into my backup socket. I was forced to cannibalize the Flex-Foot from my spare prosthesis, then retrofit it with bolts to my existing socket.

Sitting on my cot, I remove my high-tech lower leg and painstakingly scan every square inch of it, searching for any sort of a hairline crack or delamination that could prove fatal in the unforgiving world above Base Camp. Nothing. It looks perfectly sound. The holes I've drilled for the bolts show no sign of wear.

As for the crampon, which caused me so much grief during my previous bid, I carefully adjust the bail that clamps the spikes onto my Flex-Foot. After nearly an hour spent fine-tuning the fit and filing the spikes sharp, I pronounce the crampon good to go.

Around 11 P.M., I reach up and twist the lantern off. I have a luxurious five hours to sleep—that is, if I can shut off my head long enough to doze off. Staring up into the shadowy ceiling, I feel my heart pounding inside my chest. Am I doing this for the simple challenge and joy of mountaineering or to fight some holy war for the disabled? Is my bullheaded insistence on another summit bid putting other people's lives in danger? Jeff, in particular, is already exhausted from our sprint up the mountain and his push to the summit. Now, because I'm going back up, he's being forced to follow for the second time in less than a week.

I shut my eyes and run my hand to the three pouches hanging from the lanyard around my neck. Inside one, a purple velvet bag, are some ashes from the cremated body of Bill March, who died four years ago of an aneurysm. Bill was the first person I called in 1988 when I was considering an Everest climb. As expedition leader on the 1982 Canadian climb, he never made it to the top. I'd dearly love to scatter his ashes from the summit.

Sherpa Wong Chu, who led me to safety through the deadly maze of snowed-over crevasses in 1989, gave me the second pouch, which is made from a Buddhist prayer flag blessed in Tengboche monastery. In this pouch are several grains of rice that the Dalai Lama has prayed over.

When I locate the last amulet, I squeeze it tightly. Inside are locks of hair from Lizzie and Cindy as well as my wedding ring. I trace the outline of the gold band with my fingers. Then I move on to the hard lump that is also in the pouch. It is the thing that has brought me back here—that shard of dark gray stone that Greg Child handed me three years ago. How wonderful it will feel to finally be rid of this damn rock.

CHAPTER 17
Against All Odds

By the time my alarm begins chirping in the cold darkness of the tent, my stomach wants no part of it. Not now, I tell it, jumping off my cot and pulling my chilly prosthesis on. With two weeks until my fiftieth birthday, four hours of sleep just doesn't cut it anymore. Grabbing my gear, I stagger through the blackness to the mess tent, where Ming-Ma prepares me a two-egg omelet covered in Corisani. This concoction, dubbed "Sherpa oxygen" for its supposed ability to crank the cardiorespiratory system into overdrive, is made from ground-up red chili, garlic, salt, and tooth-chipping shards left over from the rocks used to grind it.

The fumes from Ming-Ma's kerosene stove do little to improve my raw throat. When Jeff stumbles into the tent, his clothes are half off and gear is hanging from his pack. All I can offer is a croak: "Top of the morning."

"You sound like death itself," he says.

I want to tell him he looks terrible himself, but instead I rasp, "Feel fit as a fiddle and ready for love."

By first light, the two of us toss sprigs of juniper onto a small fire atop a massive stone altar, an age-old custom to ward off evil spirits and honor the spirits of those who have died on the mountain. Ang Temba throws some blessed rice at us, then wraps his arms around the two of us.

"Much luck to you," he says.

Both Angela and Gareth have dragged themselves out of their bags to see us off. After the farewells have been said, I scold Gareth for not being curled up inside his tent next to his wife, Mary. We both laugh and then I look him straight in the eye, one last time.

"You sure you're still all right with this?" I ask. The two of us have been at this game long enough to know that in mountains you live and die by your decisions. When you start vacillating, you lose the ability to act decisively and you open the door to disaster.

"Yeah...yeah, I'm OK with it," he says. "I haven't changed my mind."

Angela nods to echo the sentiment. And without another moment's hesitation, Jeff and I begin the maddening task of navigating around Base Camp's shantytown of tents, craters, and rubble piles. I'm annoyed by how much energy I must expend just to reach the point at the end of camp where we can put on our crampons. After all, I know that the next ten hours of climbing must consume as little energy as possible. Everything has to be saved for the final push.

Safety demands that we negotiate the icefall before the sun hits it. The drastic variations from cold to hot generated in the first hour of morning pose the most danger to us. Sudden temperature swings can cause the overhanging seracs to let go and send ice avalanches thundering down off the west shoulders of Nuptse and Everest and onto our path.

We've been at it for nearly three hours when I hear a loud boom. The glacier shakes beneath me. Nearly a quarter of a mile away, ice crystals erupt into the air. I remain rooted to the spot, feeling the loosely cemented blocks of ice on which we stand shiver from the shock wave. This marks my eleventh trip through the icefall—five down, six up—and the place has only grown more nerve-wracking. I'll never get used to the powerful violence of this surreal world.

As the day grows warmer, I pull off my windsuit and stuff it inside my pack. Jeff, who is ahead of me capturing video footage of my ascent, is less than pleased that I've forsaken my flashy Gore-Tex one-piece for my less-than-sexy gray long johns. "Now you really look like a bloody hero!" he chides.

We move as quickly as our tired bodies will carry us through the eggshell zone, where the ice is most volatile and unstable. At any moment, the ground could open up under our feet, swallowing us along with thousands of tons of ice. Of course, strange as it may seem, this middle route is actually preferable to the more stable outer portion of the icefall, where we constantly worry about avalanches from the seracs teetering above.

After five hours Jeff and I arrive at the Golden Gate Bridge, where five ladders are lashed together across multiple crevasses. This swaying aluminum sidewalk ascends at a precarious 30 degrees up to a jumble of blocks above.

"You're definitely looking at the ultimate high-altitude machine," I announce, looking straight into Jeff's camera. "The lungs of a yak, the legs of an ostrich, and the brain of a codfish."

When I reach him at the top, I ask, "How'd that look?"

"Looked great," Jeff says, "until you started spouting all that inane drivel."

Finally we emerge from the icefall and arrive at Camp One, where we melt snow and force as much fluid into our dehydrated bodies as they'll hold. In spite of our ragged physical shape and our stopping to line up video shots, we've kept a decent pace going. Nevertheless, I'm worried that unless we get some respite from the sun, we're going to be in trouble. The few clouds overhead do nothing to block out the sun, and ultraviolet light reflects off the icy walls of Nuptse and Everest and onto the Western Cwm, which fans out all around us. The snow has turned to four inches of energy-draining slush. The heat is oppressive, suffocating. To prevent the intense UV radiation from exploding my nose and baking the inside of my mouth, I wrap around my face a green silk scarf that Angela gave me. It feels as though I'm traveling through the Sahara.

After ten hours of climbing, we arrive at Camp Two, where the always grinning Rham is waiting for us with glasses of warm

Tang. In our heat-distressed condition, this is just about the last thing we can stomach, but we slurp it down anyway. The two of us retreat inside the mess tent to rest. Exhausted after our ten-hour grind, Jeff radios Base Camp to inquire about the possibility of getting another couple of oxygen bottles brought up the mountain. Gareth's voice crackles over the radio.

"Why does Jeff need more oxygen?" he asks.

"I've decided to try and take the camera as far as I can," he replies. "If I can get a couple more bottles, I'd like to see about taking it all the way to the top."

I'm ecstatic at the news. Over the twenty years I have known Jeff, he has matured into one of the most experienced and skilled mountaineers and guides I've ever worked with. Levelheaded and a qualified emergency medical technician, he'll be priceless to have around if I get hit with another bout of lung problems.

Gareth, however, is less than thrilled.

"But that wasn't the agreement," he snaps. "The agreement was for Jeff to go to Camp Three and hand the camera off to the Sherpas."

Jeff looks at me, clearly puzzled. Trouble appears to be brewing. Suddenly I realize what is coming into play: undisclosed personal agendas.

"I think Jeff should do what he said he'd do," Gareth announces. "He can leave his camera at Camp Three and I'll come up with the Sherpas, pick it up, and continue on to Camp Four. Then we'll leave for the summit."

"Gareth," Jeff says, "you've shown no interest in running a camera until now, and you have no experience. The priorities of this expedition are for a disabled person to summit and for this to be documented as a film, right?"

"Right," Gareth concedes.

"Well, that's exactly why I'm trying to source more oxygen and am prepared to go as far as I can."

But Gareth holds firmly to his position, and the dispute becomes more inflamed. "Jeff," I finally say, "give me the radio."

When I get on the radio, Gareth again outlines his plan for Jeff to drop off the camera and for him to catch up with me after two days of climbing—to Camp Two in one day and up to the South Col the next.

"That doesn't make sense, Gareth," I say. "We're ten hours ahead of you."

"But you did it a few days ago."

"And I choked big time," I counter, closing my eyes and wondering if I could possibly have anticipated this. "Look, part of the reason we're here is to make a documentary. The longer Jeff can stay with the camera, the better the footage will turn out. You can't put in a ten-hour day, followed by a twelve-hour day, then after five hours of rest crank out another ten-hour day to the summit and expect to run a camera you have no experience with."

It becomes apparent that we're getting nowhere with this debate, so I ask Gareth to sit down with Angela and Ang Temba to come up with a solution that won't derail something that's going better than I could have dared hope. We agree to talk in two and a half hours, and I hope that in that time he and the others can think of a suitable alternative. But when I get back on the radio with him, he just reiterates the same plan.

"That's the same thing you told me the last time we spoke," I reply, trying not to let this craziness drain any more energy out of me than it already has. "Have you talked with Ang Temba and Angela to work out another option?"

"Actually, I didn't intend to come up the mountain in the first place," he says angrily. "I just wanted to see if you had the integrity to be my friend. Mary and I are getting out of here. We're leaving the expedition tomorrow."

My head spins and my stomach feels queasy. I try to talk Gareth into changing his mind, but he's adamant.

Hours later, I lie in my tent and try to understand what I might have done to cause this. The last thing I wanted was any sort of a rift. We've come too far together, worked too hard. While Jeff sleeps, my brain replays our radio transmissions over and over.

The next morning, after a breakfast of granola with powdered milk and a Sherpa Shake chaser, we start out for Camp Three. As I move up through the ice I can't stop thinking about Gareth. I've always prided myself on being a good judge of people, on understanding where outbursts come from when they occur. But this has me totally baffled. I can sense there's more to this than Gareth's believing that he was left behind. If I had more energy, it wouldn't be difficult to get to the bottom of this, but I don't. Not now. Instead, I use the pain of this wretched disagreement as fuel to quicken my pace. By the time Jeff arrives at our tiny tent perched on the top of a serac, I have the stove fired up and I'm refilling water bottles and making miso soup with ramen noodles.

At 5 A.M., we're back at it again, and within two hours Jeff and I are crawling up the thickly glazed Lhotse Face. We move upward in two-foot increments, sliding our ascenders along the fixed line. After a mere twelve feet of progress, our hearts are pounding so wildly that we have to stop to let the thumping in our chests subside. The process is slow and torturous. The past week has taken a terrible toll on my body.

The last time Jeff and I were in these parts, we had rushed up from Camp Two, climbing nearly one vertical mile of rock and ice in twelve hours. This time, we stayed overnight at Camp Three, which is what most climbers do, dividing our ascent to the South Col into two days. I thought the extra night of rest would build up a reserve of energy, so I'm depressed at how lousy I feel. I'm even more fatigued than I was the last time I clawed my way up these fixed lines. The fuel gauge reads empty.

"It all depends on how bad you want it, Whittaker," I remind myself. "This is why you refused those pain meds. So stop loading all those sandbags into your balloon and start tossing them out of the basket. You're going up, my boy! You are going up!"

As I struggle up through the Yellow Band, Jeff captures my tortured progress with his camera. Norbu and the other Sherpas catch up to us, and after a six-hour push I plod wearily into Camp Four, trying not to think about what lies above. The fly sheet to our tent flaps wildly in the wind, having been ripped by the fierce gusts that scour the ridge. Since the much-hyped storm forced teams to abandon food, fuel canisters, empty oxygen cylinders, broken tents, and anything else of little value, the South Col has been transformed into the world's highest refuse dump. Because of our paltry supplies, this is exactly what we were counting on.

Jeff checks the pressure on our oxygen cylinders; we have twelve full bottles and two that are half full. I dig through the debris and scrounge up some tea, milk, and sugar, along with a few bottles of gas for our stove. After carting the swag over to our tent, I chop ice into a stuff sack, then get the stove going and melt water for drinks and soup. The last time I sat up here, our porter resisted my efforts to help fix our malfunctioning stove. It feels great to be in control of the process.

After our meal, I pull off the liner for my prosthesis inside my warm sleeping bag and massage the blood back down into the stump. To aid my circulation, I toss down an aspirin and four ibuprofen for my damaged knees. In the dim light, my fingers dart across the carbon-graphite prosthesis as I give it one final check before reattaching the crampon. I'd trade my left foot if I knew it would ensure me ten hours of sleep, but right now sleep is a luxury I can't afford. I have to focus on the crucial task of melting ice for our meal and water bottles. I nod off for a moment, but I jerk myself awake and gather the contents for my summit pack—a spare mitt; my Swiss Army Knife for running repairs on the hill; a headlamp battery stashed inside my insulating mitt; one oxygen cylinder; four packs of a syrupy energy concoction known as GU;

and two insulated one-quart bottles of liquid, one of which contains an easily digestible carbohydrate- and fat-rich Sherpa Shake.

Sometime around 10:30 P.M., Ang Temba's voice drifts out of the radio: "Base Camp to Camp Four."

"Camp Four to Base Camp," I reply.

"Time to go. Time to go."

I force a quart of Sherpa Shake down my throat, and although my stomach convulses and I gag, I somehow manage to keep it down. We pull on our gear, and Jeff and I help each other get our oxygen bottles situated and turned on to a flow of 3.5 liters per minute. Once our goggles and oxygen masks are in place, not a speck of skin shows. Even in a light wind, at thirty degrees below zero, exposed flesh freezes in two minutes.

The Sherpas join us outside the tent and we waddle like astronauts out over the frozen moonscape toward the ice bulge ahead. This leads into a wide couloir of snow and rock that will eventually deposit us on the mountain's Southeast Ridge. The conditions couldn't be more perfect. There's almost no moisture in the air, and the winds have packed down the snow into a slab that's solid enough to climb on with our crampons.

We're moving at a good clip, but all too soon, the exhaustion returns. My legs go heavy and lifeless. Forcing myself onward, I have to stop after several clumsy steps to let my pounding heart slow. At these altitudes, even a short spurt of work sends my heart rate rocketing and makes me gasp for oxygen.

Periodically I take stock of my energy level, looking for the slightest hint that my lungs are filling with fluid. Am I looking for an excuse to turn around? After a while, I abandon these attempts at self-monitoring. I'm too cold and tired, and in any case, something tells me I'll know if there's a real problem.

Painfully clear, however, is that the frigid flesh on my stump has contracted. As a result, my leg—which is wrapped inside insulating layers of neoprene, a Styrofoam-type liner, and wool socks—is moving inside the carbon-graphite socket. Since the bottom of my stump has gone ice cold, I hope the pistoning will restore the circulation. If the blood flow doesn't warm my stump, I'll be forced to abandon my attempt once again. I am not about to gamble my livelihood just to reach the goal of the summit.

Once at the top of the couloir, we move across a snowfield and begin zigzagging between broken bands of limestone. After nearly eighteen hours without sleep, I have to concentrate on the placement of each step. Despite the copious amounts of ibuprofen I ingest each day, the 32,000 feet of climbing and 22,000 feet of descent in less than two weeks have caused my knees to revolt. In an effort to hide from the intense ache, I let myself drift farther away from my rational mind to a place where discomfort no longer exists. Because of my numbing fatigue, getting to that place is much easier than it was in a hospital bed. Each time I slip over into my subconscious, I'm climbing on autopilot. But circumstances dictate my level of awareness; at certain moments I have to jerk myself back to the present. *Hold on, Whittaker. The ride is about to get a wee bit bumpy here.*

When I fall back into my twilight zone, hallucinatory images flicker past my eyes and sounds drift through my ears. I am standing looking down at Lizzie sleeping in her bed, her face angelic. "I love you, little girl," I hear myself whisper. My hand tries to brush the hair from her temple, but as I reach out, the image dissolves....

After three hours of climbing, I creep past the outcropping of rock where I decided to turn around during my last trip up here. This pulls me out of my reverie. I've arrived here two hours earlier than I did on my first attempt. The snow beneath my crampons is wind-packed and firm, not the dodgy stuff I ran into the last time.

The upper portion of the face grows steeper and our firm footing gives way to unconsolidated powder. Lhakpa continues in the lead, compressing the snow and giving my Flex-Foot a firm place to step. Within twenty minutes, however, he is exhausted from breaking trail, and Norbu and Tashi take turns leading. Two hours later, the broad snowfield ends and we emerge onto a flat shelf known as the Balcony. Norbu helps me change my oxygen cylinder. As soon as I pull off my goggles to get a better look at what I'm doing, I feel my eyeballs becoming sticky, a sure sign that the lubricating fluid from my tear ducts is beginning to freeze. I instantly replace the goggles.

We continue upward along a wide, undulating ridge. Already we seem to be above the summit of Makalu, the world's fifth tallest mountain. Our crampons squeak in the dark Himalayan night. Traveling along the ridge provides a welcome relief. For the first time, I possess a clear sense of place that I've never experienced while trudging up the interminable face. Finally I can make out a landmark in the dark sky: the South Summit. Once again, the terrain becomes difficult, as the ridge rears up in front of us and we are forced back onto the face of unconsolidated snow that covers the icy slope. After forty minutes of travel, we locate a fixed line, which stretches alarmingly. Every time I slide my ascender two feet forward, I expend most of my energy stretching the rope and move up a measly four inches.

In a stupor, I struggle over a section of steep rock slabs coated in loose snow. Utterly spent, I'm standing on the South Summit. On all sides except one, the world drops away into an abyss. In front of me, the mountain appears as a narrow ridge. In an instant the fog inside my head clears. *There she is, Whittaker: the summit ridge!*

"This is Everest," I murmur to myself. "You're now five hundred feet higher than K2, the planet's second tallest mountain." I huddle in the notch between the South Summit and the summit ridge to rest from the wind. Pulling out a water bottle, I find that much of the Sherpa Shake has already frozen into a slush. When I take a bite from an energy bar I've stuffed inside my windsuit, I nearly break my teeth off. Nothing, it seems, can hide from this insidious cold.

Norbu reaches into my pack and connects a fresh cylinder onto my regulator.

"Time to shake a foot, Whittaker," Jeff cracks.

As we depart the South Summit to traverse the narrow ridge, I feel as though I'm leaving the trunk of a tree to crawl far out along a single branch. The mountaineer in me is awed by the boldness of Hillary and Tenzing for heading out onto this narrow ridge, using primitive equipment, to gain the loneliest summit in the world. What would Sir Edmund think if he knew an amputee was now doing it? Would he see me as a pioneer? Or would he think that I was belittling his and Tenzing's feat?

From the upper reaches of the mountain, the chances of rescue are remote. From the summit ridge, rescue is impossible. Westerly gales from the jet stream pound this slice of the mountain more than three hundred days each year, plastering snow onto its flank. Above me to the right a cornice hangs thirty feet over the Kangshung Face. When the weight of this hardened snow exceeds its carrying capacity, it simply lets go. The trick is to make sure you travel below the line at which the cornice fractures, or you're going with it.

Like the spine of some giant prehistoric creature, the ridge undulates upward for a third of a mile. But for once, the fixed lines feel firm. The mountain's Southwest Face falls away to my left, plummeting a full vertical mile down into the Western Cwm. To my right the Kangshung Face drops for nearly two. I plunge the ferrule of my ice axe into the snow and watch the axe handle disappear entirely. A crust of snow less than a foot deep is all that separates me from Tibet. When I pull the axe out, frigid air blasts up into my face.

"This is where I took my header," I hear a muffled voice behind me announce. It takes me a moment to realize who said it. Although he's only a single footprint behind me, Jeff sounds far away.

I nod, cracking away the ice that has formed around my oxygen intake pipe, and then I add, "Less than an hour to summit."

Up ahead I can see the lines running down the Hillary Step. All at once I remember the reports I recently heard of a lone English climber who became tangled in this web of ropes following a late afternoon descent. He was the last person on the mountain that season, and his body hung there for an entire winter before he was cut down and rocketed down the great Southwest Face. Visions of getting my artificial leg snagged in these lines are now consuming me. Clipping into the newest of the ropes, I promise myself that I won't let my guard down. With my good foot wedged against the rock and my prosthesis biting into the forty-foot-high ice chimney, I work my way up, digging my crampons into the rock and concrete-like snow.

Once on top, I step back onto the hard-packed snow of the ridge. For the next forty-five minutes we creep forward, one false summit after another rearing up in front of us. The end of my stump has endured beyond what I imagined it capable of, but there's nothing to be done about it now. Because I've kept moving for these past eight hours, fresh blood has continued to course down into the frigid tissue, keeping it from freezing. The continual pounding on flesh and bone, however, is starting to get to me. But I can't give into the discomfort. Not now. If I favor this leg it will be just a matter of time before I lose my footing.

Finally, up ahead, I see the ridge drop away teasingly. But this time it's no illusion, and now it comes to me, pure and startlingly clear: there's nowhere left to climb. We've come the distance. I notice a colorful stream of bunting erupting out of a snow dome. Stepping over the cluster of knotted prayer flags tethered to the ice, I pull off my oxygen mask and croak, "Who'd have thought it?"

I notice a spot on the lee of the summit, out of the wind. This spot seems like a good place to take a rest. Recognizing that I could all too easily snag my crampon on this small, makeshift shrine and rocket down the Kangshung Face, I move forward cautiously. Sinking to the ground, I pull off my neoprene oxygen mask and let the morning sun's unfiltered rays warm me. When I lie perfectly still, the thin air of this place almost seems tolerable. I shut my eyes, allowing the emotion to rush to the surface.

"You were good enough," I whisper. "Against all the odds, and all the skepticism, you were good enough."

Jeff grins as he pulls out his camera and says, "Got anything you want to record for posterity?"

"Yeah," I say, sitting up and retrieving the piece of rock from around my neck. "Greg, do you remember, in 1995, giving me some rock from the summit, and saying, 'I want you to put this back where I got it from'?" Because my throat is so parched, my words come out reedy, halting. "Well, Greg, this is for you," I continue, dropping the rock beside the prayer flags. "We took care of business."

I radio down to Base Camp to give them the news, thanking Ang Temba and the rest of the crew for keeping the faith. "I climbed this mountain for everyone who believed in me," I say, "and especially for all those who didn't." Over the radio I tell Angela once again how much it meant to me for her and Gareth to give up their summit bids so I could continue on. "This is the end of a twenty-year dream. I thank you all for sacrificing your own goals and ambitions to let me lie on the roof of the world."

Here I am, the first disabled person ever to stand atop Everest's crown. I made it. But I'm thrilled not simply because of my own accomplishment. Our group has established two other firsts, as well: Tashi Tsering is now the first human to reach the true summit twice and the South Summit once in a single season, and an amazingly robust Jeff Rhoads has become the first non-Sherpa to ascend this elusive peak twice in a single season.

With a jolt, I remember Bill March's ashes. After retrieving the zip-lock bag, I pry apart the seam, lift the bag above my head, and watch the wind scatter the powder into the sky. "It was touch and go, Bill," I say, "but it looks like we both finally made it to the top. Fly well, my friend, and thanks for believing in me when I needed it."

The Sherpa people believe that if you can't feel the hand of Sagarmatha, the goddess of the sky, on the summit, you'll soon feel her heavenly boot being applied to your backside. I can't speak with any authority about the gods, but I've come to understand that there are some things that defy any scientific or concrete explanation. And when I tuck the empty zip-lock bag back inside my down suit, it feels as if there's been a sudden change in the atmospheric pressure. The truth is that I feel as though a presence has just left me.

"You bastard!" I exclaim spontaneously as I realize, now that Bill has gone on his way, I'm all alone up here. I've wondered how a man with an artificial foot, a couple of weeks shy of turning fifty, could climb to the upper reaches of Everest twice in the amount of time most people budget to ascend the mountain once. Was the answer hanging in a pouch around my neck? Did Bill—always tireless, focused, and determined—accompany me on my journey up Everest?

But I don't have time to dwell on such questions. The summit of Everest is hardly the finish line; it's merely the turnaround point. Now I have to drag my haggard, hypoxic body down this mountain. This is a sobering realization, given that Everest claims so many of its victims on the descent from the summit pyramid.

Turning my back to the wind, I twist my artificial foot around in the snow and motion wearily to Jeff and the Sherpas. Time to head down. A few moments after we begin our retreat, I remember the tiny plastic unicorn Lizzie asked me to leave at the top of the world. She never doubted that I'd make it. I fish the small figurine out from my coat pocket, step back to the summit, and place the unicorn next to Greg's rock. "And this one's for you, Lizzie," I say as I wipe my eyes on the back of my mitten and watch the tears turn to ice.

It's time to go home.

EPILOGUE

It's been more than three years since I stood on the summit of Everest, but the mountain is never far from my mind, as it set me on a course I continue to follow today.

When I arrived back in Kathmandu on June 3, 1998, I was amazed to see the way the Nepali people were reacting to news of my successful summit bid. I was called on to attend press conferences, meetings with the Nepalese prime minister, and luncheons with the American ambassador to Nepal. The local media dubbed me "Bravest of the Brave—Emperor of the Disabled World."

The reason, I understood, was simple: in Nepal, when a person loses a foot, he becomes a beggar. Yet here was an amputee who had not only scaled the great mountain but had also been the leader of the expedition.

Still, the reaction overwhelmed me. It became clear that the disabled people of Nepal—numbering some 2.5 million—saw me as a hero and a champion for their cause. Although I was exhausted from my climb and still had a number of responsibilities to see to, I understood that with the accolades came certain expectations—expectations I couldn't ignore. The people of Nepal were in large part responsible for my success; after all, without the courage, hard work, and confidence of my Sherpa team, I could not have climbed the mountain.

It was time to give back.

In Kathmandu I visited the New Life Center for the Disabled, a group home that provides education, vocational training, and a sense of community for thirty-five children with disabilities. Without this school, the children would in all likelihood face lives as beggars or prostitutes.

Seeing the work that the New Life Center was doing, I decided to become its patron. Nepal is an impoverished country—the average annual income is only $250—and as a result there are few resources for the disabled. With support, however, grass-roots efforts like this school can make remarkable progress, particularly because a dollar goes a long way in Nepal: it costs just $1.75 to keep a child safe, happy, and educated in the New Life Center.

In September 1999 I returned to Kathmandu to gather information on disabled Nepalese and meet with government officials and concerned individuals. CBS generously agreed to let Nepalese television broadcast *Footprint on Everest*, the network's award-winning documentary about my climb. In short, I've tried to use the high profile I've attained in Nepal to draw attention to a problem that goes largely unnoticed in that culture.

But I have not restricted my efforts to Nepal. In 2001 I obtained nonprofit status for a foundation I started known as the Wind Horse Legacy. (The wind horse is a mythical creature from Tibetan Buddhism known to take prayers aloft to the gods.) The Wind Horse Legacy (www.windhorselegacy.org) is my vehicle to (1) identify and fund grass-roots disabled organizations that are doing vital work and (2) provide schools with material to encourage intelligent student discussion of disability issues.

Now more than ever, I see that there can be a higher purpose to my mountaineering. To that end, I have set out to climb the Seven Summits, the highest peak on each of the world's continents. I am committed to making documentary films of the ascents. On certain climbs, we will have Webcasts going into schools. My hope is that this will demystify disability in the eyes of children. If kids with disabilities can be accepted by their peers, perhaps society as a whole can become more accepting.

I am also developing an idea in cooperation with the Council for Exceptional Children. We want to create a national network of after-school clubs to help kids—with and without disabilities—to pursue their dreams, to know that with hard work and determination, extraordinary achievement is possible. I've learned how important it is to act on dreams; that's the very reason I started the HOGs, and why I went to Everest three times.

Recently, as I was putting the finishing touches on this book, I was reminded of just how vital dreams are. Lizzie, who is now ten years old, came with me on a climb of Little Granite Mountain, near our home in Prescott, Arizona. The two of us were hiking back to our vehicle, trying to beat nightfall, when my daughter suddenly asked, "Daddy, how high is Mount Everest?"

Although the sky was darkening, I could make out the silver speck of an airliner high above us, a long stretch of vapor trailing behind it. I stopped, sat on my haunches, and pointed up to that speck in the sky. "See that plane up there?" I said. "Well, Lizzie, the summit of Mount Everest and that jetliner share the same airspace."

Lizzie stood beside me, and I could see that she was letting her imagination sketch rock and ice ramparts between us and the speeding jet. Then she looked at me, but there was something different in those eyes, and after the slightest pause she said, "Wow."

When I stood up again I felt ten feet tall. And as we started back down the trail, her small warm hand found mine.

That one word was the nicest thing anybody has ever said to me. But I never would have received my "wow" if I hadn't lived my dream and climbed to that summit.

Now I'm going to spend a little time helping other people get their "wow" by living their dreams.

AUTHOR'S NOTE

This book is, of course, based on my own experiences and observations. I am grateful, however, for the input of family and friends who helped me as I tried to reconstruct the events of my life. Quotation marks are often used where discussions have been reconstructed from memory. In these instances, I have relied on my own recollections and, wherever possible, on the recollections of others who were present when these events took place. In some cases I have been fortunate to have incidents documented on video.

Being a college professor, husband, and father has taught me that I'm often annoying (Lizzie was six before she realized that my name wasn't "Tom Stop-it") or just wrong. Sometimes I'm annoyingly wrong. So if there's anything within these pages with which you vehemently disagree, I would love to hear from you. But I should probably warn you that once you have straightened me out, I will probably, much to your annoyance, get it wrong again.

Finally, alert readers will notice that I give the height of Mount Everest as 29,028 feet rather than the currently accepted figure of 29,035 feet. This is for the simple reason that the new figure, based on global positioning system (GPS) measurement, was not officially announced until 1999—after my three trips to the mountain.

ACKNOWLEDGMENTS

There is only one thing more exhausting than climbing one of the world's great mountains, and that is writing about it. Just as I couldn't have reached the summit of Mount Everest without the dedicated effort of my team, I never would have completed *Higher Purpose* without all the help I received—only in this case, the team was more essential to the process than I was. Before I ever set foot on Everest, I at least knew how to climb and was aware that reaching the summit would be a daunting task. Embarking on this project, however, I was a novice, and I never imagined just how difficult it would be.

Therefore, I am grateful to all those who worked to see that this book became a reality. I thank, from the bottom of my heart, Johnny Dodd for suggesting that we do the deed and for spending months transforming my drivel into a manuscript. I also thank Peter Miller, my literary agent, for shaming me into getting off the pot; Delin Cormeny, who held my hand through the process, using her special brand of intellect, diplomacy, and child psychology; and Jed Donahue, my editor, who disregarded ancient Celtic hostilities to take the manuscript Johnny and I gave him and turn it into a book. Cindy Whittaker, my wife, deserves special mention for spending countless hours typing in my additions and revisions to Johnny's text, most of which Jed wisely ignored.

In addition, I thank those individuals, too numerous to mention here, who have helped shape Tom Whittaker. This book, like my life, did not turn out as I thought it would. In some cases, people who were "I beams" in my development—and who still occupy a place in my heart—get dismissed in a couple of lines. This is especially, and unfortunately, true of the women who shared my life, loved me, believed in me, and gave me strength, joy, and purpose. Some of these women—my mother, Bobs; my wife, Cindy; and my daughters, Lizzie and Georgia—still define me through their love and their trust.

Tom Whittaker

Above all I'm grateful to Diana for pouring the gasoline and striking the match.

Special thanks goes to Big John and his lovely bride for conveying the power of the word; Todd Gold for the assignment; Captain Chuck Adams and Ian Corson for their pertinent cartography; Dr. Susan Thau for her ceaseless perspective; Ron and Grace Peters for child care beyond the call of duty; Chippy and Crippy for keeping it real; Leona and Liz for transforming sound into print; Jed Donahue for his editorial patience; Peter Miller, superagent and literary lion; and, most important, Delin Cormeny, without whom this book would probably never exist.

Finally, I can't go without mentioning my two little rays of sunshine, Christian and Ella.

Johnny Dodd